# READING THE DECADES

# READING THE DECADES

## FIFTY YEARS OF THE NATION'S BESTSELLING BOOKS

JOHN SUTHERLAND

Published to accompany the television series
*Reading the Decades*, first broadcast on BBC2 in 2002
Series producer: Mary Sackville West
Producers: John Bush, Tim Dunn, Roger Parsons
and Tim Robinson
Assistant producer: Peter Sweasey

First published 2002
© John Sutherland
The moral right of the author has been asserted

ISBN 0 563 48810 7

Published by BBC Worldwide Ltd,
Woodlands, 80 Wood Lane, London W12 0TT

Commissioning editor: Emma Shackleton
Project editor: Christopher Tinker
Copy-editor: Esther Jagger
Proofreader: Margaret Cornell
Designer: Linda Blakemore
Picture researcher: Miriam Hyman

Set in Sabon
Printed and bound in Great Britain by Butler & Tanner Ltd, Frome
Colour separations by Radstock Reproductions Ltd, Midsomer Norton
Jacket and plate sections printed by Lawrence-Allen Ltd, Weston-super-Mare

# Contents

## Acknowledgements

I would like to thank the production team at the BBC, my research assistant (and friend) Ann Totterdell, and my wife, who helped me with the preparation of this book. *JS*

# Introduction

A popular book is, from the publisher's point of view, a bet – though usually something of a long shot – that has paid off. For the literary historian it is a sociological experiment that has worked. Bestsellers fit their cultural moment as neatly as a well-fitting glove. And, typically, no other moment. Imagine Bridget Jones in a utility dress, and rayon stockings, in 1948 ('2 units of brown ale. Bad. 6 Willy Woodbines. v.gd.'). Or Joe Lampton popping Ecstasy on the London club scene. Or Jamie Oliver elbowing Fanny Cradock out of the way at the kitchen counter.

Reviewing half a century's bestsellers is like running one's fingers over a topographical map of British social history: feeling its anxieties, ambitions, aspirations, fears, prejudices, neuroses. Glass buckets dropped into the depths of yesterday. The problem is, unusually, a surplus of precisely recorded data. There are some four thousand titles which could, by a stretch, count as 'popular books of the day' between 1945 and 2002. Many more, that is, than one can reasonably digest – even with fifty-seven years to do it.

One of the pleasures of an exercise like this is that, even if one has not scrutinized every page (I haven't), one can still use the generic evidence intelligently. Why, for example, are fantasy and tales of the supernatural so phenomenally popular in 2002 and rare birds in the bestseller lists in 1950? I suggest certain explanations. Other readers will have their own explanations.

This short study is offered not as a research dissertation but as something more in the nature of an informed essay on what the British read, and why, over the last half-century. It's been fun to do – nostalgic fun, often – and I trust it will be as pleasurable for readers to have their memories jogged about what they once read or saw lots of other people reading.

A note on terminology used: particularly the terms 'bestsellers', 'longsellers' and 'fastsellers'. 'Longsellers', as I define them, are Sue

Lawley's 'desert island books': Shakespeare, the Bible and the *Oxford English Dictionary*. 'Bestseller' is something of a misnomer as it is conventionally used. The books which sell most copies in a year, every year, year-in, year-out, are boringly predictable: *The Highway Code*, telephone directories, train timetables, catalogues. A true 'bestseller' list would be duller reading than what it was made up of.

What the fascinating weekly and annual 'bestseller' (so-called) charts record are 'fastsellers'. That is, high-profile books which sell a lot very quickly and promptly make room for other titles which will also sell a lot quickly. The old-fashioned term 'books of the day' describes them better. Fastsellers never, unlike Shakespeare, the Bible or the *OED*, stick around and rarely come back. Few books can be less disturbed in the vaults of the British Library, now bursting with its 17 million volumes, than yesterday's books of the day.

# 1

BRITAIN EMERGED FROM WORLD WAR II a victorious but impoverished nation (again). The fruits of victory would be shortages, ration books, fuel cuts, utility furniture, government-issue 'marge', tinned 'snoek' (don't ask) and pilchards, rather than tinned salmon, for high tea on Sunday. 'Austerity', the word favoured by the new, nationalizing socialist government, was the order of the day. 'Misery' would have been the more honest term.

In February 1946, Whitehall imposed drastic cuts on an already exiguous national menu. Bread rationing was introduced, for the first time since the Napoleonic Wars, in May 1946. The meat allowance was cut to a meagre 8*d*-worth (3p) per person per week. Butchers did their work with scalpels and microscopes, customers jested. For a period, the government even tried to interest the British palate in whalemeat; 'Thar' she blows!' husbands feebly joked as the rubbery pulp was served up, masquerading as beefsteak.

Food rationing would continue for the British population until 1954. Clothes rationing was not lifted until 1949. 'Sweets' were 'on ration' until the early 1950s. Pubs regularly ran out of beer, which everyone suspected 'they' were watering down. A favourite formula cartoon of the 1940s was 'Wot no...?' It showed a lugubrious long-nosed face, over a garden fence, and a caption such as: 'Wot no caviar?' The population smiled, wanly. There was no caviar. Not even any dripping, some days.

Luxuries were rarities – unless acquired illicitly 'under the counter', or from some extortionate 'spiv'. When, in the opening scene of Graham Greene's 1951 novel *The End of the Affair*, set in 1946, Bendrix and Miles go for a drink to the local pub on Clapham Common, they count themselves lucky to get a couple of tots of rum. Their normal tipple, of course, would be whisky and soda. But in

1945–59

1946? Forget it; swallow whatever rotgut is available and count yourself lucky.

Although Greene does not bother to tell us, the men's overcoats would have been threadbare, the collars on their shirts 'turned', their socks many times darned and their shoes much cobbled. 'Make do and mend' was the motto of the day. If, as legend had it, German women would sell themselves for a bar of soap, their English sisters would certainly give you a date, if not a 'good time', for a second-hand pair of nylons. Even books (other than ration books) were relatively scarce. The Ministry of Supply kept paper supplies to publishers and printers on a strict quota, and would continue to do so until 1953. The British book still appeared in unsightly 'wartime regulation' format. Drab, drab, drab.

There was, of course, employment for the demobilized warriors of the nation on their return from battle. But little else. One could be grateful that there would be less blood, since so much of it had been spilled. But 'toil, tears, and sweat' remained the slogan held up to the nation. Jam (Harold Macmillan's 'You've never had it so good') was many working tomorrows away.

One could, however, legitimately add one other bodily fluid to those in Churchill's grim, promissory list. There was, in 1946, a favourite joke among servicemen about to be released, with their statutory 'demob suit', into civvy street: 'When you get home, mate, what's the *third* thing you'll do, after taking off your gas mask?'

With peace and the return of the soldiers, there was a nationwide festival of love. Copulation thrived. A Niagara of pent-up desire swept through Britain and a cohort of children, conceived in the post-war reunion of families and lovers, commemorated post-war reunion. The so-called 'bulge' would swell, like a boa constrictor's slowly digested meal, through the school system in the 1950s. The victory-offspring conceived in 1945–6 still create their demographic blip. In twenty years' time, the obituary pages of our national newspapers will need to expand 20 per cent to see them off to their final reward.

New *mores* of sexual conduct were called for peacetime love-making. Dr Eustace Chesser's *Love without Fear: A Plain Guide to Sex Technique for Every Married Adult* was published in 1947, by Collins, to answer that need. Billy Collins's Glasgow-based firm specialized in the mass production of reading matter (they were also 'respectable' verging on pious: one of the three British publishers licensed to print the authorized Church of England Bible – the others were Oxford University Press and Cambridge University Press).

Chesser's book had originally been issued in 1941, under the imprint of the medical publisher Rich & Cowan, at the whopping price of 12*s* 6*d* (62½p), 'to keep it out of younger people's hands such as typists and others'. It had been prosecuted and acquitted as an 'obscene book' in 1942; Chesser subsequently introduced some 'expurgations' of dubious material.

The guide sold massively in its liberated, mildly toned down, 'popular' Collins format at 6*s* (30p) – although typically it was not displayed in high street bookshops. It was more often purchased through the post for discreet delivery in 'plain cover', or from back-street 'speciality' shops which otherwise did a furtive trade in contraceptives, 'wank-mags' and dubiously effective abortifacients. The book circulated hand to hand, often in workplaces. But, however fearful its distribution, *Love without Fear* was very widely read – if not, as instructed, by *every* married adult.

Dr Chesser's chapter on honeymoons opens with the instruction (from Balzac): 'Do not begin your marriage with a rape'. The author advises, sagely, that men and women should wash themselves before going to bed, especially if a certain kind of 'body kiss' (details unspecified) is in prospect; bear in mind that many houses in the 1940s did not have running hot water, so that 'washing' would entail bathing in the kitchen or taking a kettle and flannel to the bathroom – hard to do tactfully. 'Foreplay' was recommended, and discreetly described. Men were firmly reminded *not* to roll over and go to sleep immediately after climax – unless, that is, they did so pillowed on their partner's breast, something that women were said particularly to enjoy. The 'partner', of course, was a spouse. It would be ten years before Chesser would, rather nervously, concede that pre-marital sex might be less than a crime against nature. His last book, *Is Marriage Necessary?*, published in 1974, a year after his death aged seventy-one, indicates how far he – and Britain – had travelled in three decades of 'sexual revolution'.

The first of the popular sex manuals, *Love without Fear* demonstrated the good that a sensible, educational book on this most sensitive of topics might achieve. Its author can lay claim to be the first

11

of Britain's bestselling 'sexologists'. Interestingly, Chesser's first book, published in 1939, was *Slimming for the Millions: The New Treatment of Obesity*. Wartime rationing would take care of the nation's over-eating problem.

*Love without Fear* was reprinted innumerably. A new issue even appeared in the summer of love, 1966 – although by this time, with the Pill available and the younger generation swinging promiscuously away, the doctor's advice seemed very grandfatherly. Chesser's sales, large by UK standards, were of course dwarfed by those of his American counterpart, Dr A. C. Kinsey (1894–1956), whose *Sexual Behavior in the Human Male* was published in 1948 and *Sexual Behavior in the Human Female* in 1953. Through his scientific 'institute' Kinsey brought a bright, cold, clinical light to bear on what was going on in the bedrooms of America. His reports, statistical and drily academic as their tone was, contained sensational revelations for the early 1950s. They went on to become bestsellers in America. Readers knew what *they* did – they wanted to know what their neighbours and children were doing. Chesser wrote a pale imitation for the British market, *The Chesser Report*, published in 1956; but his interests, as a sexologist, were always more practical and humane than Kinsey's. As his posthumous biography would reveal, Kinsey was a full-blown sex maniac; Chesser, by contrast, seems to have been a genuinely nice man.

These male authorities were partnered and, for thinking women at least, superseded by Simone de Beauvoir's *The Second Sex*, which first appeared in France in 1949. A bestseller across the Channel, de Beauvoir's book, published in translation by Jonathan Cape in 1953 and, very successfully, as a Four Square paperback in 1960, in which year it saw eight reprints, became the most popular treatise of its kind in the UK. De Beauvoir (1908–86) blazed the trail for the many feminist thinkers and ideologues who followed her.

The French *philosophe* put sex, as experienced by the woman, into an historical and – most explosively – a *political* context. 'Sexual Politics', as it would later be labelled by Kate Millett in her 1970 feminist bestseller, was born with de Beauvoir's *The Second Sex*. The flavour of the book, and the author's proto-feminist refusal to accept second place for her sex, is proclaimed in the belligerent opening sentences:

Woman? Very simple say the fanciers of simple formulas: she is a womb, an ovary; she is a female – this word is enough to define her. In the mouth of a man the epithet *female* has the sound of an insult, yet he is not ashamed of his animal nature; on the contrary, he is proud if someone says of him: 'He is a male!' The term 'female' is derogatory not because it emphasises her animality, but because it imprisons her in her sex.

Remind yourself that this fighting talk was uttered in 1949. De Beauvoir's demands for the 'Second Sex' would feed through into Françoise Sagan's 'intellectual', young-and-glamorous woman's romance which was to enjoy a cult popularity in the UK – *Bonjour Tristesse* (1954). The notion that a girl could be beautiful, brilliant and sexually independent would be something daringly new. So new, that it had to be French.

Meanwhile, for the British men who returned from the fight against the enemy from 1945 onwards, civvy street meant jobs. For the women who had been deployed in the workplace over the seven years of conflict it meant they were now out of a job – or, at least, the job description was radically changed. As with Rosie the Riveter in America, those women who had 'manned' the factory, the office, the police force or farm were suddenly 'feminized' again.

The new job description was specified in advertisements such as those for household appliances and the new 'detergent soaps', and in the 'New Look' with its tight waist and full skirts. And, most pervasively, in that never-failing source of 'soft propaganda' – women's romance. The feminine contours morphed into the new role for the woman of the day: shoulder-padded two-piece suits gave way to softer, 'fuller' contours. Femininity was decked out with nylon (silk for the masses) stockings, peroxided hair, two-inch heels and, for the younger, more casual female of the species, tight sweaters over strangulating brassieres.

The sex bomb 1940s-style was immortalized in the soft-core, steamy, Restoration period romance *Forever Amber*, a 1946 block-buster boosted by a tie-in 'film of the book', starring delectable Linda Darnell as the lusty cavaliers' busty darling, in 1947. Novelist Kathleen Winsor's 'daring' improprieties were potent aphrodisiacs in an age of state-imposed, iron-clad 'decency'. As in much popular fiction of the period, one feels in these borderline-respectable novels a kind of straining at the leash. The leash would not actually be slipped until November 1960, with the Lady Chatterley trial.

The market-leader since the 1920s in women's romance, Mills & Boon, who specialized in cheap hardbacks for 'tuppenny' lending libraries, had a good war. The staple theme of their books remained, as in the inter-war years, 'The Great Husband Hunt'. However, this does not mean that their readership was exclusively the young and unmarried. Mills & Boon has always led the field in market research, and British wives, they ascertained, enjoyed fantasizing about the husband hunt (if only they had been luckier, or hunted more expertly!) as hungrily as their maidenly sisters. Hungrily enough, at least, to dispense 2d (less than 1p) for the latest M&B. The husband hunters' prey was, ideally, square-jawed, seven to ten years older, 'professional' (i.e. earning £1000 a year), strong, silent, and dominant. No 'wimps' (as the firm's 1940s director, Alan Boon, put it). The man in the M&B universe was 'other' – inscrutable, masterful, sometimes terrible. But always the woman's true destiny: her 'mate'.

According to Alan Boon:

> the special attraction which Mills & Boon novels held for women was their 'wholesomeness', that is, the lack of pre-marital sex and 'immorality'. Indeed, before 1950, the closest physical contact, before the marriage proposal, was hand-holding, or perhaps a peck on the cheek. However, whenever the heroine falls, hits her head, and is knocked out (as so often happens), she is usually revived when the shocked hero smothers her with frantic, anxious kisses.

In other extreme moments, the occasional 'bruising kiss' – nothing 'French' – was permissible. M&B's lead writers clocked up totals to rival star cricketers (Edrich and Compton, if one's talking 1946). Three hundred titles, under a platoon of *noms de plume*, was not unusual. Leading practitioners in the genre (not all in the M&B stable – they tended to avoid 'star' writers) were Ursula Bloom ('Sheila Burns', 'Mary Essex', 'Rachel Harvey', 'Deborah Mann', 'Lozania

Prole', 'Sara Sloane'), Ruby M. Ayres, and Denise Robins ('Denise Chesterton', 'Ashley French', 'Harriet Gray', 'Hervey Hamilton', 'Julia Kane', 'Francesca Wright'). Robins specialized in romances with melodramatic titles: *Forgive Me, My Love* (1947), *Love Me No More!* (1948), *Only My Dreams* (1951), *Do Not Go, My Love* (1959).

Mills & Boon authors wrote, like so many battery hens, to a formula, and typically for a flat fee, imposed by the (male) publisher. (The formula can still be found, after innumerable adjustments for changing *mores*, on the firm's website.) Chastity ruled. The M&B universe was firmly subordinate to 'Alphaman'. The stories themselves had to observe what the house rules called 'Lubbock's Law'. Derived from the distinguished Jamesian critic Percy Lubbock, the 'law' ordained that the narrative point of view must always be that of the little woman – the 'Beta' of the species. So nature, from time immemorial, had ordained it.

Even within the domain of women's dream factory there were the familiar stratifications of the English class system. The Colonel's wife and Rosie O'Grady, sisters as they might be under the skin, preferred different brands of escapist reading matter even if the setting was the same. Take Regency Romance – a clear-cut category fantasizing a (wholly ahistorical) world of England under our fat friend, the Prince Regent, in the early nineteenth century. This variety of fiction testified to British women's long love affair with the mad, bad Lord Byron, breaker of every sexual taboo: fornication, incest, adultery – no waistcoat is big enough for all the scarlet letters Byron's breast should carry. Regency Romance, as a genre, bears witness to a folk-longing for the Edenic world before Victorian 'basics' and the evangelical revival cramped everyone's style.

The Regency Romp enjoyed a boom in the 1940s and the reason is not hard to deduce. These books, with their comfortingly safe narrative formulae, offered colour to a population suffused in wartime blackout (to protect British cities from the Luftwaffe) followed by the peacetime fuel-shortage blackouts of 1947–8 (the hardest, longest, coldest winter in living memory).

A lust for colour and blaze expressed itself also in another area of the cultural field. It explains the strange popularity, on the English stage, of the verse plays of Christopher Fry in the late 1940s (most famously, *The Lady's Not for Burning*, 1949) and the wild 'howl' of Dylan Thomas's verse. Thomas wrote the most popular poetry of the mid- and late 1940s, if any poetry since the war can truly be said to have been popular.

A national yearning for hot, sunny, faraway places – to which the only ticket during these austere times was a novel – plausibly accounts for the popularity of Lawrence Durrell's overwritten *Alexandria Quartet* (1957–8), with its exotic locations, poetic prose, and Proustian sexual intensities. Reading Durrell, one critic said, was like dining on nougat. A decade of spam made that prospect mouth-watering.

In short, the British population wanted a technicolor world where they might escape the grimly monochrome world outside the window. A world which was, until the great 'smog' crises of the early 1950s and the subsequent Clean Air Act, thick with airborne pollution. Winters were not just cold but filthy. As drink was, for the Victorian working class, 'the quickest way out of Manchester', so Regency Romance was one of the yellow brick roads out of the dreariness of 1940s suburbia.

There were two monarchs of Regency Romance in the 1940s, each queening it over her different realm. Catering for the upper tier was Georgette Heyer (1902–74). The author of some sixty works, Heyer rings the changes on the usual dramatis personae of lusty bucks, old roués, pert belles and rapacious women of a certain age and great carnal appetite. Her favoured subjects are often evident enough from their titles: *The Reluctant Widow* (1946), *The Foundling* (1948), *Arabella* (1949), *The Grand Sophy* (1950), *The Quiet Gentleman* (1951), *Cotillion* (1953), *Bath Tangle* (1955), *Sprig Muslin* (1956), *April Lady* (1957). Her novels, typically, sold between 70,000 and 100,000 each, within a couple of years of publication. She received some £3000 advance a title – generous by the standards of the time.

Heyer's fiction is carefully researched, cunningly plotted and better written than the formulaic, typically slapdash genre deserves. At their best – and they are at their best in the 1940s and early 1950s – Heyer's patch, fan, brocade, mask and (occasionally) flashing rapier romances attained to the rank of respectable literary works as well as bestsellers. Not the least legacy of Heyer's popularity was the younger British woman's decades-long affection for Laura Ashley fabrics. Sprig Muslin for the masses.

Barbara Cartland (1901–2000), the other queen of Regency Romance, catered for a less discriminating readership. She catered for decades, heaping her fans' plates high. Her first novel appeared in 1925; her first historical novel, *Hazard of Hearts*, came out in 1949. It was followed by *Knave of Hearts* and *Duel of Hearts*, in 1950. Miss Cartland survived as a living tribute to the preservative qualities of royal jelly and virtuous living. She was still writing – or employing others to write under her name, or that of her alter ego, Barbara McCorquodale – in the year of her death, 2000. Generations of susceptible women came under her spell. Supposedly her fictions were influential on the future people's princess, Lady Diana (Cartland's step-granddaughter), in her girlhood. Cartland has to her credit some six to seven hundred titles and an estimated 500 million sales, which qualifies her for that other 1950s bestseller, *The Guinness Book of Records*. She expressed an indomitable optimism, summed up in the title of her 1967 autobiography, *I Search for Rainbows*. Whatever else, she discovered her pot of gold.

Only Agatha Christie, queen of the neighbouring territory of crime and detection, rivals Cartland for lifetime sales. Unlike the ingenious Christie, however, Cartland wrote much the same novel 600 times. Her 1945–59 titles include: *Against this Rapture* (1947), *The Enchanted Moment* (1949), *Love Is an Eagle* (1951), *Cupid Rides Pillion* and *Love me Forever* (both 1953), *The Captive Heart* (1956) and *The Smuggled Heart* (1959). As a romance writer, Ms Cartland was all heart and pink chiffon. Her heroines affect such names as Delora, Magnolia, Darcia and Udela – all ending in the same vowel as 'Barbara'. They are frail but fragrant (and ultimately triumphant) creatures. Cartland said in a 1991 interview with Mary Cadogan: 'I've always written about myself. That's why my heroine is always a virgin. I'm still about the only writer who doesn't allow her heroine to go to bed with anyone until she's married him.'

But there was, for the British woman of the 1940s and early 1950s, more to life than lying on the sofa, listening to *Housewives' Choice* on the Light Programme, eating Black Magic chocolates and reading Regency Romance. The first hit of the rock and roll era was Bill Haley's 'Shake, Rattle, and Roll' in 1954 – the single which kicked off the biggest revolution in popular music since the invention of the shellac disc. The lyrics open significantly, if chauvinistically: 'Get in that kitchen, and rattle them pots and pans ... 'Cos you're a woman, and I'm a hungry man'.

Until the feminist rebellions of the 1960s women did what they were told. Cookery books instructed them how best to rattle pots and pans for their hungry man. What with world war and doing their bit in the factory, with its 'works canteen', women had forgotten the trick of it. Or, perhaps, they had forgotten their duty in the domestic scheme of things. Lessons had to be relearned. There is, from the 1940s on, a long line of bestselling, 'educational' cookbooks written by charismatic (increasingly 'celebrity') cooks.

The first in this line is Philip Harben. With his beard, his chef's hat and his consoling rotundity Harben was an incarnation of the chef – culinary Alphaman, but avuncular with it. Harben's style was no-nonsense. His was, like Chesser's, a 'plain guide' to women's kitchen duties. None plainer. His first bestseller, *The Way to Cook: Or, Common Sense in the Kitchen*, came out in 1945. A year later came *Cooking Quickly* ('"Cos ... I'm a hungry man!').

For the Coronation Year, 1953, Harben offered the patriotic *Traditional Dishes of Britain* (Queen's Pudding very prominent). Harben's prominence, as chef to the nation, was established by the growing spread of TV in the post-war years. Unlike radio, this new medium could *show* you how to do it; just like mum. A picture was worth a thousand printed recipes.

Harben yielded top spot, in the 1950s, to the sassier TV cook, Fanny Cradock (1909–84). This formidable lady (Mrs Thatcher, victrix of the Falklands, crossed with Barbara Woodhouse, dog-trainer *extraordinaire*) reconquered the kitchen territory for her sex. The luckless, remorselessly bullied Johnnie Cradock was inevitably consigned to the most menial tasks. If any: the poor fellow was 100 per cent useless. 'Do go away and have a drink!' his good lady would say, exasperatedly. It was a symbolic exile. Anywhere so long as he was not under Fanny's feet in *her* domain. Cradock's books (published, with illustrations, by the BBC) were always secondary spin-offs from her pioneering TV programmes and 'cooking shows' in which she and henpecked Johnnie would fill venues as large as the Albert Hall. She made cooking into public spectacle. Cradock's basic article of faith, as a cook, was that a resourceful woman ought to be able to cook (and hostess) a dinner for guests while wearing an unspotted black velvet dress – never that uniform of womanly servitude, the apron. Her dishes are, in hindsight (hindtaste?), awful; but she did her awfulness with verve. Like Barbara Cartland.

Elizabeth David (the Georgette Heyer of cook-books) was a much-travelled woman of the world in the pre-war period who began to compile her distinguished series in the late 1940s. Her *Mediterranean Food* appeared in 1950. It was published 'on spec' by John Lehmann, a famed bon viveur, who bought it for an advance payment of £100 – a canny purchase which ensured him many a good meal at his author's expense in subsequent years. As David said, she did not 'seriously expect that many of my readers will try stuffing a sheep, or even cooking a hare for seven hours: those recipes are included for sheer pleasure, and for the glimpse they give into a world where it is not considered pretentious, or bad form, to care about food'. The book was well received, although the RSPCA complained that her recipe for Roast Lobster was 'needlessly cruel'; the luckless crustacean was required to be thrown, living, into boiling water.

*French Provincial Cooking*, for which the publisher doubled his stingy fee, came out a year later. It would go on to be, like all David's work, a long-term bestseller in its Penguin livery. When the author returned from a holiday in Spain, in 1964, she was delighted to find her book in the UK's top ten bestsellers along with *The Kama Sutra* and Ian Fleming's *From Russia with Love*.

What class of reader was David catering for? Clearly the book-reading classes – not, like Fanny Cradock, the goggle-box classes. David belongs to the 'literature of cooking'. But neither was she writing for the upper crust. When, for example, Lady Irene Peacock published *The Adventure of Cooking* in 1950, the essence of the noble cook's 'adventure' was coming to terms with a post-war world where, astonishingly, there were no servants any more – even for Lady Irene.

David's constituency was, at core, the rising middle class: those who, for example, had done French at school but might never have been to France – yet. They had always cooked for themselves. Now they wanted to cook better. When David's books were picked up by

Penguin in the mid-1950s they became cult objects among the young, upwardly mobile and gastronomically adventurous (one of the word-of-mouth rules among her readers was: 'Never, ever, cook something for the first time when the boss and his wife are coming to dinner'). David's books were proudly displayed, alongside the newly acquired Sabatier knives and Le Creuset *marmite*. Sauce- and gravy-spattered copies of those Allen Lane veterans are still to be found in middle-class kitchens. They sold, year by year, in their hundreds of thousands. And still do.

David admitted in the 1965 revised edition of her book on Mediterranean cuisine that her recipes were, for most of her original readers, Barmecide Feasts – fantasy food. The British middle classes were, effectively, as locked up in their island by the £10 currency exchange limitation as those tight-lipped POWs in Colditz had been a few year earlier. You could blow your tenner on a single meal in Paris. 'This book', David wrote in 1965:

> first appeared in 1950, when almost every essential ingredient of good cooking was either rationed or unobtainable. To produce the simplest meal consisting of even two or three genuine dishes required the utmost ingenuity and devotion. But even if people could not very often make the dishes here described it was stimulating to think about them; to escape from the deadly boredom of queuing and the frustration of buying the weekly rations; to read about real food cooked with wine and olive oil, eggs and butter and cream, and dishes richly favoured with onions, garlic, herbs, and brightly coloured southern vegetables.

Tourism, as the industry slowly developed, enhanced the appeal of David's books. By 1961, when the first *Larousse Gastronomique* was published in translation in the UK, many of the young cooks educated into culinary expertise by David could test their own efforts against the real thing, abroad.

By the time of her death aged seventy-eight, in 1992, David was a British institution – as was her coeval, Julia Child, in the USA. David's *batterie de cuisine* was auctioned at Sotheby's in 1994. The kitchen table on which so many of her recipes had been tested was bought by Prue Leith, a celebrity cook herself, for £1000. Lesser bidders bought pots and wooden spoons, as holy relics of someone who had done as much for the British stomach as Vidal Sassoon for the British hair-do. Above all, David had raised the humble cook-book genre to a level that would have amazed her ancestress, Mrs Beeton.

Downmarket, Katharine Whitehorn's *Cooking in a Bedsitter* (1963 in paperback; called, less sexily, *The Kitchen in the Corner* on its first, hardback, appearance in 1961) gave more basic instruction for the new generation of university students. It contained such useful tips as: always wash the tin cans before putting them in the waste paper basket (they won't then stink you out at night) and – if you are cooking on a Baby Belling – make a list of what to cook first. And, most memorably, if you have friends who don't like garlic get new friends; some stinks are good.

Churchill won the war for his country, but he lost the first peace-time election for his party, in June 1945. There was a spirit of what was called 'bolshiness' stirring in the British masses, although as yet it had not erupted elsewhere than in the voting booth. Conformity still ruled in Britain in the late 1940s and early 1950s – conformity and its sartorial partner, uniformity. Men's styles remained as standardized as khaki from the quartermaster's store. Every Saturday night, at the Palais de Danse, couples robotically waltzed, quickstepped or fox-trotted (jive and jitterbug were sternly proscribed; the horrors of the creep were still to come). The men turned out in charcoal-grey 'lounge suits', the women in ball dresses or demure long skirts and starched petticoats. Some dance halls even banned high heels. It was well into the 1960s before even the Beatles stopped wearing ties.

There was book-trade as well as sartorial uniformity. Penguin, in their tasteful livery, had a good war (partly due to the canny Allen Lane's jiggery-pokery with paper allocations). Penguin were, by the mid-1940s, the nation's acknowledged popular educator. Their list embodied intellectual aspiration – self-improvement. In 1946, Allen Lane launched the first of the Penguin Classics, E. V. Rieu's translation of *The Odyssey*. (Between the wars, it was recorded, there had been eight different versions of Homer's epic published in translation in Britain. Only two had sold more than 3000 copies.)

Rieu's translation duly came out, priced 1s 6d (7½p). A retired civil servant, he was, on the strength of his Homer, appointed general editor of the Penguin Classics series. As J. P. Morpurgo puts it 'Allen Lane knew rather less Greek than his chauffeur and admitted later that he had "never read *The Odyssey*".' King Penguin (as Lane was nick-named) none the less enabled others to read it. Rieu's translation was, until *Lady Chatterley's Lover* (another Allen Lane punt), the best-selling paperback in the UK. By 1978, it had sold getting on for 2½ million copies, along with 350 other titles in the Penguin Classics list. The no.2 seller, with over a million sales, was Nevill Coghill's 1951 modernization of *The Canterbury Tales*. Robert Graves's *Greek Myths*, published in 1955, also did well for the series.

At the other end of the softcover market from Penguin are the so-called 'Mushroom Publishers' – low-overhead, pulp purveyors. The king of 1940s and early 1950s pulp fiction was 'Hank Janson'. Janson – a pseudonym for the English hack Steve Frances (1917–89) – first appeared in the bookshops in 1947. He represented a bastardized, Anglicized version of Mickey Spillane's ultra-violent thrillers (themselves bastardized versions of Raymond Chandler's PI novels) published as 'paperback originals' at 25 cents in the USA. Spillane's first title, *I, the Jury* (1947), introduced his series hero, Mike Hammer. The hard-drinking, woman-beating, whisky-swilling machismo of the aptly named Hammer was to American post-war taste. Estimates suggest, by the 1980s, global sales of 200 million for Spillane. By 1980, seven of the top fifteen all-time bestselling fiction titles in America were by Spillane. 'People like them,' he blandly explained.

Hammer is less a detective than a brutal vigilante. *I, the Jury* lays down the formula. Mike's marine buddy, Jack Williams, is sadistically murdered. Hammer sets out to avenge him, skirting the niceties of the law, vowing to his friend's corpse: 'I'm going to get the louse that killed you. He won't sit in the [electric] chair. He won't hang. He will die with a .45 slug in the gut, just a little below the belly button.' So it goes (even though 'he' turns out to be a gorgeous 'she'). Spillane astutely exploited the market he had created with *Vengeance Is Mine* (1950), *My Gun Is Quick* (1950), *The Big Kill* (1951) and *Kiss me Deadly* (1952). All the Hammer titles hit the nail.

Janson, whose first novel was *When Dames Get Tough* (1947), aped Spillane's formula. His speed of composition was phenomenal. In three weeks, in 1948, he wrote *This Woman Is Death*; *Lady Mind That Corpse*; and *Gun Moll for Hire*. (Hank, incidentally, is both the hero and the putative author of these wild adventures.) Steve Holland describes the content of Janson's fiction:

> The stories were violent, fast-paced and written in a style that was easily read. Janson was a traveller who roamed America finding women and adventure in equal quantities. The fictional America he travelled was a stark contrast to an England still in the grip of rationing (in a later interview, Frances said: 'I got all my background material by seeing as many Hollywood gangster and crime movies as I could, by reading up John Gunther's *Inside America* and various travel guides.')

Janson never approached Spillane's sales. But Janson's titles (up to a dozen a year) sold a respectable 60,000 apiece by the early 1950s. By sheer volume he had risen, as Holland points out, 'to the leagues of the multi-million sellers'. What sold his pulps was, of course, sex for the chronically sex-starved. And this it was that brought Janson to trial in 1954 for obscenity (a forerunner of the Chatterley trial six years later). After the trial, and its notoriety, Janson sales jumped to 100,000 copies per title.

A notch or two up from Janson, Dennis Wheatley, who had established himself as 'The Prince of Thriller Writers' in the 1930s, continued to please a loyal but shrinking contingent of British readers with his 'sex and occult' romances. In the 1950s they were considered as racy as a popular novelist might decently go. (Wheatley always included one 'dirty episode' in his narratives; locating them could be hugely frustrating since some public libraries unsportingly removed the offending page.) His most successful post-war titles were *The Haunting of Toby Jugg* (1948), which is about a paralysed war hero, attacked on the astral plane by a malicious warlock, and *To the Devil, a Daughter*, which, with his pre-war diabolic thriller, *The Devil Rides Out* (1935), was picked up by Hammer Films for their congenially over-the-top gothic treatment. Over a career spanning forty years Wheatley was estimated to have sold some 45 million copies of his novels.

If Wheatley's was the raciest fiction purveyed to British readers, the most innocent was that of Enid Blyton (1897–1968). A bestselling author for young readers (hers were often the first printed words they ever read), Blyton published her magazine, *Sunny Stories*, in 1926. She launched her cast of Toyland village folk in 1949: in a few years Noddy, Big Ears and PC Plod were (in their Haarmsen van der Beek illustrations) as famous as Winston Churchill. Noddy featured in the *Evening Standard*, as a cartoon mascot, for thirteen months in 1952–3 – their answer to Rupert Bear in the *Express*. By 1953 Blyton had produced eight Noddy books, with total sales of 10 million. Blyton herself was confident about what made her invincibly sunny stories so popular:

> They give children a feeling of security as well as pleasure. They know that they will never find anything wrong, hideous, horrible, murderous or vulgar in my books, although there is plenty of excitement, mystery, and fun. And the children are always real live characters, exactly like the readers…. I'm not out only to tell stories, much as I like this – I am out to inculcate decent thinking, loyalty, honesty, kindliness, and all the things that children should be taught.

A forceful, businesslike woman, Blyton managed without the services of a literary agent until 1954. Noddy became a one-character franchise industry, his image printed on toys, crockery, blankets and underwear. Sales for the Noddy books are estimated at 300 million in sixty-three languages. Noddy was, as John Lennon might have said, more famous than Jesus Christ. Or John Lennon.

A new, and amiably seditious, genre of writing for younger readers (not yet a fully emancipated 'market sector') emerged with the Nigel Molesworth *Down with Skool* series. These four illustrated books (Ronald Searle did the pictures, Geoffrey Willans the text) began as articles in the magazine *Punch*, for which Searle and Willans also created St Trinians, with its horrendous 'belles' (a series propelled into further popularity by successful film adaptations from 1955). Molesworth – 'the goriller of 3B' and 'the Curse of St Custard's' – pens his private revolutionary journal. He is, in embryo, the Angry Young Schoolboy.

One of the odder careers in popular writing of the post-war period is that of George Orwell (1903–50). This Tory anarchist – 'outside the whale', as he would put it – was, by the 1950s, up there in the charts, slugging it out with Spillane. Two Orwell titles, *Nineteen Eighty-four* and *Animal Farm*, sold year-in, year-out to become that most prized of publishers' possessions, long-term, 'bankable' bestsellers.

It is one of the ironies of literary history that in 1944, when Orwell circulated publishers with his fable of Mr Jones's farm, he could not get anyone to take the manuscript. Why? Because the Russians were our gallant ally, tearing the guts out of Germany (and saving our guts in the process). To be rude about the Russians with satires on 'state farms' would be 'bad form'. British publishers were themselves, Orwell concluded, 'gutless' (particularly T. S. Eliot, at Faber & Faber, who observed that since the pigs were more intelligent than the other animals they *deserved* to run the farm: Orwell took that very badly).

Fred Warburg was eventually brave enough to put his firm's imprint on the book. And, with the Cold War and the drawing of the Iron Curtain across Europe in 1948, being rude about the Soviet Union was what every 'gutless' British publisher now wanted to be. *Animal Farm*, far from being 'unpatriotic', became a prescribed text for generation after generation of British and American schoolchildren.

*Nineteen Eighty-four* was largely conceived in 1948 (hence the title) but was published in 1949, two years before George Orwell's death from TB. The book is coloured, gloomily, by the author's hatred of Attlee's 'totalitarian' Labour government ('Ingsoc', in the novel) and his own desperate physical condition. *Nineteen Eighty-four* made no great stir when it first appeared, although it was popular enough to warrant reprinting. By 1954 it had sold 50,000 copies in Secker & Warburg's 12s 6d (62½p) hardback edition. Sales (of the sixth impression) had slowed to 150 a month, just enough to keep it in print. Penguin brought out a paperback in the autumn of 1954 – again, nothing special was anticipated.

All this was changed overnight with the televising of Nigel Kneale's 'horrific' adaptation, put out by the BBC on Sunday evening, 12 December 1954. In the five days following the transmission, 1000 hardback and 18,000 paperback copies of *Nineteen Eighty-four* were sold and Orwell's novel was boosted into the fame which it has enjoyed ever since and will, apparently, enjoy for evermore. TB made *Nineteen Eighty-four* gloomy: TV made *Nineteen Eighty-four* a superseller.

As I recall, the production was initially slow, wordy and studio-bound in the fashion of primitive TV drama. But it built up to a satisfyingly terrific climax with the rats and 'do it to Julia' in Room 101. Perhaps too terrific for the standards of the day. The BBC clearly anticipated ruffling some feathers. Twice they gave out the warning that *Nineteen Eighty-four* was 'unsuitable for children or those with weak nerves'. This had the predictable effect of gluing even the most susceptible (and, of course, schoolchildren like myself) to their screens, with at least one fatal result. As the *Daily Express* of 14 December gleefully reported under the headline 'WOMAN DIES WATCHING "1984"':

> FORTY-YEAR-OLD ex-beauty queen Mrs Beryl Kathleen Mirfin died while watching TV's horror play "1984" on Sunday night. And last night police said her death was due to a heart attack "resulting from hyper-tension."
>
> Mrs Mirfin, her estate agent husband, and two friends saw the play at her home in Carlton Hill, Herne Bay, Kent. A friend of the family said last night: "The doctor asked if Mrs Mirfin had seen the play." ... Viewers were repelled by the scenes of torture.

The *News Chronicle* contained similar horror stories. The paper's TV reviewer solemnly opined: 'I would not like to have had the choice of this production on my conscience.'

The prompt repeat of the play on the following Thursday attracted TV's biggest-ever viewing audience. It also provoked, as the *Daily Mirror* of 17 December put it in a screaming headline: 'MORE PROTESTS OVER HORROR PLAY'. On the same page there was a comment from a staff reporter in the familiar tabloid manner: 'I NEVER WANT TO SEE IT AGAIN... says Betty Tay. I had a basinful of TV's Big Brother last night – and if it's the sort of thing the BBC is going to give us as entertainment they can keep my licence for one.'

As *The Times* pointed out in a thoughtful third leader on 16 December, Orwell's dystopian vision had been implanted in the British consciousness more instantaneously and vividly than any previous medium could have achieved: 'If anything had been needed to underline the tremendous possibilities of television, the last few days have provided it.' The BBC (whose one-channel TV monopoly ran out in 1955) capitalized on the *Nineteen Eighty-four* sensation and on Nigel Kneale's similarly gripping science-horror serial *The Quatermass Experiment* (1953).

The imaginary horrors of science fiction, typically projected into the near future, were easier to deal with than actual horrors of the near past. *The Diary of Anne Frank* (original Dutch edition, 1947; English translation, 1952) became a bestseller in fifty-five languages because, one suspects, it sentimentalized – and to some extent nullified – the horrors of the Holocaust and even events such as the bombing of Dresden. Anne made a better future possible with her statement, reiterated everywhere: 'In spite of everything I still believe that people are really good at heart.' Optimism was obligatory in the 1950s. Why else did we win the war, if not to make a *better* world?

The early 1950s saw a resurgence in popular writing about war, inspired by nostalgia for World War II and the outbreak of hostilities in Korea in 1951. A third world war was confidently anticipated. The general pattern of these bestselling war books, aimed exclusively at the 'male action' market, was the celebration of martial heroism. But British heroism, 1950s-style, had a somewhat different flavour. The country was conscious, rather unhappily, that there were now two superpowers; and neither flew the Union Jack. Compensation fantasy took various forms. A favourite was the assertion, ubiquitous in war writing of the early 1950s, that what Albion lacked in *matériel* she made up for with superior know-how.

Paul Brickhill's 'true war story', *The Dambusters*, was a UK bestseller in 1951. It is the story of how 617 Squadron, under Guy Gibson, loaded with super-boffin Barnes Wallis's bouncing bomb, daringly destroyed the Moehne and Eder dams with a pinpoint and suicidally costly raid, paralyzing Germany's industrial heartland. As Brickhill puts it, in his clenched-tooth style: 'This is a story of quality as against quantity, demonstrating that exceptional skills and ingenuity can give one man, or one unit, the effectiveness of ten. It seems that this is a rather British synthesis of talents, and perhaps this story will reassure those who are dismayed by the fact that the British and their allies are outnumbered in this not too amicable world.'

*The Dambusters* was hugely successful as a million-selling book, as a tie-in film and as a hit theme tune; it echoes in lager advertisements to this day. The bouncing bomb (deuced clever) is followed by the equally ingenious (and, in its way, symbolic) British midget submarine in C. E. T. Warren and James Benson's *Above Us the Waves* (1953). Britain: mighty midget, budget-sized superpower, battling bantam among great nations. So they dreamed.

These adventure books appealed, principally, to that now-too-old-to-serve generation of grown-up boys-at-heart addicted in their boyhood to Biggles. Captain W. E. Johns's dashing airman hero was introduced into the juvenile market in 1932. By the time of the author's death, in 1968, Johns had ninety-six Biggles books pasted on his cockpit siding. His pilot had been, successively, a World War I ace (like his creator), a freelance adventurer, a World War II squadron leader, and finally an air detective at Scotland Yard. And very old, if any young reader did his sums. There was also a Biggles for girls – Worrals of the WAAF.

The same touching faith in the superiority of British warrior skills, ineradicable 'decency' and ingenuity is encountered in other 1950s hits: P. H. Reid's *The Colditz Story* (1952), Paul Brickhill's celebrity biography of the legless fighter ace Douglas Bader, *Reach for the Sky* (1954) and Dudley Pope's *The Battle of the River Plate* (1956). All were filmed, either with Kenneth More in the lead, or with look-alikes. More created on-screen an icon of British heroism – cool, ironic, unflappable, frequently facetious in the face of danger. Jack Hawkins, the other great male action star of the decade, incarnated a set of matching British virtues: phlegmatic doggedness ('We may be slow but...'), physical massiveness and invincible 'decency'. Dirk Bogarde was the wittily erudite hero of *Ill Met by Moonlight* (1956), based on the commando exploits of Patrick Leigh Fermor (a travel writer before the war) behind enemy lines in Crete. The film of *A Town Like Alice* (Nevil Shute, 1949), another POW tale, made a star of Peter Finch.

C. S. Forester's superior Hornblower books, the saga of an English naval officer's career during the long Napoleonic Wars, had begun with *The Happy Return* in 1937. Hornblower was an unusual conception: shy, honourable, unhappily married (but loyal), gawky – an officer who has nothing in common with the glamorous super-hero Nelson other than bravery and a Christian name. During the period of hostilities and afterwards, 1793–1823, he serves in many oceans and rises steadily. Forester's books became phenomenally popular in the 1950s and 1960s, inspiring a mediocre film, *Captain Horatio Hornblower*, starring an unhappy Gregory Peck, in 1951. The series was converted into a disastrously mediocre TV mini-series in the 1990s. Over the two-decades' length of the series, Hornblower rises from midshipman to admiral. A feature of all the 1950s war docu-fictions, novels and fantasies is their celebration of the officer class. The 'worm's eye view', as the popular Ronald Shiner soldier-comedies of the time called it, is sadly lacking in these bestsellers. Britain was still a nation at the salute.

The best war book of the early 1950s, and a superseller by the standards of the time, was Nicholas Monsarrat's *The Cruel Sea* (1951). Monsarrat's novel chronicles what is, in terms of the 'big picture', a modest war effort: the seven years' patrol service of a corvette and the story of its crew. *The Cruel Sea* is written in docu-realistic mode. What was, however, most remarkable about the book was its frankness in dealing with sailors' sexual deprivations and recklessness in time of war. For much of the narrative, VD is more of an enemy than the U-boat. A special 'cadet's version' of the novel was prepared for younger readers. The book, though not the 1952 film, is graphic in its description of the horrors of drowning or burning alive in fuel oil spilled from torpedoed merchant ships. The war was close enough for novels like *The Cruel Sea* to be felt experiences, at least in the middle-aged segment of the population. In the *Listener* John Russell wrote: 'Awe, relief, gratitude and admiration are the feelings with which one closes this book.' It sold a million copies – record breaking for the time.

Other uniforms than khaki, air force and navy blue are found in popular fiction of the period. In 1948 the National Health Service came into being, and with it two new genres were born. One was the nurse–doctor romance with a hospital setting. The American pulp writer Max Brand had invented 'Dr Kildare' as a soap-opera character for American TV in the late 1940s; on British TV, the theme was picked up in *Emergency Ward 10*. The pioneer author of hospital romance was Lucilla Andrews, with titles such as *The Print Petticoat* (1954), *The Secret Armour* (1955), *The Quiet Wards* (1956) and *A Hospital Summer* (1958). Another popular hospital romancer from 1957 onwards was Kate Norway.

The second genre derived from the National Health Service was the everyday comedy of medical life. Most successful of this jolly type of novel was the series launched by Richard Gordon's *Doctor in the House* (1952), featuring the adventures of the ingenuous and newly qualified Simon Sparrow. Gordon's novels (*Doctor at Sea*, 1953; *Doctor at Large*, 1955; *Doctor in Love*, 1957) were bestsellers well into the 1960s, and after 1954 inspired a spin-off series of films starring Dirk Bogarde and (inevitably) Kenneth More. The 'cheerful chappie', insider's tone of the books (Gordon was a doctor turned novelist) looks forward to the similar achievements of the animal doctor James Herriot two decades later with *All Things Bright and Beautiful* and, further over the horizon, Father Ted. The newness (in political terms) of Gordon's medical world is summed up in the scene in which Sir Lancelot Spratt arrives in his Roller, the incarnation of 'private' practice, to bully and browbeat Sparrow and his pals, future doctors of the people.

The British people, an island race surrounded by water, were still cooped up by exchange controls on their island. The result was a compensatory lust for travel books – preferably with an admixture of high adventure. In *The Kon-Tiki Expedition*, published in 1950, the explorer Thor Heyerdahl took a balsawood raft across the oceans in an attempt to prove some far-fetched migration theories. Heinrich Harrer, not then known as a Nazi, recounted his seven years in Tibet. David Attenborough made the first of many expeditions memorialized in *Zoo Quest to Guiana* (1956). The ascent of Everest by Edmund Hillary and Sherpa Tensing, timed to coincide with the Coronation, was commemorated by the expedition's leader, Colonel John Hunt in 1953. A loyal bestseller.

The most disloyal bestsellers of the decade, as the establishment saw it, were the tell-all books by 'Crawfie', the former royal governess, who capitalized on the glamour of the royal family and the young princess who came to the throne in 1952 with: *The Little Princesses*

(1950), *The Queen Mother: A Study of Queen Mary* (1951), *Queen Elizabeth II* (1952) and *Princess Margaret* (1952).

Marion Crawford was a bright young Scot, trained at Edinburgh University's Moray House Training College, who had intended to become a child psychologist. In 1933 she was introduced to the then Duke and Duchess of York; they took to her. Miss Crawford agreed to take the position of nurse-governess to the princesses Elizabeth and Margaret, five and two at the time. She herself was twenty-five.

'Crawfie', as the little girls nicknamed her, was eminently sensible and good at her important but menial job. The schoolroom life she describes in her books is down to earth: plain food (afternoon teas with lemonade and rock cakes), a shilling a week pocket money, simple clothes, few treats. Crawfie was aided by 'Alah' (Mrs Knight, the nanny) and 'Bobo' (the nursemaid). There are cute descriptions of 'Lillibet's' (Princess Elizabeth's) early passion for horses. The York family spent quiet evenings at home, the Duke doing his petit point.

The royal grandparents, George V and Queen Mary, took a keen, if rather lofty, interest in the girls' education. George insisted that they should have good handwriting. Mary supervised timetables and syllabi. Miss Crawford described her as 'an immense help and comfort to me'; her suggestions were 'most welcome'. After the Duke's accession in 1936 life at Buckingham Palace was, however, less 'comfortable' than it had been in the Yorks' former residence at 145 Piccadilly. On 11 September 1939, a week after war was declared, Elizabeth wrote a holiday letter to Crawfie from Balmoral: 'What dreadful things have been happening lately. More history for children to learn in a hundred years.'

Miss Crawford occupied an honoured retainer's position until the publication of *The Little Princesses*, at which point she was cast into outer darkness forever. According to A. N. Wilson, in his foreword to the 1993 reissue of the book, all such acts of treachery were afterwards described by the royal family as 'doing a Crawfie'. Disloyal or not (it has been suggested that the book was authorized, clandestinely, by the princesses' mother), Crawfie's books sold massively. In her exile from favour, she went on to write a column on royalty for *Woman's Own* magazine in the 1950s. When she died in 1988, she willed all her royal memorabilia to the Queen.

The 1950s saw a notable elevation in the educational tone of Britain. In 1959, the Roberts Act imposed on local authorities the duty to provide a 'full and efficient' public library system. What this meant was a broad-band delivery system of 'good books' to the British population, juvenile and adult. For the book trade, the library sale (about 1200, countrywide, for the average hardback novel) created a kind of insurance policy. Risks could consequently be taken with new or unusual books. About 75 per cent of loans from public libraries were fiction (although these books accounted for only 25 per cent of purchases). With the paperback revolution of the 1960s, the new generation of public libraries which took over from the 2d (less than 1p) per loan corner shop were one of the two great popular educators of the post-war period. The newly strengthened public libraries were as momentous, culturally, as, in their spheres, the new NHS and the newly nationalized railways.

The most profound changes in the intellectual calibre of the reading public had, however, deeper historical roots than the post-war welfare state. The 1944 Education Act and the eleven-plus examination had opened to a whole new segment of society the advantages of grammar school education and, for the cleverest, even the privileges of university.

The rising generation of Jimmy Porters elbowed their way to the front of British society as 'new intellectuals' – 'egg-heads', as they were called at the time. John Osborne's hero in *Look Back in Anger* has, typically, got his education at a 'new' university that wasn't even 'red brick' but 'white tile'; like a 'public convenience', as he gracelessly snarls.

Education, as the nineteenth-century Conservatives had always argued, is an edge tool. It should be given to the lower classes very warily. By the mid-1950s the first generation of 'Butler kids', those who were eleven in 1944, were in their mid-twenties. They had missed the war – although they might well have been exposed to the bull and boredom of National Service. They had been issued their edge tools, and they used them, ungratefully slashing the philanthropic hands that had helped them up in the world. They were, one contemporary critic said, 'literary teddy boys' – teddy boys being the 1950s equivalent of lager louts, so-called for the Edwardian-style fashions they affected: outrageously pointed winkle-picker shoes, velvet collars and drainpipe trousers.

**Top** Reading in the bomb shelter, 1944. A decade later they will utilize their skills reading Ian Fleming or Georgette Heyer.
**Above** Graham Greene (right) relaxes with the film director Carol Reed who brought the novelist's *The Third Man*, *The Fallen Idol* and *Our Man in Havana* to the big screen.

**Above, top to bottom:**
A typical Mills & Boon
dustjacket of the 1950s;
Hank Janson (Steve Frances),
Britain's answer to Mickey
Spillane in the 1950s; and,
for the very youngest reader,
one of Enid Blyton's many
Noddy books.

**Above** The formidable
cookery writer Fanny
Cradock with henpecked
husband Johnnie at the
height of their popularity
in the early 1960s.
**Right** The groaning
table from the title page
of one of Elizabeth
David's bestselling
cookery books.
**Opposite** The famously
reticent Agatha Christie
signs copies of her novels
for French admirers.

**Above, top to bottom:**
The US paperback edition of
Britain's bestselling war novel
of the 1950s, *The Cruel Sea*;
enter 007 with *Casino Royale*
(1953); American crime
writer Raymond Chandler
became a cult among British
readers in the 1950s.

**Above** Yvonne Mitchell, Peter Cushing and André Morell in a still from
the 1954 BBC TV adaptation of George Orwell's *Nineteen Eighty-four*.
**Left** The *Daily Express* report of a Kent woman who dropped dead
while watching the TV 'horror play'.
**Below** 'I'm buying it for a friend.' A queue of eager people wait in the
November cold to buy the unexpurgated *Lady Chatterley's Lover* after
its acquittal at the Old Bailey.
**Opposite** The paperback revolution, spearheaded by 'Lady Chat'.
Penguin's edition went on to sell 2 million copies.

**Above** John Wyndham, the author of superior science fiction about the Cold War, much to British taste in the 1950s and 1960s.
**Below** Sue Lyon and James Mason in Stanley Kubrick's film adaptation of *Lolita*. Some critics thought she looked older than he did.
**Opposite** Hamish Hamilton's dustjacket for the British edition of *The Catcher in the Rye* – distinctly unlike New York.

Above, top to bottom:
John Wyndham's bestselling *The Day of the Triffids*; Frank Herbert's cult classic *Dune*; E. V. Rieu's million-selling translation of Homer for Penguin Classics.

**Above** The author and artist Tom Wolfe passing a New York subway entrance in 1966. Twenty-five years later he would satirize the city in *The Bonfire of the Vanities*.

In April 1956, as the drama critic Kenneth Tynan put it, the world changed with the first performance of *Look Back in Anger*. The Angry Young Man emerged. It was no accident that the event coincided with the Suez debacle and the resignation of the prime minister, Anthony Eden. It was the end of Empire. Whatever lingering pretensions Britain had to superpower status ('a seat at the top table') were brutally extinguished. Orders were changing. The 'Angries' even dared, in the glow of the 1953 Coronation, to be anti-monarchy (that golden tooth in the rotting mouth of England, as Osborne called it); although most publishers prudently clipped any obnoxious republicanism out of their angry authors' texts.

The salient features of the AYM genus were anger, youth and bubbling testosterone, but also ingratitude and, most worryingly, an ideology which was not just post-imperial but terroristic. The Soviet Union (rarely a source of subtle literary criticism) took a keen interest in the AYM phenomenon, seeing in it the hopeful early signs of the long-awaited English Revolution; Kingsley Amis's *Lucky Jim* reportedly sold 250,000 copies in Russian translation.

The principal ideologist of the movement – its Voltaire, or perhaps even its Lenin – was Colin Wilson. Typically, he came to public notice in a blaze of precocious brilliance and tabloid notoriety. Born in 1931 into a working-class family, Wilson was self-taught. He had not even been to a white-tile university. He spent his days, as Karl Marx had before him, in the British Museum Reading Room and camped out at night on Hampstead Heath.

A librarian at the BM, Angus Wilson (no relative, later a best-selling novelist) encouraged the strange young intellectual who dressed in what would become the AYM uniform: cords, wild hair (no Brylcreem) and big woolly jumper. In May 1956, a week after the first performance of Osborne's play at the Royal Court, Victor Gollancz published *The Outsider*, a sub-Dostoevskyan cogitation on alienation.

It was a shot in the dark on the publisher's part. Unless you were Bertrand Russell, philosophy did not sell. The author was twenty-four and a total unknown. None the less, *The Outsider* became an instant runaway bestseller. No post-war work of 'philosophy' (not all philosophers recognized it as such) sold better, faster, or – most importantly – more widely among the young. Within a year, the book had been translated into a dozen languages. Wilson was profiled in *Time* and *Life*. He was a star, a celebrity author. He was Jimmy Porter to the life.

Wilson's celebrity peaked into vulgar notoriety when, early in 1957, the irate father of the young lady he was living with burst in on the couple at a dinner party, horsewhip in hand – this, of course, is what every middle-class parent would have dearly liked to do to those rascally, long-haired Angry Young Men. The *Daily Mirror* was on the scene in minutes. Colin Wilson was on the tabloid front pages the next day. *The Outsider* sold even more copies.

In fiction, it is conventional to date the AYM movement as beginning with Kingsley Amis's anti-hero, Jim Dixon, in *Lucky Jim* (1954). Dixon, a second-rate 'don' at a third-rate redbrick university, is, in his way, a rebel, although his rebellion is largely restricted to a private gallery of gorilla faces, skiving, and authority-mocking voices.

It is just as plausible, however, to categorize *Lucky Jim* as Britain's first 'campus novel', a genre which was already well developed in America. And Amis's 'English' humour (more particularly his baroque comic effects, as when Jim awakes with a hangover, thinking some small creature of the night has made its mausoleum in his mouth – after first using it as an insect latrine) looks back to P. G. Wodehouse and Jerome K. Jerome. Whatever, *Lucky Jim* ranks as probably the funniest novel produced in the UK in the post-war period. Since 1954 it has sold consistently well, amassing huge long-term totals.

If *Lucky Jim* is the longest-selling AYM novel, the fastest-selling, in the 1950s, was John Braine's *Room at the Top*. Braine's novel, for all its 'shiny barbarism', as the cultural critic Richard Hoggart called it, has traditional aspects. It is a fable about 'growing towards the light': social mobility. The hero, Joe Lampton, is what the pop-sociologist of the 1950s, Vance Packard, would call a 'status seeker'.

We are introduced to the hero looking back from 1957 at himself ten years earlier. Lampton has arrived in a new northern town, determined to conquer it:

I came to Warley on a wet September morning with the sky the grey of Guiseley sandstone. I was alone in the compartment. I remember saying to myself: 'No more zombies, Joe, no more zombies.'

My stomach was rumbling with hunger and the drinks of the night before had left a buzzing in my head and a carbonated-water sensation in my nostrils. On that particular morning even these discomforts added to my pleasure.... My clothes were my Sunday best: a light grey suit that had cost fourteen guineas, a plain grey tie, plain grey socks, and brown shoes. The shoes were the most expensive I'd ever possessed, with a deep, rich, nearly black lustre. My trenchcoat and my hat, though, weren't up to the same standard; the coat, after only three months, was badly wrinkled and smelled of rubber, and the hat was faintly discoloured with hair oil and pinched to a sharp point in front.

Later, I learned, among other things, never to buy cheap raincoats, to punch the dents out of my hat before I put it away, and not to have my clothes match too exactly in shade and colour. But I looked well enough that morning ten years ago.

Over the following years he loses the brilliantine, the thick Yorkshire accent and, arguably, his 'soul'. Joe Lampton succeeds in his clamber to the top by brute energy and masculine charm; women are just so many sexual rungs on life's ladder. But, most of all, he succeeds because he is educated above his parents' station. Jude need be obscure no longer; 1944 has changed all that. The story of Lampton's rise in the world is as simple as something out of Samuel Smiles, the Victorian prophet of Self-Help and Self-Improvement. The difference is that Smiles never said it helped to be an utter bastard.

Braine (1922–87), a grammar school boy, worked as a librarian before becoming a famous writer. *Room at the Top*, his first novel, was turned down by four publishers before being accepted by Eyre & Spottiswoode. The book sold 5000 copies in its first week and earned Braine – who, as a librarian, was on £600 a year – £10,000 in two months. This, in 1957, was football-pool wealth. *Room at the Top* had sold getting on for 750,000 copies by the end of the 1950s, and was made into a film, starring Laurence Harvey, which won two Oscars.

Braine's novel generated lucrative spin-offs. The first film was followed by another tied-in novel and movie, *Life at the Top* (1963; Joe is cuckolded; who's sorry now?). The last throw was a 1970s TV mini-series, *Man at the Top*. This willingness to take more than one bite of a bestselling cherry was indicative of a growing book-trade trend in the 1950s.

One of the striking features in *Room at the Top* is its total repudiation of London and all that the Great Wen stands for. Joe is as much Yorkshire as that county's pudding and cricket team – not that he has much time for flannelled fools. This regional chauvinism was picked up in the next AYM blockbuster novel, Alan Sillitoe's *Saturday Night and Sunday Morning* (1958), a novel which, as the Pan paperback strapline put it, 'makes *Room at the Top* look like a vicar's tea party'.

Sillitoe's hero, Arthur Seaton, works at the Raleigh cycle factory in Nottingham. Like Joe, Arthur is a sexual buccaneer: he runs a married woman and an innocent lass simultaneously. He drinks to heroic excess (this is his 'Saturday Night'). Unlike Lampton, he does not rise on the social ladder. The 'top' does not call to him. At the end of the novel Arthur accepts his destiny as a working-class husband (Sunday, bloody Sunday). But his last utterance in the novel is ominous. This is not the last that British society will hear of Arthur Seaton:

> And trouble for me it'll be, fighting every day until I die. Why do they make soldiers out of us when we're fighting up to the hilt as it is? Fighting with mothers and wives, landlords and gaffers, coppers, army, government. If it's not one thing it's another, apart from the work we have to do and the way we spend our wages. There's bound to be trouble in store for me every day of my life, because trouble it's always been and always will be.

Sillitoe (b. 1928) refined his conception of working-class rebellion in *The Loneliness of the Long-Distance Runner* (1959, later brilliantly filmed with Tom Courtenay in the lead). Sillitoe's hero, a type popularized by Brendan Behan's 1958 autobiography, *Borstal Boy*, deliberately loses a cross-country race by stopping just short of the finishing tape. He will not play the system's games. More than that, he will do his best to sabotage those games. Sillitoe's hero, like Orwell's in *Nineteen Eighty-four*, is called 'Smith'. In other words, 'Everyman'.

Keith Waterhouse's AYM novel *Billy Liar* (1959) crossed Arthur Seaton with James Thurber's Walter Mitty. It, too, made a good film, starring Tom Courtenay and Julie Christie. In terms of literary quality, the most impressive (if grimmest) novel produced by the AYM school was David Storey's *This Sporting Life*. A miner, Arthur Machin, almost makes it to the top via the gladiatorial combat of northern Rugby League, only to be defeated and broken by the system and an insuperably frigid woman. The film made a star out of Richard Harris.

One of the many British institutions subjected to sceptical examination in AYM novels is marriage. Can Eustace Chesser's revered state of matrimony survive? Stan Barstow's *A Kind of Loving* (1960) is sceptical on the subject. Vic Brown, an upwardly mobile factory office worker, gets a working-class girl, Ingrid, pregnant ('in the pudding club', as the homely idiom of the time put it). Vic has the Faustian choice: marriage and 'the ball and chain', or freedom? He does the 'right thing', but very grudgingly. Life, he concludes, 'is no fairy tale'. Ten years later, one suspects, he might have jumped the other way – but ten years later Ingrid would have been on the Pill.

The AYM was a short-lived school. But the surly *non serviam* (up yours) mood which it articulated would crystallize into the satire and anti-Establishment movements of the 1960s. Across the Atlantic, the AYM hero is partnered by the Beatnik, immortalized in Sal Paradise, Carlo Marx and Dean Moriarty, the heroes of Jack Kerouac's *On the Road*. Kerouac's novel, published in September 1957, is virtually simultaneous with Braine's. But whereas Lampton wears a Bogart outfit (trenchcoat and fedora) picked up from 1940s *film noir*, Kerouac's guys wear faded jeans, workmen's shirts and sneakers. They have rucksacks on their back, and a joint hanging from their lips. They tumble along, like the tumbling tumbleweed. They owe their style, in short, to the Western, or cowboy movie. It would be a year or two before the British reading public – and British youth – caught up with the Beats.

The problem for heroes like Lampton, Seaton, Porter and Dixon is essentially E. M. Forster's 'Only Connect'. How can they retain the authenticity of their 'roots' – their class origins – and, at the same time, rise in the world? Does one not lose more than one gains in deserting one's class? Is Joe not – underneath all that flash and violence – just an old-fashioned snob, an oick with ideas above his station? This problem was pondered in the bestselling work of British popular sociology of the 1950s (another title of 1957, *annus mirabilis*), Richard Hoggart's *The Uses of Literacy*.

Hoggart (another Yorkshireman, born in 1918, educated at a Yorkshire University, Leeds, and teaching at Jim Dixon's university, Leicester) saw British culture as threatened by a number of sinisterly conspiring forces. The expansion of mass education – begun with Forster's Universal Education Act of 1870 and culminating with the Butler Act of 1944 – had spread literacy. But literacy for what? Papers like *Reveille* with their triviality and masturbatory pin-ups? Sex-and-violence pulps like Hank Janson's and Mickey Spillane's?

In the same book Hoggart wrote sensitively about the plight of the 'scholarship boy', the privileged but deracinated working-class beneficiary of grammar school education:

> He cannot go back; with one part of himself he does not want to go back to a homeliness which was often narrow; with another part he longs for the membership he has lost, 'he pines for some Nameless Eden where he never was'. The nostalgia is the stronger and the more ambiguous because he is really 'in quest of his own absconded self yet scared to find it'. He both wants to go back and yet thinks he has gone beyond his own class.

Hoggart articulated the discontents of a whole generation of newly arrived middle-class young Britons – more importantly, he gave them a way of making intellectual sense of their plight. It was a plight made more anxious by Nancy Mitford's witty lexicons in *Noblesse Oblige* (1956) of 'U' and 'Non-U' speech. 'Toilet' or 'lavatory'? 'Napkin' or 'serviette'? It was class suicide to choose the wrong usage.

The working-class heroes of the Angry Young Man movement exude a pugnacity wholly lacking in J. D. Salinger's self-pitying young man, Holden Caulfield. None the less, *The Catcher in the Rye* (1951) has lasted long in the all-time English-speaking-world bestseller lists (where, in fiction, it currently ranks around no.15), principally by virtue of its attractions as a school text. Late attractions, one should add. When Salinger's novel first came out in Britain it was regarded as unfit even for adult readers in its unvarnished American form. Some five hundred changes were made by the publisher Hamish Hamilton to the American text, to accommodate stricter British standards about such things as the F-word (even when so bowdlerized).

When we first encounter him, with those memorably surly opening words, 'If you *really* want to hear about it', Caulfield is running away from his exclusive East Coast boarding school. He is actually running, of course, from middle-class, 'affluent' America. His destiny. The story covers the subsequent few days of his doomed flight from the 'phoney' world towards the duck pond in Central Park, a place associated in his mind with childhood happiness. (It was here that the demented Mark Chapman, for whom *Catcher* was a sacred text, would, thirty years later, assassinate John Lennon.) We finally deduce that Holden is telling his experiences not to us, the paying public, but to some highly paid therapist. His shrink. Will he grow up less mixed up? Unhappily, Salinger has never given us a sequel – although, legend has it, there is one locked in his safe, in his reclusive New Hampshire home.

Holden is, in the parlance of the 1950s, not just 'mixed up' but a 'crazy mixed-up kid'. For 'kid' read 'adolescent'. Adolescence, as a social concept, took off with the psychologist G. Stanley Hall's books on the topic in the early twentieth century. As a hot-button topic in popular culture the heroically confused adolescent is a post-World War II phenomenon. As a defector from the world of his parents, Caulfield is the principal character in the first in a line of 'I narrative' (i.e. confessional) books, in which a young person more or less defiantly spills their guts to the reader: Anthony Burgess's *A Clockwork Orange* (1961, sensationally filmed by Stanley Kubrick ten years later) and Jeanette Winterson's *Oranges Are Not the Only Fruit* (1985) are the best of the genre. Burgess's hero drops out from his decent middle-class family life to become the teenage leader of a gang of ultra-violent 'droogs'. The heroine of Winterson's confessional work defects from her mother's extreme religious sect to become a lesbian and a writer. The significant feature in these books, and many like them, is that the moment of truth in life – the point at which a life-changing decision has to be made – is in the teens.

Sometimes that moment occurs even younger, as in Colin MacInnes's tract for the late 1950s, *Absolute Beginners* (1958).

MacInnes, in the way that good writers often do, saw the youth revolution of the 1960s coming. More importantly his novel, and others like it, performed an invaluable social service by showing the rebel ('juvenile delinquent', 'teddy boy', 'dropout') from the inside, sympathetically. Writers like Salinger, Burgess, Winterson and MacInnes (none themselves 'absolute beginners' when they wrote their novels) give youth a soul and a sensibility. As Linda says in Arthur Miller's 1949 play, *Death of a Salesman*, 'Attention must be paid.' These novels pay it.

Novels like *Nineteen Eighty-four* and *The Catcher in the Rye* have sold over the decades by virtue of being adopted as classroom reading matter. The same eligibility as a provocative UK sixth-form or US twelfth-grade 'discussion' text has put William Golding's *Lord of the Flies* (1954) in the category of long-term supersellers; in 2002 it still sells around 250,000 copies annually. Golding's novel up-ends the optimism of Ballantyne's optimistic fable of Victorian colonialism, *The Coral Island*. The tale of a group of English schoolboys, with no adults to supervise them, reverting to savagery on their 'idyllic' desert island, *Lord of the Flies* is also a kind of reverse *Colditz Story*. The English virtues of decency, comradeship and pluck are not inextinguishable. They are skin-deep. Golding had difficulty getting this first novel published and it was poorly reviewed on publication – 'dull and tendentious' was the general verdict. The book has outlived its early critics and survives as one of the twenty all-time bestselling novels of the twentieth century.

Golding's dystopia opens with an atomic war; the children are being evacuated to the safety of Australia when their plane is shot down. Since the USSR had acquired 'the Bomb', in 1949, the world had lived under the shadow of the four-minute warning. The end was very nigh. The two superpowers possessed enough nuclear weaponry to annihilate all living things on the planet apart, zoologists hypothesized, from some hardy cockroaches and molluscs buried deep in estuary slime.

Nuclear anxiety accounts for the sales success of the most popular practitioner of British science fiction in the 1950s, John Wyndham. Wyndham specialized in what Brian Aldiss called, memorably, 'the cosy catastrophe'. Holocaust, that is, which none the less ends happily with the family still together, 'bonded' even closer by crisis. Apocalypse has a silver lining.

John Benyon (1903–69) – Wyndham was a *nom de plume* – made various false starts in life before embarking on writing sf for American pulps in the 1920s and 1930s. He served in the Army during World War II. On demob, in 1946, he began writing sf again – but now for a middle-class readership. His first success was with *The Day of the Triffids* (1951). In that novel the population of the world is blinded by laser beam satellites in space; Wyndham, like Arthur C. Clarke, anticipated 'Sputnik'. A synthetic and horribly intelligent plant, the Triffid, takes over, destroying and consuming humanity. The Triffid, of course, is a descendant of H. G. Wells's Morlocks in *The Time Machine*: sf is the most light-fingered of genres. In an early version of the story, run in America, the deadly Triffids originate in Russia. Vegetable nukes. In the UK, *The Day of the Triffids* was published a couple of weeks before the Attlee government fell. Some readers saw its vision of a ruined, post-apocalypse Britain as an allegory of the abject failure of the welfare state.

Wyndham followed up with his best novel, *The Kraken Wakes*, in 1953. The title is taken from Tennyson's poem about a mysterious, sleeping, undersea monster that no human has ever seen – nor is it seen in Wyndham's narrative. Having been woken by mankind's nuclear explosions, the Kraken acquires atomic weaponry and sets off what we know as global warming, by melting the ice caps and flooding out the human race.

In *The Chrysalids* (1955, set in New Zealand), the human race has reverted to sadistic Puritanism in order to purge itself of genetic mutations after nuclear war. There is an echo here of Nevil Shute's 1957 post-nuclear fantasy, *On the Beach*, which was successfully filmed in 1959. In Shute's fantasy, a colony in the antipodes has a few months' grace before the clouds of nuclear contamination arrive to destroy them. How will they spend that brief reprieve? In *The Midwich Cuckoos* (1957), the most charming of Wyndham's novels, invaders from space ('body snatchers', as the 1956 film would call them) impregnate, simultaneously, all the fertile women in a village that is suspiciously like the Archers' Ambridge. The novel has been twice filmed, in heavy-handed fashion, under the melodramatic title *Village of the Damned*.

What is striking about Wyndham's science fiction is its witty scenarios, its Cold War resonances and its literary quality; not surprisingly, he was taken up in the 1960s by Penguin – the book trade's most honorific seal of approval. In literary historical terms he did what Ray Bradbury did in America with his *Martian Chronicles* (1951) and *Fahrenheit 451* (1954). He made science fiction respectable to readers for whom it was a déclassé genre associated with giant ants, little green men and Flash Gordon doing battle with Ming the Merciless. But, as Aldiss points out, the salient feature of a Wyndham scenario is its reassuring sense that England, middle-class England, can survive – even the four-minute warning and nuclear catastrophe. A much bleaker scenario is projected in J. G. Ballard's 1960s 'catastrophe' novels (among them *The Drowned World* and *The Drought*). No survivors in that wasteland.

The belief that British 'quality' – as Paul Brickhill puts it in *The Dambusters* – can compensate for superpower 'quantity' is at the heart of Ian Fleming's ultra-English Bond books, the first of which, *Casino Royale*, came out in 1953. James Bond would be the most successful British series hero since Sherlock Holmes. Fleming's fantasies of omnipotent British style were emotional balm for a country which had, as the unkind American politician put it, lost an empire and not yet found a role.

Ian Fleming (1908–64) in his early forties, with Eton, Sandhurst and a good war in naval intelligence behind him, found himself at a loose end. He set about becoming a bestselling author methodically. He read John Buchan, Peter Cheyney (a now forgotten hack, in vogue as a thriller writer in the 1930s and 1940s) and Edgar Wallace ('King of the Thrillers'). The strongest influence was Sapper's (the *nom de plume* of H. C. McNeile) Bulldog Drummond – one of the so-called 'clubland thugs' popular in 1930s low-brow fiction.

The resulting concoction, James Bond, was partly Richard Hannay, a kind of 'counterspy', and partly Raffles, the consummate, urbane, 'perfect English gentleman'. But he was professional in ways that these amateur heroes of popular fiction were not. Bond is not just James Bond (Fettes and Oxford) but 007 – the double zero denoting the licence to kill, a soldier of the Queen. He is as much a serving member of the armed services as the guardsman outside Buckingham Palace.

Fleming was lucky that during his wartime service at the Admiralty he had made friends at the distinguished publishing house of Jonathan Cape. Cape's imprint (after much soul-searching) on these 'shockers' gave the Bond books a unique seal of approval. In the 1960s Cape would publish Len Deighton; by that time spy fiction was modish and chic. It was Fleming, principally, who had made it so.

Bestselling fiction, especially 'genre' or 'category' fiction, is marked by 'me-tooism'. There is rarely anything genuinely novel in these novels. *Casino Royale*, when it appeared in 1953, struck a genuinely fresh note, even with its opening sentence: 'The scent and smoke and sweat of a casino are nauseating at three o'clock in the morning.' 'Three O'clock in the Morning' was the title of a smoochy popular song of the period. It suggested huge nocturnal depravity. The British, in 1954, were an early-to-bed race, if only to save on the electricity bills. TV, for example, signed off – with the Queen and cocoa, or Horlicks for the insomniac – at ten o'clock; radio an hour later. Casinos were as unknown in Britain as opium dens, and just as frightening. Not until the gaming acts of the 1960s and 1970s would even the lowly betting shop become a feature on the British landscape. A million Britons would buy *Casino Royale* within five years. Fewer than one in ten thousand would have, with their own nostrils, snuffed the heady casino stench that Fleming describes.

In fact, this first Bond novel was slow to take off. After fifteen months in the bookshops it had sold only 8000 copies. But it did well enough to encourage the novelist to write a string of sequels. *Casino Royale* was followed, in swift succession, by *Live and Let Die* (1954), *Moonraker* (1955), *Diamonds Are Forever* (1956), *From Russia with Love* (1957; Fleming's initial intention was to kill off Bond with this title), *Doctor No* (1958), *Goldfinger* (1959), *For Your Eyes Only* (1960), *Thunderball* (1961), *The Spy who Loved Me* (1962), *On Her Majesty's Secret Service* (1963) and *You Only Live Twice* (1965).

Over the ten years of his writing life (he was only in his fifties when he died) Fleming's books would sell an estimated 40 million copies. Their cultish appeal was immensely enhanced when President Kennedy listed them among his favourite reading in a 1961 article in *Life* magazine. Their popularity was extended to a mass audience by the string of films which began in 1962 with *Doctor No*, starring

Sean Connery as 007. With the films, sales of the novels rocketed. Fleming was, in the early 1960s, earning over £250,000 a year in royalties. By the summer of 1964, nine of the Bond titles in their Pan paperback form had sold over a million copies apiece. Some 21 million Bond books were in circulation in the English-speaking world.

The films played up the jokily 'sophisticated' aspect of the novels – to the point of self-parody when the part was taken over by Roger Moore and, much later, to ultra-parody in Mike Myers's delightful spoof, *Austin Powers*. The films sustained the Bond boom long past the death of his creator; though they did not enrich Fleming himself, who signed away the rights for a pittance. The books were posthumously continued by other hands – most successfully by John Gardner and Fleming's most eloquent admirer, Kingsley Amis.

The Bond narratives are rigidly formulaic. Typically they open with 007 'going to pieces, slowly'. The only thing that will revive him is action. Action of an extravagantly demanding kind duly presents itself. He is called on to save the civilized world. Bond 'pulls himself together'; girds his loins (loins, for a certainty, will be much exercised in the action to come). This is what Kingsley Amis called the 'sit down 007' phase, as his superior, 'M', briefs him on the next mission impossible. The game is afoot. It quickly becomes a duel to the death with some dastardly (and invariably foreign) criminal mastermind (Blofeld, Doctor No, Drax, Goldfinger, Largo, Mr Big) or sinister (invariably foreign) organization (SMERSH or SPECTRE).

The plot is (invariably) mind-boggling. Goldfinger, for example, aims to steal all the gold in Fort Knox. Hugo Drax in *Moonraker* and Emilio Largo in *Thunderball* intend to visit atomic destruction on British and American cities. In *On Her Majesty's Secret Service* Ernst Blofeld intends to infect Britain with a virus which will wipe out its crops and livestock (there had recently been a devastating foot and mouth outbreak in Britain). In *You Only Live Twice* the gloriously indestructible Blofeld is enlivening his retirement by enticing Japanese depressives to commit suicide *en masse* in his garden of poisonous plants.

The struggle will be enlivened by beautiful (and willingly warm) women, ice-cold martinis (famously shaken, not stirred), five-star hotels and three-star meals, sophisticated gambling with the high rollers, and probably some ingenious torture (after his death, Fleming was revealed to be a flagellomaniac: he was, after all, an Etonian). As Amis points out, 'no woman can hold Bond'. He holds several, to their great satisfaction. He even converts the lesbian Pussy Galore in *Goldfinger* to straight sex; Oddjob, the homicidal Korean butler, is a pushover by comparison. Bond marries only once and his bride, Tracy, is shot dead almost before the marriage is consummated – would he have remained faithful, one wonders?

There were, of course, the inevitable denunciations of Fleming's hero. The *Spectator* labelled Bond, in its review of the film of *Doctor No*, as 'every intellectual's favourite fascist' (whether the Conservative magazine disliked intellectuals more than fascists was uncertain). In the *New Statesman*, in 1958, Paul Johnson launched his notorious 'Sex, Sadism, and Snobbery' assault on the Bond novels. They celebrated, Johnson sneered, 'the sadism of a schoolboy bully, the mechanical two-dimensional sex-longings of a frustrated adolescent, and the crude, snob cravings of a suburban adult'. And, of course, they sold by the ton. The *New Statesman* should have been so lucky.

At the deepest level, James Bond is a chauvinist creation. He incarnates the sense that John Bull may be the smaller dog, nowadays, perhaps even the underdog. But his bite is that of a superdog. Bond is not just sexier and more stylish but smarter than his big American (or even Soviet) counterpart. British readers devoured the Bond books and felt great again. And again. And again.

One of the odder outcomes of the Cold War was the Russian invasion of the American bestseller lists and, to a lesser but still considerable extent, the UK popular market. In 1957–8, three heavyweight novels fought it out at the top of the charts. The most influential, in terms of ideas, was Ayn Rand's *Atlas Shrugged*. Rand, a youthful exile from the Soviet Union, loathed everything that had happened in her native country since 1917. Her book is a ferocious vindication of market capitalism. Vaguely science fiction, and overwhelmingly a treatise, it fantasizes the 'wealth creators' of America – the CEOs, bosses and managers – going on strike. They will no longer, like Atlas, carry the load. The novel ends with a capitalist sermon delivered by Rand through her hero, John Galt. Rand's novel popularized her philosophical school, Objectivism, and recruited disciples, including the young Alan Greenspan, for years afterwards. It never, however, made the same inroads in the UK (although, one may suspect, Mrs Thatcher was sympathetic to Rand's tenets). When Rand died, her coffin was decorated, by her own instruction, with a gigantic floral dollar bill.

At the top of the cumulative 1958 American bestseller list is Boris Pasternak's *Doctor Zhivago*. This novel, which was effectively smuggled out of the Soviet Union, was written by one of the few great writers in the state who had survived Stalin's savage purges. It is, essentially, a narrative of love, survival and ultimate loss during Revolution. Optimists saw the fact that Khrushchev's regime tolerated its publication as welcome signs of a 'thaw'; though some, like Nabokov, suspected that the smuggling out of the book was a put-up job by Moscow.

The novel won Pasternak a Nobel Prize – which he could not go to Stockholm to collect, any more than he could collect his vast royalties. *Doctor Zhivago* was, partly as a result of all this publicity, one of the bestselling novels of the year in the UK. It went through eleven printings and was serialized in the *Daily Express* (which cannot have pleased the Kremlin). The novel's long-term popularity was ensured by David Lean's epic 1965 film, starring Omar Sharif as the hero and Julie Christie as his lifelong love, Lara.

Close behind *Doctor Zhivago*, at no.3 on the 1958 list, was Vladimir Nabokov's *Lolita*, whose publishing history was as complicated as that of Pasternak's novel. Nabokov (1899–1977) wrote his study of an obsessed paedophile in the early 1950s. Despite the clear literary merit, no American publisher would touch this journal of a middle-aged pervert seducing (raping?) his twelve-year-old stepdaughter ('Do you think I'm mad?' one of them retorted).

To get it into print Nabokov was obliged to place his novel with the notorious Parisian publisher of 'dirty books', Maurice Girodias, whose Olympia Press also had Henry Miller, William Burroughs and D. H. Lawrence on its list. *Lolita* came out in the French capital in 1955. Its literary qualities persuaded an American publishing house to take the risk of bringing it out in the USA three years later. *Lolita* was banned by innumerable public libraries, but Putnam were rewarded with huge sales. For six months (until, to Nabokov's chagrin, it was displaced by *Doctor Zhivago*) it was the bestselling novel in America. It would be a year before any British publisher would touch it, although many British tourists consumed the book's forbidden prose in France. The movie rights from *Lolita* enabled Nabokov, an expatriate Russian who hated the USSR as cordially as, if less ideologically than, Rand, to retire from his teaching position at Cornell University. Stanley Kubrick paid a hefty $150,000; the film, starring James Mason and a decently post-pubescent Sue Lyon, came out in 1962.

By the mid-1950s, austerity had receded in Britain. Things were looking up. Who knew – one might even oneself get to drink a martini (shaken, not stirred), smoke Balkan Sobranie and eat coquilles St Jacques at the Ritz. Certainly snoek and Woodbines were things of the past, for the middle classes at least. None the less, general prosperity did not bring all the expected results. It was not what H. G. Wells had promised in *The Shape of Things to Come* – a gleaming utopia. As individuals of every social class in Britain got richer, better fed and more lavishly entertained (by now they had indeed, as Harold Macmillan said, never had it so good), somehow the country, particularly its cities, looked shabbier.

The paradox was explained, wittily, by J. K. Galbraith (b. 1908) in what would be the bestselling work of popular economics of the decade, *The Affluent Society* (1958). Among the many terms which were put into circulation by pop-sociology and pop-economics in the 1950s and 1960s – 'organization man', 'man in a grey flannel suit', 'power elite', 'military industrial complex' – the most influential and current was 'affluent'.

With his paradox of 'private affluence and public squalor' Galbraith put the economic problem of the age succinctly: you could have individual wealth or public services. Not both. Which did Britain want? A good car and poor railways? A plush house and filthy streets? Or vice versa. It was a dilemma in which the electorate were caught between the futures offered first by Harold Wilson and then by Margaret Thatcher until, finally, settling on the 'third way' of Tony Blair which cannily promised (but did not deliver) both.

If Galbraith's was the cleverest popular book of the 1950s, the worthiest was Trevor Huddleston's *Naught for Your Comfort* (1956), a work which brought the outrage of South African apartheid to the notice of the British reading public. In the same year as the book's publication the Revd Huddleston, who had worked as a priest in the

47

African township of Sophiatown, was banned from South Africa. As Archbishop Desmond Tutu later put it: 'If I had to choose one person who got the anti-apartheid movement onto the world stage, that person would be Trevor Huddleston without a doubt.' And he did it with a book.

The mid-1950s saw the emergence of the bestselling 'non-book' – that is, the book which was really about nothing at all but which everyone wanted to read, or at least purchase. The most successful was *The Guinness Book of Records*. The founding idea for this all-conquering non-book came to Sir Hugh Beaver of the Guinness Brewery, in 1951. He got embroiled in friendly controversy over whether the golden plover was the fastest game bird on the wing. Sir Hugh noted, sagely (with a glance at the huge vats of his local brew), that 'records were just the things that started pub and bar arguments all over the world and it was about time that somebody produced a book full of records to settle this kind of dispute'. Who had eaten the most goldfish in an hour? What was the maximum number of adults ever jammed into a VW automobile? Who has the longest moustache in the world? No more need drinkers argufy over such questions.

The McWhirter twins, Norris and Ross, were commissioned to compile the first *Guinness Book of Records*, which appeared in 1955. The book was given edge by Roger Bannister's four-minute mile, achieved the year before. The UK was interested in records, particularly when Britons (God Save the Queen) broke them. The first issue comprised a mere two-hundred pages and cost 5s (25p). Guinness took a huge punt with a first print run of 50,000 copies. W. H. Smith was not in the punting mood. They initially ordered six copies, nationwide. Within a week, they upped their order to 10,000. Within a year, sales had soared to almost 200,000. A US version was produced, called *The Guinness Book of Superlatives*. It sold well in Irish Boston. In time *The Guinness Book of Records* would itself merit a place in *The Guinness Book of Records* as 'the world's all-time bestselling copyright book', selling 20 million copies in twenty years.

# 2

The 60s

LADY CHATTERLEY'S LOVER, an ostentatiously 'literary' novel of the late 1920s, became the all-time bestseller of the early 1960s. 'Sleepers' one has heard of; 'Lady Chat' was the Rip van Winkle of popular books. D. H. Lawrence (hopefully, but without serious hope) had tried his paean to 'John Thomas and Lady Jane', the English penis and vagina, on English publishers in 1930. All turned it down. The British authorities did not look kindly on purveyors of filth – or, in the legalese of the day, books with a 'tendency to deprave and corrupt'.

Lawrence eventually published his last novel in depraved and corrupted Paris, where it became an instant off-shore bestseller. English tourists lined up to buy: 'Lady Chat' ranked with the Folies Bergère and Montmartre as one of the naughty pleasures of the French capital. All this changed when in 1959 Roy Jenkins successfully introduced his Obscene Publications Bill. The Jenkins Act, as it was popularly known, decreed that if a dirty book could be shown to have 'redeeming social merit' it might none the less be published. How to ascertain that saving merit? Expert witnesses, 'sexperts', would be called to pronounce on the matter. Similar legislation had recently got *Lady Chatterley's Lover* and much else into print and runaway bestsellerdom in the USA.

It was a sign of changing *mores* in the UK when Weidenfeld & Nicolson had, in 1959, published *Lolita*. Despite its paedophile narrator-hero, the book escaped prosecution. It was prudently published in hardback, at the then sky-high price of 22s 6d (£1.12½). It helped that Nabokov's refined pervert never uses four-letter words, nor does Humbert describe his crimes other than in a hyper-literary way. Take, for example, this description of his groping his sub-teen step-daughter:

> The day before she had collided with the heavy chest in the hall and – 'Look!, look!' – I gasped – 'look what you've done,

49

what you've done to yourself, ah, look'; for there was, I
swear, a yellowish-violet bruise on her lovely nymphet thigh
which my huge hairy hand massaged and slowly enveloped –
and because of her very perfunctory underthings, there
seemed to be nothing to prevent my muscular thumb from
reaching the hot hollow of her groin – just as you might tickle
and caress a giggling child – just that.

Despite the meringue-like fineness of the prose, *Lolita* went through
four editions in a year. It was not the prose, perhaps, that the mass of
readers were after.

Penguin, among the most venerable of British publishers, resolved
in 1960 to commemorate the thirtieth anniversary of D. H. Lawrence's
death with a ten-volume set of his works. They further resolved
to include in it *Lady Chatterley's Lover*. It helped that Lawrence's
book had been written with a defiantly moralistic intention: to
'hygienize' English attitudes to sex. As he put it in an accompanying
essay on the book, 'That ghastly crudity of seeing in sex nothing but
a functional act and a certain fumbling with clothes is, in my opinion,
a low degree of barbarism, savagery. As far as sex goes, our white
civilization is crude, barbaric, and uglily savage: especially England
and America.'

The provocative element was that Penguin's 1960 paperback edition
of *Lady Chatterley's Lover* would, unlike *Lolita*, cost only 3s 6d (17½p).
This meant that the man in the street – the millions of men in any
British street, not even a back street – might buy it.

Allen Lane's firm played their Chatterley game cleverly. They
stored 200,000 copies of the novel in their warehouse and dispatched
twelve early copies to the Director of Public Prosecutions, challenging
him to prosecute. The great machine of English law duly obliged, and
the trial was set for November 1960. Prosecuting was Mervyn Griffith-
Jones, who had successfully done Hank Janson five years before.
His method was the same for *Lady Chatterley's Lover*. If this were
not a dirty book, pray, what was? The text contained, the pedantic
Griffith-Jones calculated: '30 "fucks" or "fuckings"; 14 "cunts"; 13
"balls"; 6 each of "shit" and "arse"; 4 "cocks" and 3 "piss"'. Less a
novel than a lavatory wall, or so the prosecution contended.

In his opening address to the jury, Griffith-Jones delivered himself of the legendary rhetorical question: 'Is this a book that you would have lying around in your own house? Is it a book that you would even wish your wife or your servants to read?'

The defence, backed up by thirty-five expert witnesses, testified more cunningly to the wholesomeness of Lawrence's novel. The prophet of the phallus wanted merely to make sex clean again – to purify the fine old Anglo-Saxonisms so pedantically catalogued as 'filth' by Griffith-Jones. The love between Lady Connie and her game-keeper, Mellors, was not, the Bishop of Woolwich (John Robinson) testified, 'adultery'. No, no. It was 'an act of holy communion', even though the Church of England as yet had no liturgy to cover their bonking in the woods.

After twelve days of courtroom argument and front-page headlines *Lady Chatterley's Lover* was acquitted. Handcuffs dropped from the wrists of every author in England. They could now deprave and corrupt at will. There had been huge publicity for the trial. It was a standby topic for cartoonists, comedians and leader writers for weeks. You could raise a laugh simply by saying the word 'gamekeeper'.

*Lady Chatterley's Lover* sold 2 million for Penguin in two years. Before people became brazen about displaying it, copies were passed over the counter in plain brown bags ('discretion assured,' as the phrase went). The Chatterley Trial, about which C. H. Rolph wrote a bestselling 'special' for Penguin, was followed by a series of other prosecutions against John Cleland's eighteenth-century 'erotic' master-piece, *Fanny Hill* (1963); Alexander Trocchi's bawdy Bildungsroman, *Cain's Book* (1964); William Burroughs's 'Beat' classic, *Naked Lunch* (1964); and Hubert Selby Jr's ultra-violent *Last Exit to Brooklyn* (1968). The trend was, with a few hiccups, as with *Oz 28*, the 'schoolkids' issue, in 1971, one-way: towards 'liberation'.

The 1960s was a decade of 'liberation' in other areas than books. In the UK National Service, with its hated conformity and discipline, was finished (with Vietnam looming, the 'draft' would continue in the USA, poisoning relations between the generations). Hair sprouted and cascaded, rebelliously, from young male heads. Legs extended, endlessly, from female mini-skirts. Footballers, those working-class heroes, successfully broke the terms of contract that had kept them to a maximum of £20 a week (how bizarre that serfdom of Beckham's predecessors now seems). Civil Rights legislation in America in 1964 would – nominally, at least – emancipate previously persecuted minorities including women, who were in fact a 51 per cent majority. In 1967, the Sexual Offences Act in the UK would legalize homosexual intercourse between consenting adults.

Young people wanted things that had previously been the privilege of their elders: cars, stylish clothes, gramophone records – above all, sex (sex rendered, at last, 'free' by virtue of Carl Djerassi's contraceptive pill). A sign of the times – more specifically of how far you could go – is evident in the rise and fall of *The Little Red Schoolbook*, originally published in Denmark in the late 1960s. Denmark had been a pioneer in liberalizing laws. When Lord Longford (alias 'Lord Porn') went there in the mid-1960s to research his report on the deleterious effects of pornography, he claimed to have found a Danish farm where animals could be hired for sexual purposes. Could degradation sink further? (Yes, alas.)

*The Little Red Schoolbook* was translated and published (208 pages, 3s or 15p) in Britain by an underground publisher, Richard Handyside, whose list contained titles by Fidel Castro and Che Guevara – Handyside was radical. The 'Little Red Book' of the title alluded, provocatively, to the manual written by Chairman Mao for his young Red Guards. The British version had sold some 50,000 copies by 1971. It told children what their 'rights' were and advised them on how to resist adult tyranny. It described, soberly, how drugs might be safely used. Most provocatively, *The Little Red Schoolbook* gave instruction on advanced techniques of masturbation. On pornography it sagely recommended that 'it is quite possible that you can get some good ideas from it and may find something interesting that you have not tried before.'

This was too much for Mary Whitehouse, the decade's *censor librorum*, who alerted the police. Scotland Yard raided Handyside's premises and charges were brought before the Clerkenwell magistrates in April 1971. British publishers formed a defence league. *The Little Red Schoolbook* was defended by John Mortimer, QC, who later, in 1978, created the bestselling character 'Rumpole of the Bailey' – a wry self-portrait; in 1971 he was simultaneously defending *Oz 28*, the 'schoolkids' issue, at the Central Criminal Court. Despite all efforts, Handyside was convicted and fined, largely because *The Little Red Schoolbook* did not make clear that in the UK, unlike Scandinavia, the age of consent for young women was sixteen. Mrs Whitehouse declared herself 'greatly relieved'. An 'immensely depressed' Handyside brought out an expurgated edition of his book in November, which relieved his depression by promptly selling 100,000 copies. This trial, and the concurrent *Oz 28* trial (which Mortimer also gallantly lost) signalled what was the hot-button issue, even in a decade of wholesale 'liberation': young children and sex.

Liberation, as it advanced, stretched the gap between generations to breaking point. As Philip Larkin (1922–85) glumly put it, in his late 1960s poem 'This Be the Verse':

Sexual intercourse began
In nineteen sixty-three
(Which was rather too late for me) –
Between the end of the Chatterley ban
And the Beatles' first LP.

Despite his gloom, Larkin, boosted by his popularity with English teachers and examination boards, would enjoy three decades of fame as Britain's most admired poet and unofficial laureate – few Britons in the 1960s could have named the official laureate, Cecil Day Lewis. Even so, his sales demonstrated that 'popular poetry' was, in the late twentieth century, a gross contradiction in terms. Larkin's most popular volume, *The Whitsun Weddings*, came out in February 1963. Published by Faber's, the slim volume sold 4000 copies in its first two months. Over the next six years, *The Whitsun Weddings* sold a further 9000. These were handsome sales – for poetry.

Poetry remained the runt in the literary litter, as it had been for most of the twentieth century. John Betjeman, a future laureate in 1972, did well with his blank-verse autobiography *Summoned by Bells* (1960), which made W. H. Smith's annual bestseller list. Betjeman (1906–84) was, the nation discovered, a natural on television. His eccentricities (a love of teddy bears, for example) and his crusading devotion to preserving the England he loved (Euston Railway Station, Victorian Gothic churches and the suburban amenities of Miss Joan

Hunter Dunn, famously) endeared him to many more Britons than would have counted themselves serious readers of poetry. He abhorred what he called 'ghastly good taste'.

The demotic 'Liverpool poets' Roger McGough, Adrian Henri and Brian Patten enjoyed a more glitzy success in the late 1960s on the coat-tails of the city's mop-haired pop group. Their groupy anthologies, *The Liverpool Scene* and *The Mersey Sound* (both 1967), sold well. Whether they would have done so had it not been for the Beatles' first LP is another matter. None the less, the Liverpool poets recruited a new audience for verse with lively public performances, very different from the traditional, church-like 'poetry reading'. In the USA Rod McKuen and Allen Ginsberg demonstrated that, if you targeted the young, poetry might, like rock and roll, attract huge crowds.

None of these poets achieved the sales of the lyricist-turned-comic belletrist John Lennon, with his superselling surrealist fantasias *In His Own Write* (1964) and *A Spaniard in the Works* (1965). These books, as well as testifying to the author's fascination with Salvador Dali, whom he later befriended in New York, remind one that the Fab Four style grew out of the British art schools rather than the universities. In his introduction to *In His Own Write* Paul McCartney wrote: 'None of it has to make sense and if it *seems* funny then that's enough.' Lennon's books seemed funny to hundreds of thousands of fans.

In the 1970s Pam Ayres, after an appearance on the talent-spotting TV show *Opportunity Knocks*, enjoyed some success with her wry, light verse such as *Thoughts of a Late-night Knitter* (1978). But poetry, unless accompanied by some musical instrument such as Bob Dylan's guitar, was a minority taste in an age of increasingly mass consumption.

The most unlikely bestselling poet of the period was the prime minister's wife, Mary Wilson, whose *Selected Poems* came out in 1970. Mrs Wilson was also the author of a bestselling 'diary', mercilessly lampooned in *Private Eye*. *The Times* of September that year gave Mrs Wilson's verses front-page treatment, commenting: 'What seems unavoidably designed to become the most successful (financially at least) slim volume of poetry published this century was launched yesterday with pop of champagne and puff of publicity.' The former PM attended the Oxford Street book launch, and 60,000 copies of her poems were sold in the first month – about three times what Larkin cleared. Some of Mrs Wilson's verses, such as the following on an unemployed man, combine a touching loyalty to her husband's party with rhymes worthy of McGonagall (the worst of poets, who enjoyed something of a revival in the 1960s thanks to the efforts of the comedian Spike Milligan):

> He lives on the steps of Central Hall
> And buys his food from a coffee stall;
> A tattered bundle protects his head
> From the gritty pavement of his bed.
>
> Every morning you'll see him there –
> Dirty and smelly, with matted hair;
> His feet are bandaged, his clothes are rags,
> All his possessions in paper bags.
>
> 'Lay-about, drop-out!' you glibly say,
> And hastily look the other way;
> But the Gates of Hell stand open wide
> For those who pass on the other side!

The Dives, Lazarus and Good Samaritan references remind us that Mrs Wilson, as well as being a prime minister's wife, was a clergyman's daughter.

Along with *Lady Chatterley's Lover*, the most predictable best-seller of the 1960s was the *New English Bible*, whose New Testament section was published in 1961 (the Old Testament would follow in 1970). The Anglican Church had resolved on a new translation by committee in 1947. Two publishers were licensed to bring out the new Bible: Cambridge University Press and Oxford University Press. The aim of the project was, as one of the translating committee put it: 'to make the New Testament intelligible to an intelligent reader' ('reader', not 'worshipper'; the Bible was now, truly, a 'book').

Theology, like everything else in the 1960s, was liberating itself. John Robinson, the bishop who had testified to the sacramental purity of Lady Chatterley's misconduct in the Old Bailey trial, discovered himself an overnight celebrity. He exploited this new pulpit with a bestselling work of divinity, *Honest to God* (1963). The book sold out its first edition of 6000 copies on the day of publication and would eventually clear the million mark and be translated into seventeen languages. Robinson's notoriety as an atheist in bishop's gaiters was confirmed when he published an article in the *Observer* entitled 'Our Image of God Must Go' – which many (mistakenly) read as meaning that the Creator himself must be voted out like a Conservative prime minister who had outstayed his welcome. Robinson's point (one which had been expounded at length by the Continental theologians, Bonhoeffer and Tillich) was that God is not 'up there' but 'inside us'. Arguably, Robinson's treatise did for English divinity what Lawrence's novel did for English fiction.

The Chatterley trial had two immediate effects. It emancipated fiction. No more would writers be obliged, like Norman Mailer in his 1948 bestseller *The Naked and the Dead*, to invent euphemisms like 'fug' (the 'three-letter, four-letter' word). The yawning gulf between Martin Amis and his father, Kingsley, in terms of what earlier generations would have called 'foulmouthedness' is a measure of the cultural distance travelled in November 1960. And, of course, Martin Amis is positively Austenish alongside writers of the 1990s such as Irvine Welsh or James Kelman.

In 1969 *Portnoy's Complaint* took explicitness all the way from the bedroom to the bathroom. Another 'last frontier' was crossed in Philip Roth's portrait of the artist as a young Jewish masturbator. Outrageousness peaks when young Portnoy violates the family liver and replaces it in the fridge for his unwitting nearest and dearest to eat later – a refinement of onanism that not even *The Little Red School-book* recommended. In Britain Brian Aldiss, otherwise famous as the country's leading practitioner of science fiction, followed up with *The Hand-Reared Boy* (1970), another semi-autobiographical work which featured Mrs Hand and her five daughters. The novel ran into trouble with British publishers, for whom some cows were still sacred. The herd was, however, shrinking fast.

A less contentious effect of the Chatterley acquittal was to jet-propel the 1960s 'Paperback Revolution'. Britain became in this decade a book-buying rather than a book-borrowing nation. Mills & Boon, always ahead of the curve, took the momentous step of moving from hardbacks (for 2*d* lending – less than 1p) to paperbacks (for buying, at 2s 6d or 12½p). After November 1960, 'paperback' became synonymous with 'exciting reading': books on the edge of permissibility. Soft, glossy, illustrated covers were 'sexy'. Paperbacks, too, tended to close the national divisions between Britain and America. The two countries still had their distinctive preferences where hard covers, particularly non-fiction, were concerned. On paperbacks, however, there was much common ground – partly, one suspects, because these were books favoured by the young and the would-be young. And in the 1960s the youth of America, Britain and Europe, especially in the international student movement, were combining their forces in a great revolt against authority.

Books specifically concerned with sex, previously prohibited or available only in prohibitively expensive hardback or 'expurgated' form, were, after November 1960, on open display as shiny paperbacks: *The Kama Sutra*, *Fanny Hill*, *My Secret Life* and *The Perfumed Garden* became favourite 'loo books' among the middle classes. Why be ashamed of *any* bodily function? A minor bestseller of the decade was the *Private Eye* memoir of Le Pétomane, the virtuoso of broken wind. Henry Miller's *Tropic of Cancer* and *Tropic of Capricorn*, twin bibles of the Beats, were finally, after two decades, published in the UK and the USA. There were other breakthroughs. *Giovanni's Room*, first published in hardback in 1957, became a big-seller in 1960s budget-price paperback. James Baldwin's novel blended high literature with high camp and, to cap it all, the author was the USA's top-ranked African-American novelist and a self-proclaimed gay. Black, pink and proud. Essentially, Baldwin's novel is about the pain of 'coming out' (it is set in France: the criminal law on homosexuality would not be relaxed in the author's native country until later in the 1960s). The book was less to the taste of radical blacks, who were emerging in the USA. James Baldwin wanted to be a white man's wife, Eldridge Cleaver sneered in his bestselling polemic *Soul on Ice* (1968).

John Updike's *Couples* (1968) did for the Brahmin white-collar communities in New England what Grace Metalious's *Peyton Place* (1957) had done for the blue-collar suburbs ten years earlier. It tore away veils of 'American dream' to show a seething cauldron of adulterous sex beneath. Updike's raunchiness pressed hard against permissibility, even in a post-Chatterley era. J. P. Donleavy's *The Ginger Man*, which was published overseas in 1955 but banned in Britain for five years, combined the explosive ingredients of Irish Catholicism and a bachelor American's wild sexual adventures in tight-gutted Dublin. Like *Portnoy's Complaint*, it was both dirty book and comic masterpiece.

All these works would be classified as 'literary' or, as the book trade put it, 'upmarket'. The most cynically 'downmarket' exploitation of the new freedoms was Harold Robbins's *The Carpetbaggers*, published first in the UK by Anthony Blond, as a hardback with some prudent excisions, in 1963. This sex'n'violence roman à clef, based loosely on the life of Howard Hughes, sold in the millions for Four Square paperbacks which brought it out in 1964. The following nauseating scene, in which the hero's father and Indian mother are tortured to divulge the whereabouts of gold they haven't got, is typical of its assault on the reader's sensibility:

> The man pressed the burning coal against Sam's neck and shoulder. Sam screamed in pain. 'They ain't got no gold!' His head fell sideways. The man withdrew the burning coal and the blood welled up beneath the scorched flesh and ran down his chest and arm.... Holding Kaneha by the hair, his knife to her back, the oldest man pushed her towards Sam. They stopped in front of him.
>
> 'It's been fifteen years since I skinned an Injun, squaw man,' he said. 'But I ain't fergot how.' He moved swiftly around in front of her, his knife moving up and down her skin.
>
> A faint line of blood appeared where the knife had traced from under her chin down her throat through the valley between her breasts across her stomach and coming to a stop in the foliage of her pubis.

The brute is later identified by the tobacco pouch he has made out of his luckless victim's skinned breast. Poor D. H. Lawrence. 'Savagery' was, by 1963, cultish and profitable in ways that the pious author of *Lady Chatterley's Lover* could never have foreseen. And he, unwittingly, was responsible. To have had anything to do with books like *The Carpetbaggers* before 1960 would have meant prison. Now ten-year-olds could (and did) buy them with their Smarties from the cornershop bookstand.

The new 'explicitness' vitalized the soggy mass of women's romance, recruiting into its readership newly 'liberated' women who wanted much more than Church, Children and Cooking. Rosie the Riveter was back – in a Pucci pantsuit. The pioneer in this new genre was Jacqueline Susann (1921–74). Two things are universally known about her. The first is that her 1966 novel *Valley of the Dolls* was, for years, listed in *The Guinness Book of Records* as the bestselling novel ever. Estimates of global sales range between 20 and 40 million. The second fact universally known about Jackie Susann is that Truman Capote said, on TV, that she looked like a 'truck driver in drag'. He then humbly apologized. To the truck drivers of America, that is.

As the 'female Harold Robbins' Susann laid the blueprint for the 'bodice ripper' and the 'sex and shopping' (or, more raunchily, 'F*cking and Sh*pping') genres. Other novelists – Rosemary Rogers, Danielle Steel, Jackie Collins and Judith Krantz, the most faithful of Susann's disciples – took up where she left off. Even Joyce Carol Oates's 2000 'literary' bestseller about Marilyn Monroe, *Blonde*, finds its roots in Susann's novel.

Jackie Susann began writing in her forties, a period when she realized she was never going to make it on film, stage, radio or TV, or in modelling. 'Forty,' she once said, 'is Hiroshima.' She began with a book about her poodle, saucily entitled *Every Night, Josephine* (1963). This was followed three years later with *Valley of the Dolls*, which promptly made no.1 in America. The narrative is not all glitz and vulgarity. Pathos underlies the romantic glamour of Susann's saga of three young women making it, and not making it, in showbiz. Notably pathetic is the story of big-bosomed Jennifer North, based on Marilyn Monroe, who kills herself with an overdose of 'dolls' – pills. Neely O'Hara, the gutsy street-girl based on Judy Garland, also ends unhappily. The third of Susann's heroines, Anne Welles, with whom the author most closely identifies herself, finds a happier solution to her dilemma: should she marry a millionaire, a gentlemanly press agent or a stud-novelist? Life can be so hard for beautiful people.

Susann was no Shakespeare – had he ever made no.1 on the *New York Times* bestseller list? she would sweetly inquire. Her manuscripts arrived, as one of her editors wearily complained, 'barely in English'. Where Susann and her publicist husband Irving Mansfield excelled was in the promotional tour and the celebrity talk show. Her heavy make-up with huge false eyelashes and bright orange lips, the satin pantsuits and mountainous raven hair rendered her a natural for PR appearances: if, perhaps, somewhat like a truck driver in drag.

As Elaine Showalter would put it in *A Literature of their Own* (1977), Jacqueline was ultra-feminine but in no sense feminist. Feminism took naturally to books. Women read. They do not, normally, gather in large groups, as do men. There is no female equivalent of the football crowd. Books (the literature of their own) articulate women's issues and facilitate communication. They constitute, in the largest sense, woman's debate with women.

Betty Friedan's *The Feminine Mystique* (1963) is plausibly seen as a starting point in the women's movement of the late twentieth century. What Friedan argued was that the 'ideals' of traditional womanhood, something propagated for centuries by 'women's romance', were imprisoning. New definitions were necessary. She provided them.

Betty Friedan, née Goldstein, was born in 1921 in Peoria – that epitome of small-town America. The daughter of first-generation Russian–Jewish immigrants, young Betty was a high-achieving psychology student at Smith College. She was not conventionally pretty; nor, as time went on, did she want the cumbersome baggage that came with good looks. On graduation, Miss Goldstein (she would later co-found the magazine *MS*, consigning 'Miss' to the dustbin of history) went into journalism. She worked mainly for trade union papers and leftist magazines.

Her synopsis of what would later become *The Feminine Mystique* was turned down by several publishers on the grounds, as one editor pointed out, that it appealed to 'sick' women. Meanwhile her life went on in much the same way as other women's. Betty married Carl Friedan in 1947. While working on a New York newspaper in 1949, she was fired when she unwisely notified her superior that she was pregnant. The injustice radicalized her in new directions.

The five-year process of writing *The Feminine Mystique* was stressful. In 1960 she had three children, all under twelve. Her husband later 'complained that when he came home "that bitch" was writing her book on the dining-room table instead of preparing the meal in the kitchen'. Publication of *The Feminine Mystique* in 1963 coincided with the breakdown of Friedan's marriage. The completion of the book (and the thinking that went into it) gave her courage, she claimed, to divorce Carl in 1969. His next wife would be a non-intellectual who could make chicken soup: 'That's love,' he declared. He never got that kind of love from Betty – or a 'blow job', he ungallantly divulged in 2000.

In her book Friedan addressed what she called 'the problem that has no name', that is, the oppression of women under high capitalism. American women, she declared, were trapped in the 'concentration camp of suburbia'. The kitchen was a cell. The 'mystique' of 'the American woman' was a sham: what Marxists would call 'false consciousness'. It needed to be 'demystified'. Friedan's book was a runaway bestseller, purchased and read by millions of American women and, furtively, many men. The National Organization of Women (NOW) was formed in 1966 as a response to the programmes outlined in Friedan's incendiary book. In September 1968 the city of Atlanta saw the symbolic dumping of brassieres in trash cans; apocryphal legend claims they were burned.

Feminist writing, by the mid-1960s, was a bestselling genre. Women consumed books about women, by women, in large amounts. The trick for the publisher was to find something sufficiently rousing. Titles tended to be battle cries. By 1970 the *New York Times* books supplement was routinely doing several round-ups a year on women's books. Highlight publications of the period included Oriana Fallaci's *The Useless Sex* (1964), Shulamith Firestone's *The Dialectics of Sex* (1970), Mary Daly's *The Church of the Second Sex* (1968), Juliet Mitchell's *Women's Estate* (1971), Kate Millett's *Sexual Politics* (1970), Robin Morgan's *Sisterhood Is Powerful* (1970: the publishers would not allow Morgan her original title, 'The Hand that Cradles the Rock').

Feminism, as ideology and polemic, created a launch pad for popular fiction. Sylvia Plath wrote her autobiographical novel about growing up American, middle-class, privileged, discontented and female in the late 1950s. *The Bell Jar* was, however, published under the pseudonym 'Victoria Lucas' when it came out in 1963. The author did not want to mortify her mother and living relatives. Even 1960s feminism had its soft edges. It was not until after her suicide at the age of thirty in 1963 that the novel came out under her own name.

As Sylvia Plath's *The Bell Jar* it sold steadily and in large numbers over the subsequent decades.

Ten years after the author's death, Esther Greenwood was almost as famous as Holden Caulfield – at least, among women readers. The vivid opening paragraph catches the novel's mood of morbid, introspective vitality:

> It was a queer, sultry summer, the summer they electrocuted the Rosenbergs, and I didn't know what I was doing in New York. I'm stupid about executions. The idea of being electrocuted makes me sick, and that's all there was to read about in the papers – goggle-eyed headlines staring up at me on every street corner and at the fusty, peanut-smelling mouth of every subway. It had nothing to do with me, but I couldn't help wondering what it would be like, being burned alive all along your nerves.

Plath would, in the event, choose gas rather than electricity for her exit strategy. One recalls Elaine Showalter's sardonic recycling of Virginia Woolf's maxim: 'The ultimate room of one's own is the grave.' For militant feminists of the decade, Plath – woman novelist, woman poet and woman – articulated their battle slogan: 'Give me liberation, or give me death.'

A more ambivalent attitude to the new freedoms of women was expressed in Mary McCarthy's bestselling and cold-eyed saga *The Group* (1963), which follows the careers of a clique of young women during and after their years at Vassar University in the late 1930s. McCarthy had been working on the novel for years before the feminist interventions of the 1960s. One section, 'Dottie Makes an Honest Woman of Herself', which contains a description of a diaphragm being fitted in penetrating gynaecological detail, had caused a scandal when it was published in *Partisan Review* in 1954. By the time she finally completed the novel, McCarthy confessed herself to be 'losing faith' in the 'idea of progress'. Were things *really* better than they had been a quarter of a century ago for young women? *The Group* caused offence among the author's Vassar contemporaries with its depictions of drunkenness, lesbianism, and sexual delinquency in their Ivy League dormitories. McCarthy's novel made the no.1 spot on the *New York Times* bestseller list and film rights were sold for $162,000 – a vast sum at that period. The film, starring Candice Bergen and directed by Sidney Lumet, came out in 1966. It did nothing for McCarthy's literary reputation.

Feminist rigour seeped into other fiction of the 1960s. Ira Levin's fable of women rendered brain-dead by suburban life, *The Stepford Wives* (1972), would sell among feminist groups because many assumed, wrongly, that Ira was a woman's name. The new sense of what it was to be a woman inspired a generation of young novelists. These women, and many of their readers, were products of the new university system. Fay Weldon's (b. 1933) first novel, *The Fat Woman's Joke*, came out in 1967. Margaret Drabble's (b. 1939) *The Millstone* (1966) took a revisionary line on 'unwanted' pregnancy – that traditional doom of young women; the Pill and legalized abortion changed the world for young women in the 1960s in ways that their mothers could never have dreamed of. Angela Carter (1940–92), the most gifted of this generation of young women writers, introduced magic realism to British readers in 1967 with *The Magic Toyshop*. Carter's idiosyncratic views on feminism would be articulated in *The Sadeian Woman: An Exercise in Cultural History* (1979).

The four decades after World War II were golden for British fiction, but particularly for fiction by women authors who wrote well, sold well and were well up with the modern wave. The roll call would include Doris Lessing, Iris Murdoch, Margaret Forster, Edna O'Brien, A. S. Byatt and Penelope Mortimer. Typically these women authors chose subject matters that would appeal to their own sex. Drabble and Forster both recalled in later life that they wrote on domestic themes in their early novels because they were, at that period of their lives, confined at home with children (as were many of their fans). Penelope Mortimer's *The Pumpkin Eater* (1962) probes, sceptically and at times bitterly, the woes that are contained in motherhood. *My Friend Says It's Bullet-proof* (1967) is the first British novel to deal centrally, honestly and humorously with mastectomy.

The most successful writer of thrillers for male readers in the 1960s was Alistair MacLean (1922–87). His bestselling career started with what is claimed to be his best novel, and was his personal favourite,

*HMS Ulysses* (1955). This chronicle of a 'mutiny ship' which redeems itself by extraordinary heroism on the Russian convoy route in 1943 was clumsily written, but had a persuasive authenticity to it. At nineteen, in 1941, the author himself had joined the Royal Navy, and knew whereof he wrote. *HMS Ulysses* laid down the MacLean bestselling formula. It features a single-sex, invariably male society or 'crew' in an enclosed situation, typically some kind of 'vessel', governed by 'manly' codes of action under crushing stress. Archetypally, in MacLean's thrillers, the closed society is that of a ship, the values naval, and the stress that of war.

In his later, peacetime, scenarios the MacLean fleet diversifies: we have the refugee boat (*South by Java Head*, 1958), the nuclear submarine (*Ice Station Zebra*, 1963), the Caribbean luxury liner (*The Golden Rendezvous*, 1962), the cargo craft (*Bear Island*, 1972), the oil rig (*Fear is the Key* and *Seawitch*, both 1977). Other closed situations which MacLean experimented with were the hurtling train (*Breakheart Pass*, 1974), the sealed-off weapons establishment (*The Satan Bug*, 1962), and, famously, the commando squad on a mission in enemy-held territory, as in *The Guns of Navarone* (1957) and *Where Eagles Dare* (1967).

High-grossing films of these last two, featuring a galaxy of box-office stars, boosted MacLean himself into stardom. The contention in MacLean's action scenarios is that one daring mission, by a small band of brave men, can change the course of war (or, in *Ice Station Zebra*, cold war – in both senses). He never learned the art of writing well, but he wrote well enough to communicate his core belief: 'Manliness transcends all.'

*Lady Chatterley's Lover* was not the only 'sleeper' to make it into the 1960s bestseller lists. In 1967 the BBC launched a mini-series adaptation of *The Forsyte Saga*, a rambling sequence of novels by the middle-brow author John Galsworthy (1867–1933) which had enjoyed a vogue in the 1920s. Galsworthy's addictively melodramatic chronicle of a family from Victorian times through the Edwardian era to World War I provoked one of TV's most spectacular manias. The episodes went out on Sunday evening, and all over the country vicars prudently changed the hour of evensong so as not to lose their already dwindling congregations to the tube. Babies were named Jolyon (played by the charismatic Kenneth More) and Fleur (Susan Hampshire); Soames, as immortalized by the grim-looking Eric Porter, was less in vogue at christening services. The novels themselves reappeared in W. H. Smith's list of bestselling books for the year.

By the end of the decade, TV was a mighty engine in the British book trade. Kenneth Clark's 1969 series, immodestly entitled *Civilisation* (he was promptly dubbed 'Lord Clark of Civilisation' by *Private Eye*), created the non-fiction bestseller of the year. In the book version of *Civilisation* Clark records that he has not tried to elaborate or 'improve' his scripts. To do so, he says, would take a year's work and would deprive the book 'of a certain ease and speed, which might be counted in its favour'. Intelligently, he realized that this kind of book was, generically, the servant of the dominant medium – TV.

Clark's anatomy of what it was to be truly civilized created a perfect match of high connoisseurship and coffee-table book (British coffee was, by the late 1960s, moderately drinkable). Connoisseurship diverged into other areas: Egon Ronay's *Good Food Guides* (from 1959 onwards) began the long task of cultivating the British palate into something like Continental expertise. The books sold like hot croissants. Connoisseurship was also the theme pushed by Robert Carrier, in his campaign to create a renaissance in British cuisine. Carrier, who first established his reputation in the Sunday colour supplements, published his *Great Dishes of the World* in 1963 and, by the 1980s, it would have sold 2 million copies. Great food, Carrier asserted, was quite at home in the UK – whose cooking was traditionally (and justly) disparaged by its more sophisticated European neighbours. The 1960s gave birth, among other things, to gay pride, black pride and – in Carrier's book – culinary pride.

Britain's relationship with the book evolved in many ways over the decade. Reading matter clamped between covers remained a principal form of the nation's entertainment. But the book, as it had since Caxton, served higher purposes. It remained a principal conduit through which the population might acquire lifelong education. Books also articulated a growing sense of civic self-awareness among Britons. 'Liberation' meant that they could take control of their lives and their environment. In the 1960s they increasingly did so.

Penguin Specials had first been launched during World War II, to mobilize the nation for conflict with titles such as *Why Are We*

*Fighting?* In the 1960s, these Specials articulated civic concerns. Less 'Why are we fighting?' than 'What kind of world are we making?' The 1964 American Surgeon General's Report on Smoking and Health, which authoritatively linked tobacco and cancer, elicited a Special on the country's favourite vice, as did the national debate on capital punishment: Arthur Koestler's *Hanged by the Neck* (1961). The state strangling of murderers was abolished in 1969, in line with the legalization of abortion and the Sexual Offences Act – all of this came about in the last four years of the decade.

The most effective of the Penguin Specials was the least obviously sensational. Colin Buchanan produced his government report *Traffic in Towns* in 1963. Buchanan argued, humanely and eloquently, for 'quality of life' in the face of the road-building juggernaut which was defacing British cities and the explosive growth in British car ownership (a phenomenon which, elsewhere in the book trade, made *The Highway Code* a year-in, year-out bestseller). The Buchanan Report went on to become the most surprising bestseller ever printed by Her Majesty's Stationery Office. An abridged version was duly published by Penguin – unprecedented for a government report – and the report was translated into several languages.

Popular fiction was like a thermometer in the mouth of the 1960s, registering current anxieties, hopes and fantasies. Harper Lee's novel *To Kill a Mockingbird*, about a gallant white lawyer defending a 'Negro' (the preferred term in those days) falsely accused of rape, was published in 1960 as the Civil Rights Bill was being hatched for Congress. The film of the book, starring Gregory Peck, came out in 1962, two years before the Bill became law. *To Kill a Mockingbird* was being read everywhere, while the implementation of the new law was still struggling in redoubts of bigotry such as Arkansas. Lee's novel, the only work she ever published, went on over the years to become an all-time American bestseller, boosted by its prescription for school-children as a handy lesson in citizenship and civil rights.

One of the indices of the sophistication of the modern British and American book trades was their growing speed of response to current events. New printing technology allowed books to respond with almost the speed of newspapers (on their part, newspapers were struggling to catch up with TV news). Clive Irving's 'instant book' on the

Profumo affair, *Scandal*, appeared, it seemed, barely hours after what it chronicled. The defence minister, John Profumo, had been hounded from office for adultery with an alleged call-girl, Christine Keeler, who was also sharing her favours with a Russian naval attaché, Eugene Ivanov. The minister made the disastrous mistake of lying about it to Parliament. The subsequent hue and cry ruined him and brought down Macmillan's government. The rich whiff of scandal also made an unlikely bestseller out of Lord Denning's report to the government in 1963, and an even more unlikely celebrity out of Denning himself.

The Cuban missile crisis in October 1962 brought the world closer to annihilation than it had been since the flood in Genesis. The episode produced some rapid-response bestsellers, notably Fletcher Knebel and Charles W. Bailey's *Seven Days in May* (1962). It fanta-sizes a takeover by super-patriot generals who intend to launch pre-emptive nuclear strikes on the USSR. The novel sold a massive 2 million copies and remained in the *New York Times* bestselling list for forty-nine consecutive weeks. President Kennedy confided to a friend that he considered a Seven-Days scenario 'quite possible'. He knew 'a couple of generals who might wish to turn the book's fiction into a reality'.

Other 'scare' books in this most nervous of periods included Richard Condon's *The Manchurian Candidate* (1959), in which Amer-ican prisoners in the Korean War are brainwashed to assassinate the president. A movie was made from the novel in 1962, but banned after the shooting of John F. Kennedy the following year. In Eugene Burdick and Harvey Wheeler's *Fail Safe* (1962) a series of accidents precipitate a nuclear exchange between the USA and the USSR. The hot line had, under Kennedy and Khrushchev, just been installed; it was hoped that, even if war broke out, its proliferation might be controlled. In *Fail Safe*, the two leaders agree to sacrifice Moscow and New York and leave it at that. The concept of 'proportionate response' was popularized. The best work in this nervous cluster was not a novel but Stanley Kubrick's blackly comic film *Dr Strangelove* (1963). The films, if not always the novels they were based on, were eagerly consumed in the UK.

More cheerfully, the moon landings in 1969 propelled into the American bestseller lists the first work of straight science fiction, Michael Crichton's *The Andromeda Strain* (1969). With its computer printouts and docu-science gimmicks, the novel chimed perfectly with the techno-optimism of the period. Neil Armstrong's small step for man also ensured classic status (and bestsellerdom) for Kubrick's prophetic *2001: A Space Odyssey* (1968) and Arthur C. Clarke's novelization of the film (which had, in fact, been based on one of the British sf maestro's earlier short stories). The *Star Trek* TV-novelizations boomed, as did membership of 'Trekkie' cult-groups.

There was, as the decade came to an end, a growing confidence (some might have called it hubris) in the omnipotence of American science and technology. Alvin Toffler envisioned a utopia via technology in *Future Shock* (1970), a book which became a runaway bestseller and inspired the setting up of Future Shock institutions. Gazing into his crystal ball, Toffler foresaw large portions of the world's population at the turn of the century (i.e. now) living on the ocean floor, or on pontoon cities, grazing contentedly on the harvests of 'aquaculture' (fishburgers?). Global climate would, he prophesied, be micro-controlled. One would be able to turn sunshine off and on, like a set of patio lights. Riffling through one's yellowed 1970 paperback, it is what Toffler did *not* foresee that strikes one most forcefully: global warming, depletion of the ozone layer, AIDS, women's liberation. Most strikingly, in his 600 pages, Toffler makes no more than a dozen passing references to the computer.

In Britain, two public events inspired a tidal wave of opportunistic books for a short-lived market. One was the death of Churchill in January 1965. This event had been so long in coming that publishers, like the obituarists, had had ample time to prepare their wares. The titles that did well, in the aftermath of Britain's first state funeral since the death of George VI, were *Winston Churchill as I Knew Him* (1965), by Lady Violet Bonham Carter; *The Wit of Sir Winston* (1965); *Winston Churchill: The Struggle for Survival* (1966), by Lord Moran, Churchill's physician, who revealed – scandalously, some thought – that in his last term as PM Churchill had been disabled by strokes; and Randolph Churchill's authorized biography of his father, the first volume of which was published in 1966.

No one, apart from manager Alf Ramsey, seriously expected England to win the 1966 football World Cup – as well expect a mountaineer to climb the North Face of the Eiger in concrete boots, quipped

Michael Parkinson, then a sports writer on the *Sunday Times*. But, to the nation's joyful amazement, England did win, in a thrilling final against Germany at Wembley. It was like a real-life episode of *Roy of the Rovers*, the comic-book hero of soccer-mad boys, started in 1954. England's victory inspired innumerable books and a strong-selling line which lasted for years, though there was something of a check when England lost to Germany next time round. Among the more notable and bestselling were Bernard Joy's *World Cup Football Championships* (1966); David Coleman's *World of Football* (1970); Jack Rollin's *England's World Cup Triumph* (1966); Kenneth Wolstenholme's *The Boy's Book of the World Cup* (1966); Bobby Charlton's *Book of European Football* (1969: contributors included Denis Law, Jackie Charlton, Matt Busby, Ray Wilson and George Best, or their 'ghosts'); and John Arlott's *Soccer: the Great Ones* (1968).

Spy and secret agent fantasies retained their popularity in the 1960s with Bond, inevitably, the brand leader. But, interestingly, there developed a line of bestselling 'anti-Bond' spy books. Foremost was John le Carré (b. 1931), with his international bestseller *The Spy Who Came in from the Cold* (1963). Le Carré's 'looking glass world' (as he would call it, in his next novel) was as seedy as the world of 007 was glamorous ('candyfloss', le Carré called the Bond books; he offered something much grittier).

In *The Spy Who Came in from the Cold* Leamas is a burned-out operative who is blackmailed into undertaking some double-cross espionage work. It will be, he is assured, his last mission. He can then 'come in'. Le Carré, unlike Ian Fleming, had experience of 'dirty' post-war espionage rather than the buccaneering WWII variety that the creator of Bond drew on. Le Carré's narrative ends with the hero being shot on the Berlin Wall dividing East and West which went up in 1961 (and would come down in 1989), deserted by both sides and every master. Le Carré's novel was the first spy thriller to head the American bestselling fiction list. (It did so in 1964, ahead of Terry Southern's bawdy rewrite of Voltaire, *Candy*, and Saul Bellow's *Herzog*. It was a strong year for fiction.)

The contention that one's real enemy is behind one, in the upper echelons of the British secret service, not across the Iron Curtain, permeates Len Deighton's string of bestselling spy thrillers, which began with *The Ipcress File* (1962). In this novel Deighton introduced his bolshy, resolutely NCO operative, Harry Palmer (as he is named in the films; in the novels he is anonymous). Deighton's novel contained an Appendix with technical information testifying to the author's supposed inside expertise in spycraft. Both *The Spy Who Came in from the Cold* and Deighton's novel were successfully filmed, starring Richard Burton and Michael Caine, respectively.

In the USA, this mood of scepticism about leaders was fuelled by the Vietnam morass. Joseph Heller's anti-war satire *Catch-22* (1961) was appropriate less to the 1941–5 conflict in which the hero serves, reluctantly, than to that unfolding, messily, in Southeast Asia. The appeal of Heller's airman, Yossarian, was that his main efforts were directed not to killing the enemy but to getting his own backside safely out of the firing line. (He toys with feigning lunacy: but Catch-22 decrees that if you claim to be mad, you can't be mad.) The book appealed to draft dodgers and draft-card burners, an increasing segment of American youth, especially on the campuses. Vietnam also helped inspire the new genre of journalism, with works such as Norman Mailer's bluntly rhetorical *Why Are We in Vietnam?* (1967). Catch-22 was the smart answer.

If books on cooking had dominated the 1940s and 1950s – hungry decades – how not to suffer the effects of cooking was now big book business. The 1960s were, indeed, the fat years. People had learned to cook, and to eat too well. It was a threshold moment in 1962 when Dr Herman Taller's *Calories Don't Count*, published a year earlier, made it to the top of the US non-fiction bestseller list. Taller's manual outsold everything that year including the big novel of the early 1960s, Irving Stone's *The Agony and the Ecstasy*, a lumbering 'biofiction' about Michelangelo.

The implication of Taller's book was profoundly reassuring. You could eat like a horse and none the less remain as thin as a rake. Effectively, all you had to do was avoid carbohydrates (the dreaded potato). *Calories Don't Count* sold 2 million copies. It is the nature of slimmers that they try, try and try again. And they buy, buy and buy again. Good news for the book trade, who can print, print and print again.

The first recorded 'diet book' had been published in 1864. Entitled *A Letter on Corpulence*, it was written by an English coffin- and cabinet-maker, William Banting. Finding himself no longer able to tie his shoelaces, Mr Banting took the advice of a Dr William Harvey. The doctor advised his fat patient to avoid 'starchy foods' and 'saccharine matter', just like Dr Taller a century later. But starchy foods were hard to avoid. Britain had, from time immemorial, had its 'chippies' and corner sweet shops: purveyors of fast food, junk food – above all, fattening food.

In America, this kind of eating was rationalized, industrialized and popularized in the postwar period. In 1948, Richard and Maurice McDonald opened their first restaurant selling cheap hamburgers, a dish pioneered for fast customer delivery at the 1904 World's Fair. The Big Mac was born. This mouth-watering combination of ground meat and processed cheese contained 60 grams of fat. Classically, it was washed down with a milk-shake and accompanied by 'fries', which tripled the fat intake. In 1957, Colonel Harland Sanders opened his first Kentucky Fried Chicken outlet. Fried, of course, meant sweltering in fat. In 1958, the first Pizza Hut was opened by two college students, Frank and Dan Carney. Their speciality was dough, slathered in cheese and other fatty toppings.

Despite Taller's reassurances, American women in particular decided that calories did count. In 1963 the first Weight Watchers meeting, based loosely on the '12-step' technique pioneered by Alcoholics Anonymous, was organized in New York by housewife Jean Nidetch. About four hundred people attended to hear about the 'meal plan for ladies' which had enabled Ms Nidetch to lose almost 50 pounds. In 1968 Nidetch published her bestselling *Weight Watcher's Cook Book*. Taller's bestseller inspired a stampede of 'me-tooism' among publishers hoping to strike it rich. The main struggle over the next few years was between advocates of self-help like Ms Nidetch and those who put their trust in the wise, all-knowing doctor. In 1967, the physician Irwin Stillman published *The Doctor's Quick Weight-Loss Diet*, which advocated a crash intake high in protein – it also included the advice to drink ten large glasses of water a day, which would keep the slimmer well exercised running to the bathroom. An estimated 20 million people tried the diet.

Over the next forty years other doctors would enrich themselves with diet books for the massive masses. They included *The Scarsdale*

*Diet* (1978: only 700 calories a day); *The Pritkin Diet* (1979: low fat, high fibre, exercise and 'lifestyle' changes); *The Cambridge Diet* (1981: this all-liquid regime was prohibited by the US Food and Drugs Administration following thirty deaths – they were, presumably, the thinnest corpses in the morgue). Finally, as Susie Orbach memorably put it, fat became a feminist issue. Dieting, not food, was the enemy, a message powerfully proclaimed in Susan Powter's 1993 polemic *Stop the Insanity*. But there was money in insanity – there always is. By this point, some half a billion diet books had been published following Taller's breakthrough in 1962.

In the UK, the post-war fat years were slower in coming. But by 1964 the *British Medical Journal* declared 'obesity' to be the country's main 'nutritional disorder'. Affluence had truly arrived. Anxiety about obesity was suddenly a major merchandising opportunity. A vast number of 'remedies', 'supplements' and 'slimming diets' were promoted to the engorged English nation: Dramal, Metercal, Complan, Carrugan, Limmits, Formula 21. The value of the market in the mid-1960s was estimated at £20 million a year. By 1967, it was estimated that at any one time one in ten Britons was on a diet and that one in four women dieted at least once a year. Everyone wanted to be Twiggy.

How-to slimming books boomed. Early bestsellers tended themselves to be slim volumes, suitable for carrying as aides-memoires in the handbag: for example, Jane Collins's *Pocket Calorie Guide to Safe Slimming* (1960). Another short book (in Collins's Nutshell series), *Sensible Slimming* (1964), by Dr Bryan Y. Kingsworth, adopted an aggressively no-nonsense approach: 'Is Fatness Your Fate?', 'Let's Face It, You Overeat!'.

Professor John Yudkin's *This Slimming Business*, published by Penguin in 1962, instructed the nation about calories in a less hectoring spirit. Yudkin's book was unusual in being directed not merely at fashion-conscious women, but at the British population in general. It was a health, not a fashion issue. One of the country's leading authorities on nutrition, Yudkin directed his criticism principally against refined sugar ('empty calories'), provoking Britain's major producer, Tate & Lyle, and their mascot, 'Mr Cube', to counter-attack. Sugar, they maintained, was good 'energy food': efficient, palatable, fast-acting and cheap.

One aspect of 1960s liberation was a new and radically non-conformist variety of children's literature. The biggest bestseller in this new wave of books for children was Roald Dahl (1916–90), the 'anti-Blyton'. Dahl, despite his Norwegian name, was a product of the British Establishment. His school reports at Repton, however, did not foretell any great achievement in authorship: 'I have never met a boy who so persistently writes the exact opposite of what he means, he seems incapable of marshalling his thoughts on paper,' observed one despairing teacher.

Dahl chose not to go to university, going instead to work as an executive for Shell Oil. In 1939 he enlisted in the RAF in Nairobi and had a short if lively war: after being invalided out he ended up in January 1942 at the British Embassy in Washington DC as an assistant air attaché. There he met C. S. Forester, the creator of Hornblower, who encouraged him to write up his wartime adventures for the *Saturday Evening Post*. Dahl earned his first $900 as a writer and promptly lost most of it in a poker game with Senator Harry S. Truman.

After the war Dahl began writing 'sick' but humorous 'tales of the unexpected' for adults, which were very successfully adapted for TV from the late 1970s. One, typically, describes a bullied wife's sadistic revenge on her husband, whose brain and one eye are preserved, after the decay of his body, in a tank of fluid. His second collection of stories, *Kiss Kiss*, was published in the USA in February 1960 and marked a breakthrough point in his career. By April, 16,000 copies had been sold. The British publisher, Michael Joseph, read the book and offered a £350 advance for the British rights. *Kiss Kiss* sold around 20,000 copies in hardback in Britain, about ten times what Joseph would normally expect for a collection of short stories.

Domestically, things were going badly for the author. In 1960 his baby son, Theo, suffered brain damage. In 1962 his oldest child, Olivia, died. In 1965 his wife, the actress Patricia Neal, suffered a devastating stroke. Dahl himself was racked with acute arthritis. He wrote in many kinds of pain.

In the 1960s Dahl started writing up the stories he had been inventing for his own children over the years. He had to overcome some resistance from his American publishers, but the eventual result was *James and the Giant Peach* (1961) and *Charlie and the Chocolate*

*Factory* (1964). *The Twits* (1979) and *The BFG* (1982) followed. By 1968, James alone had earned his author a peachy million dollars. Dahl's books for children became worldwide bestsellers; sometimes in unlikely places. The initial Chinese print run for *Charlie and the Chocolate Factory*, for example, was 2 million copies. By 1990, the year of Dahl's death, his lead titles had all cleared the 10 million mark and it was estimated that every third British child bought or was given a Dahl book each year.

Whatever one thought of Dahl's writing for children – and some found it too razor-edged for impressionable minds – it represented a distinct advance over traditional children's literature. It was, undeniably, better stuff. And there was, as the 1960s progressed, a similar uplift in the quality of all levels of popular book purchased and consumed by the British reading public.

Some cultural events stand out as bench-marks. In 1969, the Booker Prize was launched. Its early years were famously bumpy, and some early winners were eccentric. But, as winner after winner passed into literary history, the publicity generated by the prize ensured large sales and generally raised the tone of the popular novel. 'Quality' fiction, across all the major genres and readerships, features prominently in W. H. Smith's bestseller lists for the decade: Giuseppe di Lampedusa's *The Leopard* (1960), Evelyn Waugh's *Unconditional Surrender* (1961), Mary Renault's *The Bull from the Sea* (1962), Morris West's *The Shoes of the Fisherman* (1963), John le Carré's *The Spy Who Came in from the Cold* (1964), Norman Mailer's *An American Dream* (1965), Graham Greene's *The Comedians* (1966), Len Deighton's *An Expensive Place to Die* (1967), Iris Murdoch's *The Nice and the Good* (1968), J. R. R. Tolkien's *The Lord of the Rings* (1969).

Quality fiction at budget price was provided, inevitably, by Penguin, who in the mid-1960s launched their Penguin English Library. These were budget-priced classics, retailing at around 6*s* (30p) a volume. They differed from their predecessors such as Everyman Books by presenting themselves to the customer in a sexy paperback format with illustrated covers and containing a scholarly (but not dauntingly so) critical apparatus. They were aimed at the general, not the student or academic, reader. The first title in the series was *Wuthering Heights*, edited by the distinguished critic David Daiches. Eventually, the list would grow to some six hundred titles. PEL's success inspired that sincerest of praise, imitation. World's Classics and a revamped Everyman Paperback series soon joined Penguin in the 'classics' section of high street bookshops. Britain was, manifestly, reading 'good books' again.

These good books were, in the terminology of the decade, 'Establishment'. Ranged against them were anti-Establishment (alternative or underground) literature. Every dissident, protest or drop-out group had a literature of its own in the 1960s. The most popular philosopher of the decade, judged by sales, was Herbert Marcuse. His *One Dimensional Man* (1964) put a potent jargon into circulation among the well-read young: 'repressive tolerance', 'the closing of political discourse', 'one-dimensionality'. Marcuse's thesis was paradoxical: the more comfortable and 'liberated' life was under capitalism, the more tyrannical. Catch-22, as Heller would say. Marcuse was a German emigré, a leader of the so-called Frankfurt School. He was, in the 1960s, living on the West Coast of America where his most admired student was the black activist Angela Davis, along with Eldridge Cleaver and George Jackson a bestselling African-American author in her own right. It was from California that the most articulate sub-Marcusian manifestos of youthful rebellion and style statements emanated.

The UK too had its gurus and rebel scholars dispensing new forms of philosophy, psychology, sociology and anthropology for the people – young people, mainly. Foremost was the psycho-philosopher-poet R. D. Laing (1927–89). Born, educated and trained as a psychiatrist in Glasgow, early in his career Laing experimented with what he called the 'Rumpus Room' technique. This was an area in the hospital in which medical staff and schizophrenic inmates would change roles – the patients, that is, would wear the white coats. This idea is also central in Ken Kesey's novel *One Flew Over the Cuckoo's Nest* (1962; filmed in 1975). In the 1960s, the idea of the patients running the lunatic asylum had its proponents.

Laing's main contention was that madness is not physiological (a wiring fault in the brain) but socially constructed. To be mad is to be a victim of oppression. This led to his daring proposition, very congenial to the *enragés* and *engagés* of the 1960s, that madness is a 'sane' response to a deranged society: arguably the only sane response.

Laing had been profoundly influenced by Colin Wilson's 1956 book *The Outsider*, not least because it demonstrated how potent the printed word could be in propagating dissident doctrine to a mass audience. In the same year, 1956 (as Kenneth Tynan noted, a momentous date in British culture), Laing moved from Glasgow to the Tavistock Clinic in London. Here he continued to develop his idiosyncratic line of psychotherapy. He also began writing what would be influential and bestselling books for the general reader: *The Divided Self* (1961), *The Politics of Experience* (1967) and *The Bird of Paradise* (1967).

The importance of R. D. Laing for the radical young of the 1960s was that he connected psychoanalysis with street revolution. If madness was socially constructed, you needed not mental hospitals but barricades. The cure for mental illness came out of the barrel of a gun. Laing's books also pondered, intelligently, the altered states induced by psychotropic and – in the jargon of the decade – psychedelic drugs. This line of literary investigation had been opened up by Aldous Huxley's 1954 treatise *The Doors of Perception*. By the 1960s, thinkers like Laing were well through the door.

The most influential youth guru of the 1960s was Marshall McLuhan, though he himself was not of their generation. McLuhan (1911–80) was born in Manitoba, Canada, a country which he later regarded as a sad handicap to aspiring intellectuals like himself. On graduation from college McLuhan seemed destined to be a middling university professor who would achieve only small successes in life, rather than a thinker who would leave an indelible mark on the 1960s.

Three influences formed what would later be called McLuhanism. The first was reading G. K. Chesterton's *What's Wrong with the World?* in 1932. From that time McLuhan adopted the English Catholic sage's abrupt, epigrammatic style and his extempore mode of composition. He would write *The Gutenberg Galaxy*, his masterwork, in less than a month. As a result, one wit said, McLuhan's writing looked as if McLuhan had never read it.

The second major influence on McLuhan was postgraduate study at Cambridge with F. R. Leavis. The third was his realization, in the 1950s, that communication systems were at the heart of the modern world. McLuhan articulated his thesis in three major works: *The*

*Gutenberg Galaxy* (1962), *Understanding Media* (1964) and *The Medium Is the Massage* [sic] (1967). All sold massively, mainly in soft cover to young readers. No professor had ever achieved such sales, or such stardom, with what were essentially dry academic monographs. He was taken up by other stars in other fields: Abbie Hoffman (king of the hippies), John Lennon, Susan Sontag. Famously, Woody Allen invited him to play a cameo role in *Annie Hall*. McLuhan's colleagues in universities were, on the whole, more sceptical. Or, perhaps, just envious. Inside every Professor Dryasdust there is a celebrity don scrabbling to get out.

The 'youth market' emerged in the 1960s as something identifiable within the larger constellation of the 'reading public'. The most literate and book-hungry among the youthful were the so-called hippies. The movement of the late 1960s was international, as were the books spun off from it (perversely, even Abbie Hoffman's *Steal this Book!* of 1971 sold well in America and the UK). The ultimate hippy how-to book was *The Whole Earth Catalog*. An item was listed in the *Catalog* if it met four criteria: '1. Useful as a tool; 2. Relevant to an independent education; 3. High quality or low cost; 4. Easily available by mail.'

In *The Whole Earth Catalog* one novel is listed – Frank Herbert's *Dune* (1965). In it the author fantasizes life on a pseudo-Mars, in which a dry, parched environment is kept in perfect ecological balance by pseudo-humans who harvest a mysterious 'spice' (drug, that is) from the desert, a crop guarded by fearsome sandworms (the fuzz, that is). *Dune* sold 2 million copies in paperback between 1965 and 1977, making it the bestselling sf title ever. It was made into a film in 1984, starring Sting and directed by David Lynch. It enjoyed some cult success, but twenty years after the event its time was well gone.

The other sf title of this era which became a bestseller, especially with the hippy young, was Robert Heinlein's *Stranger in a Strange Land* (1961). A Martian ('Valentine Michael Smith') falls to earth. He has, it transpires, extra-sensory powers: his mind can be at the same time individual and collective. Smith is a hermaphrodite, young and beautiful. A perfect candidate, in other words, for the communes which were all the rage among the young in the 1960s. This hippy from another planet introduces congenial earthlings to his 'grok' ritual

(Charles Manson and his family solemnly 'grokked' before going out on their homicidal rampages).

Science fiction had long been a popular but rarely bestselling genre. The first no.1, 'true' sf bestseller in the USA was Michael Crichton's *Jurassic Park*, in 1989. In the UK it was Robert Harris's *Fatherland*, in 1992. Like other genres such as the woman's romance and the Western, the bulk of sf has always tended to be published first in low-priced paperback, requiring authors, for whom royalties would be proportionately low, to over-produce. There was never time for any one title to be a bestseller.

At its heart, the sf market in the 1960s and 1970s was rock-solid, homogenous and ravenous. It was also preponderantly male and well educated; Jack Williamson and James Gunn, two academics who also wrote sf, estimated that by the end of the 1960s there were around a thousand science fiction and fantasy courses being offered in American higher education. An Ace Book survey in the mid-1970s identified the average reader of its sf paperbacks to be fifteen to thirty years old, urban, male, with a high school and college education. Such readers tended to buy six to twelve sf paperbacks a month and their favourite authors were Arthur C. Clarke, Robert Heinlein, Isaac Asimov, Frank Herbert and Ursula LeGuin (a rare woman author in the genre).

The oddest bestseller among hippies was J. R. R. Tolkien's *The Lord of the Rings*, which grew out of a formidable knowledge of old European mythologies. The Oxford Professor of Anglo Saxon had conceived his drama of Frodo, Gandalf, and the Hobbits as long ago as the 1930s. It was originally intended for the delectation of his fellow donnish 'inklings', as they called themselves; C. S. Lewis was another inkling, whose 'Narnia' novels enjoyed cult success in the 1960s. After a spectacular piracy episode in America in the mid-1960s which publicized it, *The Lord of the Rings* trilogy became first a cult classic, then a passport to the underground. London's most trendy club for the hip young in those years was called Middlearth. The more fanatical followers taught themselves Dwarvish. The Beatles were as deep into Tolkien as into the doctrines of the Maharishi. All this extra-mural fame was somewhat bewildering to the Oxford academic, by then in his seventies. He would have been even more amazed, in 2002, to see his fable – along with the Harry Potter saga – regarded as the most popular *children's* book in the Western world. The children had taken over the kindergarten.

Science fiction sold well in the 1960s, and so did science fact. Popular science had evolved into a highly profitable line for the British book trade. These books, typically by a leading authority in the field, were targeted at the literate, self-improving, middle-class reader: the heart of the reading public. Desmond Morris's *The Naked Ape* was far and away the most popular work in this genre. Among other things, the book's popularity signalled the final acceptance of Darwin's theories a century after the momentous publication of *The Origin of Species*. We were descended from monkeys: official. Not that all resistance was dead. *The Naked Ape* enjoyed the distinction of being burned by religious fundamentalists – a guarantee of instant bestseller-dom. For every book that goes up in smoke, ten thousand are subsequently sold (ask Salman Rushdie).

*The Naked Ape* opens with the *faux-naïf* statement: 'There are one hundred and ninety-three species of monkeys and apes. One hundred and ninety-two of them are covered with hair. The exception is a naked ape self-named *Homo sapiens*.' It is an idea picked up vividly by Stanley Kubrick in the prelude to his 1968 film, *2001: A Space Odyssey*, a work which ponders how exactly the naked ape contrived to steal a march on the other 192 dumbos. (Kubrick's film drew, principally, on 'The Sentinel', a story by Britain's leading science fiction writer, Arthur C. Clarke. The 'naked ape' episode was, apparently, the director's idea.)

Born in 1928, Morris was trained in zoology. After graduate work at Oxford on the ten-spined stickleback, young Desmond decided that he had bigger fish to fry. There was, in the late 1950s and 1960s, an insatiable appetite for natural history. On BBC TV (with tied-in books) this appetite was supplied by the French diver Jacques Cousteau; by Armand and Michaela Denis; by the decade's best-known ornithologist, Peter Scott; and by the BBC's brilliant and highly telegenic discovery David Attenborough. Authors included Gerald Durrell (whose *The Overloaded Ark*, published in 1953, was the first of many bestsellers) and Joy Adamson, with her books on lions.

In 1956 Granada TV decided to take on the BBC in this lucrative field by launching an ambitious series of programmes on natural history. Desmond Morris, by now a leading academic zoologist, was chosen to present them. He would, over the next few years, do 500 episodes of *Zootime* for Granada. Like other erudite popularizers of science and culture, notably Jacob Bronowski, Morris had a 'common touch'. He could make the complex comprehensible. *The Naked Ape*, published in 1967, became an instant worldwide bestseller in twenty-three languages. It would sell some 10 million copies over the next few years, boosted by a TV tie-in. Naked apes loved *The Naked Ape*. Morris's book explained such things as why, at rush hour on the London Underground, passengers with their faces just centimetres from each other will do anything to avoid eye contact. It explained why smells are so terrifying (millions are made every year through the selling of 'deodorants'). The piquant word 'Naked' in the title helped (the book might not have sold so well if it had been called 'The Hairless Simian'). The book was also helped (in its original edition) by a vivid cover illustration of *Homo erectus* emerging, stage by stage, from apedom.

Joy Adamson's 1960s bestsellers were co-authored with her husband George, a game warden in a Kenya national park. In 1956 his hunting party startled a lioness and her cubs in the deep bush. She charged, he shot and killed her. He brought one of the lion cubs back to Joy. The couple, who were childless, adopted the animal and named her Elsa. When she was three years old, the Adamsons decided to reintegrate Elsa into her natural environment rather than send her to a zoo. Elsa was taken back into the bush and patiently trained to be wild, or 'free'. The experiment worked.

In 1961 Joy wrote a book about what they had achieved with Elsa. The model she had in mind was Michaela Denis's *Leopard in My Lap*, which had recently done well. Joy, Austrian by birth, was never entirely easy with the English language. She used George's diaries, photographs and warden's journals and duly took her bundle of type-script and pictures to England. Publishers were unimpressed. Thirteen turned it down before it was taken by Sir Billy Collins, who subsequently had an affair with the author. An advance of £1000 was offered, after which *Born Free* was extensively rewritten in-house. The first edition sold out and within months it was translated into twenty-five languages. It made Joy Adamson £500,000 in the first ten years after publication and inspired two follow-ups: *Living Free: The Story of Elsa and Her Cubs* (1961) and *Forever Free: Elsa's Pride* (1962). The 1965 film *Born Free*, starring Bill Travers and Virginia McKenna, along with John Barry's hit theme song boosted sales of the books and made a celebrity of Joy. The Adamsons' 'liberated' zoology appealed to the spirit of the age. The books were a kind of Dr Spock for big cats.

The couple's lives were more complex than readers and filmgoers realized. George was occasionally violent and perennially spendthrift. Joy was serially unfaithful; they separated in 1970. She, enriched by the *Born Free* royalties, travelled around the world, lecturing on wildlife issues and promoting Elsa Clubs. The message of the books took on a quasi-religious tone. *Born Free* was prescribed for the Religious Education syllabus in Northern Ireland. Passages were read aloud in churches in America. On 3 January 1980 the sixty-nine-year-old Joy Adamson, who always said she liked animals more than people, was murdered at her camp on the Kenyan nature reserve where she had lived for three years. The murderer was never discovered.

Zoology, largely because it is so telegenic, did very well in the UK. But mass readership in Britain was slower than in the USA to catch on to the environment as a worrying political issue. In America, the wake-up call was sounded by Rachel Carson. Following a career with the US Fish and Wild Life Service, Carson, a trained biologist, popularized her views on ecology and what modern industrialism was doing to destroy it with *The Sea Around Us* (1952). She was particularly concerned about the unrestricted use of chemical pesticides since World War II. Her powerful critique, *Silent Spring*, was published in 1962, challenging government and the agricultural industry to reform their ways. It stands out as the first of many 'whistle-blowing' books, a genre brought to razor-edge perfection by Ralph Nader with his assault on the US motor industry, *Unsafe at Any Speed*, in 1965. Both authors demonstrated the social power of the book in the modern age. Both were ruthlessly counter-attacked by the industries they accused. Unfortunately, Carson died in 1964 aged fifty-seven, before she could witness the huge effect of *Silent Spring* and the reduction in use of (particularly) DDT and other harmful pesticides which it achieved. Nader lived to see safer cars on American roads.

Eric Berne's *Games People Play* introduced the new school of transactional psychology to a general readership. The book became an international bestseller, claiming a high spot in American bestseller lists in 1965. Berne's basic thesis was that all human interactions involve 'pose', 'role' and, as he put it, game-playing. He did not mean soccer. 'Games', he asserted, 'are a compromise between intimacy and keeping intimacy away.' It was very much a doctrine for the decade, with such consummate performers as Richard Nixon and Harold Wilson leading the free world.

Eric Berne was born Leonard Bernstein in Montreal, Canada, the son of a doctor and a writer. The Bernsteins came to the New World to escape persecution in the Old World. Berne's subsequent fascination with 'game-playing' may be connected with the new self which the immigrant must invent in order to survive in his new homeland.

Leonard Bernstein graduated from McGill University Medical School in 1935. The young psychiatrist emigrated to the USA, where he became an American citizen and changed his name to Eric Berne. After war service as an army psychiatrist he moved to California, where he published his first book, *The Mind in Action*, in 1947. He was by now a disciple of, and undergoing analysis by, Eric Erikson, America's most renowned psychoanalyst.

Over the next few years, Berne moved away from Freudian models to establish his own school of 'transactional analysis'. This was a mode of therapy which replaced the classic 'talking cure' with more active group therapies. In their interactions adults should, Berne maintained, discover the 'child within' and a whole repertoire of earlier selves that make up the mature ego. The human mind is like a snake which does not shed its skins, but keeps them like clothes in the wardrobe for subsequent use.

When writing for his peers, Berne employed the jargon of high psychoanalysis. For the masses he avoided such terminology but did so without condescension. He wrote his famous book in his last years, in the aftermath of his second divorce, at a time when his personal life was chaotic. He died in 1970, aged sixty, having just completed the sequel to *Games People Play*, the catchily entitled *What do You Say After You Say Hello?*

# 3

## The 70s

THE 1970S USHERED IN SOPHISTICATED FORMS of synergy (media interconnection), verticality (the same company owned the film studio as owned the publisher who produced the book of the film) and globalization (the multinational conglomerate dominated the 1970s book trade). A vast bestseller machine emerged, with many articulated and smoothly operating parts. Stephen King's bright idea went in one end, 10 million sales and a tie-in movie popped out the other.

The bestseller had always been an American kind of book. There had been lists in that country, advising retailers and customers on 'books of the day', since 1895. There was, by contrast, no authoritative bestseller list in the UK until 1974. The British ethos was traditionally, and defiantly, different from the American. Books, the British book trade maintained, should not compete with each other in a Darwinian struggle for top place – that no.1 spot which the American book trade saw as the *summum bonum*. Books, bookish Britons believed, complement each other.

In the 1970s the British and American book trades came closer together. By the end of the century they would, at many points, converge. This did not mean colonization by the larger partner. As with popular music and the numerous 'British Invasions', it was a give-and-take thing. Mario Puzo and Peter Benchley sold big in the UK; but Frederick Forsyth, Alistair MacLean, Arthur Hailey, Agatha Christie and Alex Comfort sold big (often bigger) in the USA.

Reviewing American bestseller lists of the 1970s, one is struck by the prominence of British authors – and, chauvinistically, by the high quality of their product. In 1970 John Fowles's experimental Victorian novel *The French Lieutenant's Woman*, which would be filmed in 1981 and given another lease of bestselling life, led the field, closely followed by Graham Greene's comic picaresque *Travels with*

*My Aunt* and Victoria Holt's lush romance *The Secret Woman*. In the non-fiction category, the *New English Bible* headed the lists (what bestseller *could* be better?).

Frederick Forsyth shot straight to the top in 1971 and 1972, with his rat-a-tat sequence of *The Day of the Jackal* and *The Odessa File* – thrillers for modern times. Mary Stewart figured frequently among the decade's bestsellers; first in 1973 with *The Hollow Hills*, a narrative of King Arthur's 'hidden years', narrated by Merlin. In the same year Greene's dark and ultra-English 'entertainment' *The Honorary Consul* made the charts, as did Alistair Cooke's *America*, spun off from a Kenneth Clark-style mini-series designed originally for British TV viewers.

In 1974 Richard Adams's 'Beatrix Potter for grown-ups' animal thriller *Watership Down* and le Carré's 'Bond for grown-ups' *Tinker, Tailor, Soldier, Spy* were among America's top ten fiction titles. And Forsyth made it three in a row with his polemical, pro-Biafra thriller *The Dogs of War*; all of his first three books were picked up for big-budget films by Hollywood. James Herriot was an unlikely British best-seller in America that year, with his country vet's fictionalized memoirs.

In 1974 Jack Higgins's wartime docu-thriller *The Eagle Has Landed* (Germans abduct Churchill) was the big novel of the year, inspiring a movie starring Michael Caine. It was closely followed by James Clavell's epic of samurai Japan, *Shogun*, which span off a Richard Chamberlain-starring TV mini-series. It went down big in Japan, as well. That year also saw Hercule Poirot's swansong, *Curtain*. Agatha Christie's novel had been thirty-five years in cold storage. She wrote it and then put the manuscript in a safe during the Blitz in 1941, not expecting to survive Hitler's bombs.

A charming entrant to the bestseller lists was David Niven's witty memoir of being an English actor in pre-war Hollywood, *Bring on the Empty Horses* (1975). Niven's earlier bestseller, *The Moon's a Balloon* (1971), had founded a genre – the celebrity actor's veteran reminiscences. Dirk Bogarde, in the following decades, probably earned more from his eight volumes of autobiography than he had from his stardom as a matinee idol.

In 1976 Jack Higgins's *Storm Warning* and Mary Stewart's *Touch Not the Cat* were both high in the American top ten. Both authors by now had 'name recognition'. There were other second appearances. The American lists in 1977 were dominated by *The Silmarillion*, Tolkien's posthumous follow-up to *The Lord of the Rings*; *Daniel Martin*, John Fowles's follow-up to *The French Lieutenant's Woman*; and *All Things Wise and Wonderful*, James Herriot's follow-up to *All Things Bright and Beautiful*. In 1978, Ken Follett's docu-thriller of World War II, *The Eye of the Needle*, was the first of a string of no.1 titles for this British author in America. In 1979, General Sir John Hackett's *The Third World War of 1985* revived the Victorian genre of futurological military fantasy. Vietnam had generated a popular appetite for war stories – preferably more cheerful ones than the 1970s history books recorded.

There was, title for title, a bigger presence of American titles in the British bestseller lists, particularly fiction, in the 1970s. But given the higher volume sales in the USA, with four times the population of the UK, Britain more than held its own in the global English-speaking market.

The biggest international blockbuster novel of the 1970s came early in the decade. The background to *The Godfather* is legendary. Mario Puzo (b. 1920) had written two 'literary' novels which netted a paltry $6500 between them. 'I was 45 years old,' the author recalled, 'and tired of being an artist. It was time to grow up and sell out.' In a spirit of cynicism, he wrote a gangster saga set in 1940s New York. He got a $5000 advance based on the synopsis. The paperback rights were sold for a then record-breaking $410,000. Puzo had sold out in style.

Published in late 1969, *The Godfather* rocketed to the top of the American bestseller list. By the end of the decade, boosted by Francis Ford Coppola's 1971 film and Marlon Brando's Oscar-winning performance as Don Corleone, worldwide sales of over 15 million were claimed by the novel's publishers. *The Godfather* was the fastest bestseller ever. Even in the UK, with its very different patterns of crime.

The germ of Puzo's novel is an exuberantly paradoxical essay he published in 1966: 'How Crime Keeps America Healthy, Wealthy, Cleaner and More Beautiful'. Crime *is* the American way. The novel celebrates Mafia family life (the family that slays together, stays together) and the efficiency and high business ethics of the 'organization' – themes which would be picked up and exploited thirty years later in the hit TV series, *The Sopranos*. But irony, especially anti-American irony, never sold 15 million books and Puzo wisely kept the novel's core ideas oblique.

Pressing hard on Puzo's pre-eminence in the bestseller lists, Erich Segal's *Love Story* (1970) sold more than 10 million copies over the decade. He was, on the face of it, an unusual candidate for success in popular fiction. The son of a rabbi, Segal taught classics at Harvard before becoming really rich. *Love Story* was originally conceived as a screenplay and the narrative is exactly what the title baldly declares it to be: *Romeo and Juliet* on the American campus. Two students fall in love. He encounters parental opposition. They overcome it. Joy. She dies, beautifully, of an unidentified disease. Tears. The book's 'message' is summed up in its now proverbial maxim: 'Love means never having to say you're sorry.' The hardback edition of *Love Story* was reprinted twenty times in its first year. Students loved it; however, when it was entered for a prestigious NBA award, the judging panel threatened to resign if it were not withdrawn. The film, which came out in 1970 and starred Ali McGraw and Ryan O'Neal, was also a huge hit. Segal did not have to feel sorry about anything – except, perhaps, that people tended not to take him seriously as a classicist any more.

If *The Godfather* was the page-turner of the decade, the 'beach book' that Americans packed for their summer vacation was *Jaws* (1974) by Peter Benchley (b. 1940). In just six months as a Bantam paperback the novel sold 6 million copies. Within a couple of years it reached the maximal 10 million mark, which meant that one in ten adult Americans had bought it. In Britain, Pan's paperback edition of *Jaws* sold a million in its first year and twice as many in its second, boosted by the 1975 film. Stephen Spielberg's movie itself broke box-office records, taking almost half a billion dollars in receipts after a production outlay of $8 million. '*Jaws* mania' received America's highest popular acknowledgement in 1975: the front cover of *Time*.

The 1970s were notable for a number of bestselling animal narratives directed at the adult rather than the traditional young persons' market. Three became international supersellers: *Jonathan Livingston Seagull* (1970) by Richard Bach; *Jaws*; and *Watership Down* (1972) by Richard Adams. All, oddly enough, were first novels. All connect with a great political cause of the age, the environment. At their root is that *angst* first formulated in 1962 in Rachel Carson's Cassandra warning to the modern age, *Silent Spring*.

Benchley's novel reflects the typical 'environmental' uneasiness of the 1970s. Was it, after all, *right* to hunt the white whale Moby Dick to death and his species to extinction? In the 1952 novella that helped win him the Nobel Prize for Literature two years later, Hemingway pictures the sharks as – well, *sharks*; thieves of the sea. The sharks rob Santiago, the old man, of his hard-won catch, the giant marlin, ensuring that he will die poor.

In *Jaws* there are, by contrast, two schools of thought about the 'Great White'. For Hooper, the ichthyologist, the fish is beautiful: 'Sharks have everything a scientist dreams of. They're beautiful – God, how beautiful they are! They're like an impossibly perfect piece of machinery. They're as graceful as any bird. They're as mysterious as any animal on earth.' 'Horseshit!' responds Quint, the Hemingwayesque old fisherman. In his unlyrical view sharks are neither mysterious nor wonderful. They are 'dumb garbage buckets'. The dualism is sustained until the climax of the novel in which both men die killing the shark, which also kills them.

Bach's is a simpler fable. Its narrative comprises a fictional reconstruction of a visionary seagull's flight from A to B. In prose poetic fashion, it celebrates airy freedoms. The name 'Livingston[e]' evokes man's questing, exploring spirit. It is plausible that this dreary 'novel', which sold 2 million copies in America in 1972 and also did well in the UK, drew its appeal from the late 1960s and early 1970s resurgence of *Wandervogel* idealism, more realistically depicted in that other tract for the times, *Easy Rider* (1969), and in the Devil's Island escape story (boosted by a 1973 film) *Papillon*, by Henri Charrière.

Questing and escaping were the themes of the decade. Animal, fish, bird (or even jailbird) migration allegorized the decade's restlessness. Richard Adams's novel (the best of this bunch) took as its dramatis personae the farmer's foe and Britain's most loved and cuddly vermin, the rabbit. The origin of *Watership Down* is recalled in its dedication to the author's daughters, Juliet and Rosamond. Adams conceived the story on a car journey with his ten- and eight-year-old girls. Afterwards they 'kept pestering him until he agreed to write it down'. He did so in 1969. The book was taken on by the fringe publisher Rex

Collings in 1970. Two years later the rights were shrewdly bought up by Kaye Webb, director of Puffin Books, the children's list at Penguin. Under this imprint *Watership Down* became a bestseller – for adults.

*Watership Down* tells the story of the inhabitants of a warren who decide on a great migration after one of them, Fiver, has a vision of a field covered with blood (the developers with their bulldozers are imminent). Under Hazel's command, and after many adventures and vicissitudes, the rabbits eventually win through to a rodents' promised land, Watership Down. Adams's novel topped UK bestseller lists in 1973 and 1974, the first 'children's book' to enjoy that pinnacle position. Its long-term sales were boosted by a British-made cartoon film version in 1978. Adams had further, if less spectacular, success with *Shardik* (1974), which has a bear 'hero', and *Plague Dogs* (1977).

A vision of animal creation less red in tooth and claw is offered by James Herriot (1916–95), whose Yorkshire vet's stories were all-conquering in the mid-1970s. In 1975–6, no fewer than eight of his titles featured in the hardback and paperback UK bestseller lists. Herriot's anecdotal reminiscences are, on the face of it, amateurish literary efforts, tinged with nostalgia for a country way of life now forever gone. In fact, they bear witness to the natural skills of a born raconteur who knows his animals, his county and human nature.

The formula behind the Herriot books is simple: *Dr Finlay's Casebook* crossed with *Dr Dolittle*. Although they are frequently classified as 'fiction', Herriot's books are, more properly, 'embellished memoirs'. Underneath, one senses a life's hard graft in what unbookish people call 'the real world'. Fans, with their fanatic detective zeal, soon discovered that Darrowby, the fictional small town in which the stories are set, is Thirsk, on the North York Moors, where James Herriot (real name Alf Wight) had his practice. A tourist centre (pilgrim's shrine would be the truer term) has since been set up in Wight's house by the local council.

James Herriot's experiences with his eccentric and lovable colleague Siegfried Farnon recall Richard Gordon's successful series that started with *Doctor in the House*. Both men could tell a good story, and had a wealth of good stories to tell, furnished by their professional careers. Herriot's books came thick and fast in the 1970s, along with superior TV adaptations. *All Creatures Great and Small* (1975), a huge hit, was followed by the similarly hymnal *All Things Bright and Beautiful* (1976) and, thereafter, always one and sometimes two books a year. All were cut from the same pattern – 'a funny thing happened to me on the way to the pregnant cow'. All were bestsellers in Britain and, after PBS picked up the TV serial, in the USA as well, where they slotted neatly into the same notch as that other ultra-English export, *Upstairs, Downstairs*. The Herriot books represented, in the mid-1970s, an elegy for a lost England: unchanged since the enclosures and, as we once fondly (but erroneously) thought, unchangeable forever. Herriot celebrates a rural world before battery farms, agro-chemicals and the Common Agricultural Policy.

A 'small world', in other words. That quality was celebrated – just as everything else, including the bestseller, was getting frighteningly bigger – in one of the most influential treatise books of the decade, *Small Is Beautiful* (1973) by E. F. Schumacher. Its influence lasted: a 1997 *Times Literary Supplement* poll ranked it as one of the 'hundred most influential books published since the Second World War'. Schumacher's is 'heterodox economics'. The book's subtitle indicates the author's thesis: 'Economics As If People Mattered'. Quality of life is as important as the bottom line. Like many of the most influential thinkers of the post-war period, such as Eric Berne and Jacob Bronowski, Schumacher was a refugee from pre-war Europe. In the late 1940s (like Bronowski, again) he had worked for the newly nationalized Coal Board. Dealing with very large and inherently intractable structures convinced him of the truth of what would be the core belief expressed in *Small Is Beautiful*: 'If a society grows beyond its optimum size, its problems must eventually outrun the growth of those human faculties which are necessary for dealing with them.' That stage had, in the Western world, been well passed by 1970. Schumacherian concepts of 'renewable resources' and 'sustainability' influenced thinking about global planning for the next three decades.

If Alistair MacLean was the middle-brow bestseller machine of the 1960s, his top spot was usurped in the 1970s by Arthur Hailey. Hailey's was a remarkable, but quintessentially British career. He did not start writing fiction until the age of thirty-five – by which time he had seen much of the world and had made any number of false starts in life. Born to a working-class Leicester family in 1920, Hailey left school at fourteen and entered the RAF three years later. He rose through the (non-commissioned) ranks during World War II. Despairing of Britain and socialist austerity he emigrated in the early 1950s to Canada, where he wrote his first novels. On the strength of his earnings he moved to California in 1965 and, as his fortune continued to prosper, to tax exile in the Bahamas in the 1970s.

Hailey's first successful fiction, *Flight into Danger*, was published in 1958. It employs a gimmick that would be much imitated (there is, as popular fiction everywhere witnesses, no copyright in gimmicks). Everyone on board an airliner, including the pilot, is disabled by food poisoning – only one passenger, who knows nothing about flying planes, remains conscious. Nail-biting suspense follows.

Hailey followed with a hospital melodrama, *The Final Diagnosis*, in 1959. It did well. Bigger things were to come. His first blockbuster was *Hotel* in 1965 – filmed lavishly two years later. It was followed by *Airport* in 1968 – filmed, with no expense spared, in 1970. These novels established Hailey's superselling formula. In *Airport*, multiple crises are woven together: a snowstorm has 'socked in' the airport (clearly Chicago); there is a mad bomber aboard an incoming plane; a stewardess is pregnant by the pilot. Reviewers of the book and film made hay with it: 'The best film of 1944,' sneered one; 'A Grand Hotel in the sky,' wisecracked another. But readers in their hundreds of thousands, and cinemagoers in their millions, adored Hailey's 'all life is there' melodrama.

Hailey's big 1970s novels would be set in the USA. Each of them would make the coveted no.1 spot on the *New York Times* bestseller list, certifying their author as the top novelist of the decade. *Wheels*, a multi-plot melodrama about how cars are made in Detroit, appeared in 1971. The most thoroughly researched and genuinely informative of Hailey's novels to date, it follows the career of maverick auto-boss Adam Trent – based, unfortunately as later events would prove, on *wunderkind* John Z. DeLorean. *The Moneychangers* (1975) 'uncovers' the mysteries of the US banking system. *Overload* (1979) does the same for the West Coast electrical supply industry. All Hailey's novels did well in the UK, although not one in a thousand readers can have identified the author as a local lad made good.

What Hailey did so profitably in these novels was to fix on a contemporary universal experience – something which everyone who could afford $2 for a paperback has, does, wants, or is likely to be affected by. With the arrival of mass tourism and the jumbo jet, for the first time in the 1970s vast numbers of 'ordinary' people travelled by air and congregated in airport lounges; often they passed the weary hours of waiting with Hailey's 'airport fiction', as the genre was called. In America in the 1970s most Americans drove a Detroit-made car, stayed at a hotel, used a bank, and carried credit cards. Everyone used electricity. At the same time, these universal experiences involved mystery – private areas sectioned off for 'staff only'. This was where Hailey's research came in. He spent, he claimed, four years on each of his works; and fully one year was devoted to study of his subject. Hailey communicated to his readers what made these things tick. His books retain their appeal: 160 million copies had been sold, world-wide, by 2002.

The biggest, wholly British, fiction superseller of the early 1970s was that rare thing in popular fiction – something original. *The Day of the Jackal* invented and popularized the docu-thriller – the adventure story based on secret (now it can be told) history. It was the runaway British bestseller in 1971 and went on to sell strongly in the USA. By 2002, worldwide sales were estimated at 9 million and still going strong.

The genesis of the novel is book-trade legend. Frederick Forsyth received a gentleman's education at Tonbridge School but left at seventeen to take a commission in the RAF, where he became the youngest fighter pilot in the service. This phase of his career is commemorated in the aeronautical ghost story *The Shepherd* (1975). From 1961 Forsyth, now twenty-three, worked for the news agency Reuter's, following in the footsteps of Ian Fleming. But whereas Fleming's formative experiences had been in Moscow in the 1930s, Forsyth picked up his insider's gossip in Reuter's Paris bureau in the early 1960s, at a period when the French capital was seething with resentment against the granting of independence to Algeria, which many patriots regarded as a sell-out. Forsyth stored it all away.

Forsyth took Fleming as his model, but brilliantly modified the traditional thriller by hybridizing its narrative with historical fact. The novel opens, for instance, with a vivid description of an 'historical' assassination attempt on President De Gaulle on 22 August 1962. The account which Forsyth gives of the composition of his book links him with those other great amateurs of the classic British thriller – John Buchan, 'Sapper' and, of course, Ian Fleming:

> My first novel, *The Day of the Jackal*, must remain, I believe, one of the most accidental novels ever written. I decided, in January 1970, with little hope of success, to try my hand at a single one-off novel, for no better motive than that I happened to be broke and without many prospects after twelve years in journalism. I dashed off *The Day of the Jackal* in thirty-five days, virtually without notes, relying on my memory and keeping the plot in my head. That, so far as I was concerned, was that. If it failed, so what. If it succeeded in making a few pounds, so much the better. The compulsion to write another one was a minus quantity. I seem destined to remain a quite damnably lucky amateur.

All authors should be so damnably lucky. Four British publishers turned the manuscript down. But, with hindsight, one can see exactly why, once published, *The Day of the Jackal* took off meteorically. The fantasy of an upper-class English killer, codename 'Jackal', setting out to bump off the French president struck a sympathetic chord with Britons in 1971. Many of them desperately wanted to get into Europe. And who had barred the way? One man, Charles De Gaulle, who had memorably said that if Britannia wanted to join the Common Market, she would have to come *nue*, naked. A lot of Europhiles would have been right behind the Jackal.

The docu-thriller would prove a rich 1970s vein. Forsyth himself exploited it with rapid follow-ups, *The Odessa File* (1972), *The Dogs of War* (1974), *The Devil's Alternative* (1979) and *The Fourth Protocol* (1984). The new genre was, however, bigger than one author. Close on Forsyth's heels came Jack Higgins (one of the many pen names of Harry Patterson, b. 1929) with *The Eagle Has Landed* (1975). Written by an Irishman who would later pen a series of thrillers around his IRA hero, Sean Dillon, Higgins earned a record pre-publication advance for his book in America. *The Eagle Has Landed* was, despite its British origins, first published in America – the richer market pulled it across the Atlantic. It went on to do phenomenally well, selling 18 million copies over the next ten years.

Like Forsyth's *Jackal*, Higgins's *Eagle* is a pseudo-documentary 'secret history'. Its contents are described in the 1970s paperback blurb, with its 'military' precision of reference:

> At precisely one o'clock on the morning of Saturday, November 6, 1943, Heinrich Himmler, Reichsführer of the SS and Chief of State Police, received a simple message: 'The Eagle has Landed.' It meant that a small force of German paratroopers were at that moment safely in England and poised to snatch the British Prime Minister, Winston Churchill, from the Norfolk country house where he was spending a quiet weekend by the sea. This book is an attempt to recreate the events surrounding that astonishing exploit. At least fifty per cent of it is documented historical fact. The reader must decide for himself how much of the rest is a matter of speculation or fiction.

The most talented of those who exploited Forsyth's docu-thriller breakthrough was Ken Follett (b. 1949). A young English writer who had studied philosophy at University College, London, Follett had drifted for some years as a provincial journalist, writing pulp thrillers on the side. He broke into international bestsellerdom with *The Eye of the Needle* (originally called *Storm Island* in the UK) in 1978. The chronicle of a top German spy known as the 'Needle' after his penchant for the stiletto as a killing weapon, Follett's docu-thriller too is usefully summarized by its 1970s paperback blurb: 'His code name was The Needle. He was a tall, handsome German aristocrat of extraordinary intelligence – England's most dangerous enemy. He knew the secret that could win the war for Hitler.' The secret, of course, is Overlord: the Allies' invasion plan. The Needle's villainy is foiled by a beautiful English woman, though the foiling is somewhat complicated by the fact that she falls in love with the tall handsome German aristocrat of extraordinary intelligence.

In overview, the 1970s was a great decade for old-fashioned thrillers with fashionable new twists and flavours. Flying less high (but with the same kind of material) as Forsyth, Follett or Higgins was Desmond Bagley (1923–83), the leader of the British second division. And coming up fast on the outside lane Dick Francis (b. 1920) topped the British lists in 1979 with *Whip Hand*, the latest in a long sequence of ex-jockey's thrillers begun with *Dead Cert* in 1962. Over the years, Francis's horsey whodunits would become a firm favourite with, among others, Kingsley Amis, Philip Larkin, the Queen Mother and millions of ordinary Britons.

Francis's writing routine was as disciplined and repetitive as his training had been when he was a champion jockey. Every January he would deliver a new manuscript to Michael Joseph, under whose publishing colours he always wrote, and the novel would duly appear a few months later. And it would, as duly, top the British bestseller lists. Francis's novels were reassuringly amateurish, untaxing and rigidly formulaic. A good read, and nothing more. But, at the end of the day (reading in bed, that is), what more did one want? In 1999 the biographer Graham Lord provoked a fuss by alleging that Francis's wife, Mary (a former reader with Michael Joseph – she had turned down *The Day of the Jackal*), was the power behind her husband's pen. The allegation was not denied; nor did it much bother Francis's by now veteran fans. No complaints were forthcoming from Clarence House.

From the British publisher's point of view, the most reliable writer of male-action thrillers was Wilbur Smith. Born in Africa in 1933, he was educated at Rhodes University where the colonial idealism of Cecil Rhodes burned indelibly into his personality. Smith became a full-time writer in 1964 after the publication of his first novel (and first bestseller) *When the Lion Feeds*. A grand panorama of South African history, it follows the adventurous life and heroic exploits of a settler named Sean Courtney. His hero is swept up into the Zulu War battle at Rorke's Drift, the gold rush, a veritable holocaust of big game hunting and some relaxing romance after the day's bloodshed. Subsequent instalments in the Courtney saga (Smith likes to connect his fiction into large sequences) take in the Boer War and the growth of the South African mining industry, through which Sean becomes a rand-millionaire.

What Smith offered in his novels was two-fisted adventure. Or, as the *Evening Standard* put it, he created 'A man's world, where hate can swell like biceps and frontiers beckon as seductively as a woman.' His own life conformed to the outdoor excitements of his fiction. A writer in the Jack London mould, Smith, made wealthy by his fiction, travelled the world: the ski slopes, the safari trail and the deep sea fishing grounds called to him. And, on his return, he wrote about them for the Englishman whose life contained no more adventure than a daily dash for the 68 bus to work.

There is, in all Smith's fiction, a concern with 'wilderness': the environment not yet wholly ruined by man. He favours titles which invoke the beauties and perils of the natural world – *When the Lion Feeds*, *A Falcon Flies*, *The Leopard Hunts in Darkness*, *The Eye of the Tiger*, *Elephant Song*, *Cry Wolf*. His stories centre on acts of daring, extreme peril and lush romantic love with Alphaman in the driving seat.

Smith had six titles high in the UK bestseller lists in the 1970s. His string of hits began with *Gold Mine* (1970) set, as the title signals, in the mining world of present-day South Africa; the price of the precious metal had rocketed at this period – Smith's fiction is often topical in this way. The novel was filmed as *Gold*, starring Roger Moore, in 1974. *Eagle in the Sky* (1974) chronicles the epic struggles of Israel for survival. The hero, David Morgan, is a jet-fighter pilot involved in a passionate relationship with the voluptuous Debra; the novel's popularity was boosted by the 1973 Yom Kippur War. There followed the *The Eye of the Tiger* (1975), a tale of underwater adventure. *A Sparrow Falls* (1977) is the last instalment in Sean Courtney's saga, coming into the twentieth century and World War I. Sean's story ends with this novel, but his family chronicle was continued with *The Burning Shore* and the launch of the 'Courtneys of Africa Saga' in 1985.

Smith's *Hungry as the Sea* (1978) is an adventure yarn set among supertankers and international shipping. A lone mariner takes on the consortiums. It features shipwreck, hurricane and the hero Nick Berg's even more tempestuous involvements with the lovely Samantha. *Wild Justice* (1979) is an international terrorist hijack thriller (the crime of the moment), the narrative as jet-propelled as the planes. As always Smith's hero, Peter Stride, triumphs against the forces of evil. Good (and masculine muscle) prevail. As the 1970s came to an end Wilbur Smith began a new saga, that of the Ballantyne family, with *A Falcon Flies* (1980). It had been a high-flying decade for the author, as well.

Although none of his adventure stories made no.1 in any year's UK charts, cumulatively he out-totalled all rivals, with the possible exception of Forsyth.

Smith's thrillers were resolutely old-fashioned: Rider Haggard for modern times. A newer-fangled sub-genre which sold consistently well in the 1970s was the 'nightmare that wouldn't die', Nazism resurgent, thriller. The Eichmann trial of 1961 had alerted the world to the fact that many of the senior Nazi criminals had escaped justice (had they been *helped* to escape justice?). No one, for example, could avoid noticing that the great hero of the 1969 American moon landing was a former Nazi scientist, Wernher von Braun. What other scientists from that horrific regime were still at large? Popular fiction of the decade fantasized old Germanic monsters in white coats hatching plans for a fourth Reich in the jungles of South America. Mengele, the vile concentration camp doctor, featured in popular novel after novel, as (*in propria persona* or under thin disguise) did the famous Nazi-hunter Simon Wiesenthal.

Novels like Forsyth's *The Odessa File* (the bestselling novel in the UK in 1972, and in the USA in 1973) detailed, with meticulous plausibility, the Nazis' escape routes and their networks of still loyal 'comrades'. In America Robert Ludlum devised a string of popular thrillers around the 'nightmare that wouldn't die' plot. Two themes predominated. The first was that these refugee Nazis were obscenely rich, with their ill-gotten gains. Secondly, and even more horribly, they had taken with them into exile the secrets of their eugenic experiments, enabling them to breed a new master race.

In Ludlum's *The Holcroft Covenant* (1978) one signature will suffice to release the billion dollars of Swiss-held Nazi booty, which will permit the re-creation of the German Reich. In Peter Lear's *Golden Girl* (1977) the athlete heroine is 'a bright, beautiful manufactured monster, bred from Nazi stud-farm stock', generated out of a test tube to win at the 1980 Moscow Olympics. There were any number of other thrillers along these two lines.

The best of the 'nightmare that wouldn't die' sub-genre were William Goldman's *Marathon Man* (1974) and Ira Levin's *The Boys from Brazil* (1976), both of which were successfully filmed. Levin began his career as a writer of whodunits. *The Boys from Brazil* opens

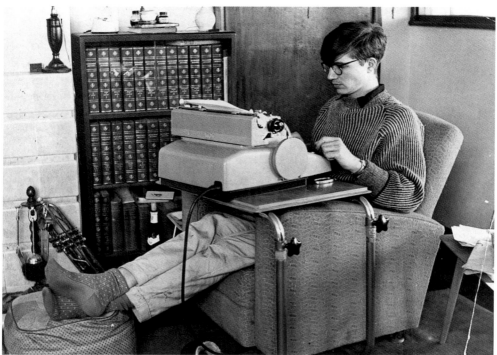

**Top** 'Which of us sells the most?' Ian Fleming and Barbara Cartland.
**Above** The Angry Young Man: Colin Wilson quietly typing, the *Encyclopaedia Britannica* close at hand.

**Opposite** Sylvia Plath, whose confessional first novel *The Bell Jar* was published under the pseudonym Victoria Lucas in 1963. It would become a classic text for the emergent feminist movement.
**Right** Felix Topolski's striking portrait of Jacob Bronowski at the time of his triumphant BBC television series and its tie-in book. He did not live to see its huge success.
**Below** The indefatigable Jackie Susann (right) – or 'a truck driver in drag' as Truman Capote described her. The author was perhaps less a love machine than a PR machine – all her novels were no.1 bestsellers.

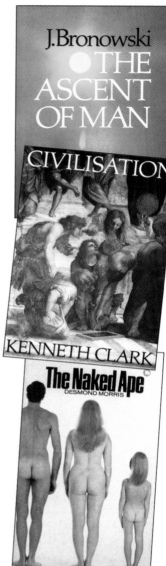

**Above, top to bottom:** The TV tie-in comes of age. Jacob Bronowski's *The Ascent of Man*, Kenneth Clark's *Civilisation* and Desmond Morris's *The Naked Ape* headed British bestseller lists for years on end, educated the British public in the higher things of the mind and in the process made media superstars of their authors.

**Above** A young Frederick Forsyth moodily contemplating the plot of his next internationally bestselling docu-thriller.
**Below** Jack Nicholson's Randle Patrick McMurphy goes head-to-head with Louise Fletcher's Nurse Ratched in Milos Forman's 1975 film adaptation of Ken Kesey's *One Flew Over the Cuckoo's Nest*.
**Opposite** Definitely *not* Fanny Cradock. Germaine Greer saw no conflict between being an outspoken feminist and being a good cook.

**Above, top to bottom:**
De Gaulle in the gun sights in Forsyth's *The Day of the Jackal*; the iconic cover of Greer's *The Female Eunuch*; one of Dick Francis's annual bestsellers, *Whip Hand*.

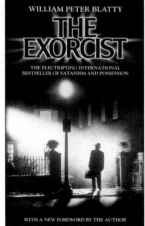

**Above** Writer and broadcaster Alistair Cooke, seen here at a signing session for one of his many bestselling books, has been Britain's beloved transatlantic correspondent for more than fifty years.
**Below** Jeffrey Archer promoting his bestseller about Fleet Street, *The Fourth Estate*, in the interval between his triumphant 1987 libel case and his conviction for perjury in 2001.
**Opposite** Before the *fatwa*. Salman Rushdie holds aloft the 1989 bestseller that would forever transform his career.

**Above, top to bottom:**
Jonathan Lynn and Antony Jay's *Yes, Minister* was a hit on the small screen and in the bookshop; Douglas Adams's brilliantly dotty *The Hitch-hiker's Guide to the Galaxy*; the evocative movie image that helped make Blatty's *The Exorcist* a superseller in paperback.

# JANE FONDA'S WORKOUT BOOK

by Jane Fonda

with photographs
by Steve Schapiro

**Above** Forty may well have been 'Hiroshima' for Jackie Susann. For Jane Fonda, however, middle age provided an opportunity to show how great you could still look, fifteen years after *Barbarella*. Her *Workout Book* (1982) and the accompanying video blazed a trail for celebrity lifestyle publications.

with a clever exercise in reader hoaxing. Why is an apparently random selection of men being simultaneously murdered round the world? The Simon Wiesenthal figure in the novel thinks there must be a reason, but he can't put his finger on it. It emerges that the 'Angel of Death', Mengele, has planted a hundred of Hitler's cloned offspring on to unsuspecting adoptive parents.

*Marathon Man* features a Nazi dentist coming to America to reclaim his ill-gotten gains – diamonds stolen from Jews during the war and now held in a New York safety deposit box. It means his leaving the safety of South America. But with the loot, he can further the aims of new-Nazidom. Goldman's novel, as the title indicates, trendily exploits the 1970s running, jogging and marathon-racing vogue. It was the 'fitness decade', when authors like Jim Fixx would enrich themselves with jogging books. In Goldman's thriller the hero escapes from the villainous Szell, who is torturing him with a dentist's drill ('Is it safe?' he asks, time and again), by taking to his heels and outjogging the bad guys.

There is a deep tinge of occultism in the 'nightmare that wouldn't die' fiction of the 1970s. Black magic and black Nazi uniforms harmonize naturally. The theme of Anthony Burgess's fine novel *Earthly Powers* (1980) was that new forms of superstition would rush in to fill the vacuum left by traditional religion. A godless age would, perforce, become a superstitious age, incapable of living without the comfort of theology whether true or false. Gods we must have. If not Christian, then pagan. Theologians worried as children in playgrounds all over the world chanted Obi-Wan Kenobi's 'May the Force Be with You'.

Burgess's thesis was borne out by the international popularity of Erich von Däniken. A Swiss national, and before he became a best-selling author the manager of a five-star hotel, von Däniken achieved fame with his first book, *Chariots of the Gods* (1967). He argued that astronauts from other galaxies had, in prehistoric times, dropped in on planet earth. They had performed 'miracles' for our bewildered ancestors and had been worshipped as gods. The 'chariots' often referred to in ancient mythology were, in fact, flying saucers. The Ark of the Covenant was, von Däniken speculated, a nuclear reactor bestowed on the human race by these benevolent aliens. Von Däniken's scrutiny of ancient documents and his decodings of old Mayan and Egyptian pictograms, allegedly showing stickmen aliens in spacesuits, were adduced in support of his thesis.

His books went on to sell 60 million copies worldwide, boosted by the author's indefatigable promotional efforts. And, of course, the inextinguishable gullibility of the reading public. He sold spectacularly well in the UK in the 1970s with *Gods from Outer Space* (1970), *The Gold of the Gods* (1972), *In Search of Ancient Gods* (1973), *Miracles of the Gods* (1974) and *Signs of the Gods* (1979). Von Däniken evidently believed that if you had a good title, why for God's sake fix it? His most recent book is *Odyssey of the Gods: An Alien History of Ancient Greece* (2000). His books, derided by legitimate archaeologists, made him fabulously rich and enabled him to set up his own institute. His ideas fed into movies, and back into novelizations, with blockbusters like *Close Encounters of the Third Kind* (1977). Indirectly, they stimulated interest in L. Ron Hubbard's cross-over science fiction and theology, Scientology. Hubbard's manual, *Dianetics*, first published in 1950, was one of the perennial bestsellers of the 1970s although it never appeared on the lists.

Occult fiction – new varieties of 'horror' – made a powerful comeback in the 1970s. Known in the trade as 'frighteners', one or two titles feature every year. The most successful, and a trailblazer, was Peter Blatty's *The Exorcist* (1971), which sold an estimated 12 million in the USA in the 1970s and some 2 million in the UK, boosted in both markets by William Friedkin's 1973 film. The book's theme is simple and Manichaean: the age-old struggle of good and evil. Regan, a good little eleven-year-old, is possessed by the devil. Good girl becomes unspeakably evil girl. Under the influence of her demon, Regan twists the head off her single-parent mother's lover and impales what's left on a spiked railing. Finally, in an orgy of horror, Regan is exorcized. Good girl again.

A large number of these 'frighteners' centred on possessed, demonic or downright satanic children. 'Problem children', that is, gothically magnified. It is tempting to link them with Benjamin Spock's ubiquitous *Baby and Child Care* which, with 25 million sales in the decade, outsold most other books – certainly all horror novels. Spock, too, was big on problem children – although his remedies tended to be less drastic than exorcism.

'Frighteners' made natural partners with movies. Stephen King came to pre-eminence in the 1970s with *Carrie*, the story of an ordinary American schoolgirl with, as it emerges, extraordinary powers which, in a bloody climax, enable her to nuke her whole neighbourhood telekinetically. At the time he wrote it King was an undistinguished mass producer of gothic for the pulp fiction market, but his career was catapulted into bestsellerdom by Brian de Palma's 1976 film adaptation. Hollywood's new expertise in special effects created a huge market for elaborate and imaginative horror scenarios. Stephen King obliged.

King was born in 1947 in Portland, Maine, a recurrent setting in his fiction. His father abandoned the family in Stephen's childhood, something to which the author frequently refers. After an ordinary American high school and college career King graduated from the University of Maine to work as a schoolteacher. He had been writing genre fiction (sf, horror and Westerns) from childhood. In 1971 he began writing a story about a girl called Carietta. In January 1973 he submitted *Carrie* (as it now was) to the publisher Doubleday, who sold the paperback rights to New American Library for $400,000. Thereafter, Stephen King was big-time. None bigger. Unlike Blatty, a one-bestseller author, King was the Midas of horror in whose hands all schlock turned to gold. He was lucky to have his novels adapted by the most creative of film *auteurs*. Stanley Kubrick did *The Shining* (1980; haunted hotel), John Carpenter did *Christine* (1983; haunted car), David Cronenberg did *The Dead Zone* (1983; haunted teacher). As the decades rolled by, King would establish himself as the bestselling male author of the century.

Burdened with the sobriquet 'the British Stephen King', James Herbert achieved instant popularity (in Britain, at least) with his first novel, *The Rats* (1974), a gothic vision of London over-run by a plague of super rodents. No pied piper is available and the capital welters in an orgy of fur and blood. Herbert followed up with *The Fog* (1975), *The Survivor* (1976), *Fluke* (1977; his most interesting novel, told from a dog's eye view) and *The Spear* (1978), a frightener about Nazism resurgent through the magical powers of (what else?) a spear. Herbert was born in the East End of London (a locale he evokes well in *The Rats*), the son of street traders. There is a punk-like grittiness about his fiction.

He himself claims to have been principally inspired by the American horror comics he read in his youth and maintains that the essential appeal of his fiction is that it is not snobbish. Horror for the proles.

Horror fiction was big business in the 1970s, but sometimes the normal sequence – the 'film-of-the-book' – was reversed, with the big-budget film being written up as a bestselling book. *The Omen*, the story of an 'imp of Satan', was, in 1976, the first true 'novelization' (afterthought 'book-of-the-film') to head the American bestseller lists. The author (i.e. novelizer) was hired hand David Seltzer; the studio retained copyright. The first novelizations to feature on British lists were George Lucas's *Star Wars* (1978; 'ghosted', of course), Stephen Spielberg's *Close Encounters of the Third Kind* (1978, also 'ghosted'), *The Amityville Horror* (1979, Jay Anson), *Alien* (1979; the no.2 fiction paperback of the year, by Alan Dean Foster, the most gifted of the 1970s novelizers).

These pseudo-novels are less interesting in themselves than as evidence of growing consolidation within the entertainment industry. In this respect, *Star Wars* is significant. In November 2001, a Channel 4 TV viewers' poll voted George Lucas's film no.1 of the hundred greatest films. It is dubious, on simple artistic criteria, whether it deserves that palm. And, examining the 1970s *Star Wars* phenomenon, it makes sense to see it less as a free-standing film than as a franchise industry.

Like the McDonald's hamburger, *Star Wars* could be consumed, in numerous varieties, by the whole family, from the youngest to the oldest of both sexes. It was less a film or novel than a marketing strategy, designed to scoop up cash and pocket money; and it was helped by the commercial fact that in the modern USA there is virtually no product which cannot be copyrighted, patented, registered under a trademark or sponsored. The consumer could watch, read, listen to, drink or play with *Star Wars* products. It came as a Twentieth Century-Fox film, and as a range of book, pictorial and print items, from the Ballantine and Random House division of the RCA conglomerate. LP records and myriad wall posters, comics, drinks, drinking vessels, toy laser guns, light sabres and board games were everywhere to be had. In 1978 American children could even buy Darth Vader ice-lollies ('Popsicles'), a fraction of whose price, as with all the other brand-named commodities, trickled back to the 'Star Wars Corporation'.

The turnover was incalculable. By 1979 the film alone was estimated to have made $200 million on its modest $6.5 million production cost.

As soon as the film hit the American screens, in June 1977, the novelization, nominally by George Lucas, shot to the head of the best-seller lists and sold 3½ million copies in three months. In Britain the novelized *Star Wars* was put out by the paperback imprint Sphere, who reportedly gave a massive $225,000 for the rights. It was a good investment. The book promptly made the British bestseller lists, and stayed there for months.

Why did *Star Wars* succeed so spectacularly? Lucas's explanation was simple: '*Star Wars* is a movie for the kid in all of us' (the kid within, as Eric Berne would say). There are other explanations. In the mid-1970s America was emotionally battered. The country had, in Vietnam, lost a war for the first time in its history. Watergate had brought the presidency into disrepute. Escapism was in order – more welcome in that it was an escapism which fantasized the 'Republic' (led by old-fashioned all-American heroes like Han Solo and Luke Skywalker) winning against the Evil Empire of Darth Vader, Moff Tarkin et al. (Most villains in *Star Wars* have English, or vaguely European accents.)

The oil shock of 1973, when OPEC (the Oil and Petroleum Exporting Countries) quadrupled the price of oil, precipitated recession and double-digit inflation in the Western world. It also gave rise to a wave of disaster scenarios in popular entertainment. The big disaster films of the 1970s were *Earthquake* (1974), *Airports '75, '77*, and *'79* (a trio based on Hailey's original disasterless melodrama), *The Poseidon Adventure* (1972, devised by novelist Paul Gallico), *The Towering Inferno* (1974, 'partly based' on Richard Stern's *The Tower*, 'largely based' on T. N. Scortia and F. M. Robinson's *Glass Inferno*), *Juggernaut* (1974), and the remake of *King Kong* (1976).

Given the supremacy of Hollywood, these scenarios resurface either in original novel form or as novelizations in British bestseller lists: usually not in the top spots, but as healthy, surefire money-spinners. Such was Hollywood's appetite for this material that when Arthur Hailey put out *The Moneychangers* for film rights in 1974 the word came back, 'Tell Hailey we want disasters.' He duly obliged with *Overload*, which chronicles a disastrous power cut in California.

If you read popular fiction, the outlook was by the mid-1970s apocalyptic. There were flavour-of-the-decade novels about climate change (Arthur Herzog's *Heat*, 1977), storms (Jack Bickham's *Twister*, 1978), flood (Richard Doyle's *Deluge*, 1976), a new Ice Age (George Stone's *Freeze*, 1977), and earthquake (Alistair MacLean's *Goodbye California*, 1977). Goodbye human race. The most enduring of the disaster scenarios was J. G. Ballard's dystopian vision of a car-wrecked London encircled by homicidal motorways, *Crash* (1973).

There were, of course, more cheerful tones to be found in British and US bestseller lists. The American bicentennial in 1976 made a bestseller of E. L. Doctorow's superior novel *Ragtime* (1975). It also propelled Alistair Cooke's affectionate portrait of his adoptive country, *America*, into a long-term presence in US and UK lists. Britain too had an anniversary to celebrate. In 1977 Queen Elizabeth II reached her silver jubilee year – twenty-five years on the throne. A quarter of a century of increasing prosperity and, assuming one overlooked the troubles in Ulster, peace. The jubilee produced a harvest of books, of which the bestselling (and best) was Robert Lacey's *Majesty* (1977), a satisfyingly well-researched book which is sympathetic to HM without being obsequious.

Jubilee celebration, with all its pomp and historical resumé, stimulated a wave of 'nostalgia' bestsellers. The most durable was the astonishingly successful *The Country Diary of an Edwardian Lady*, which topped UK bestseller lists for the best part of three years. It consisted of Edith Holden's Warwickshire 'nature notes', accompanied by her own charming illustrations, for 1906. Holden's was the first of many 'nostalgia' volumes, designed for browsing in rather than reading.

As the Queen of England celebrated her jubilee, the Queen of Detective Fiction left the stage. Agatha Christie died in January 1976, aged eighty-six. Her first novel (a Poirot mystery, *The Mysterious Affair at Styles*) had come out in 1921, half a century earlier. Eighty-odd titles followed. Half her output featured Poirot, the omniscient Belgian sleuth, with his English 'Dr Watson', Arthur Hastings. A quarter featured Miss Marple. As a plotwright (her forte) Christie specialized in puzzle pieces. Some have an exotic setting (*Murder on the Orient Express*, famously); others, such as *The Murder of Roger Ackroyd*, have a cosy English rural setting.

Her career was boosted early, in 1926, by her famous 'disappearance' and, as some assumed, suicide attempt following marital difficulties. It generated headlines in the newspapers and inspired the 1978 film, *Agatha*, starring Vanessa Redgrave and Dustin Hoffman. Christie's subsequent life was sedate after her second marriage, in 1930, to the archaeologist Max Mallowan. She became a British institution and was made a Dame of the British Empire in 1971. In the USA she was the most predictably bestselling of crime writers. At the time of her death her American sales were reckoned at half a billion. If you read one Christie, chances were you would go on to read all eighty.

Dame Agatha was prolific in the 1970s. In *Passenger to Frankfurt* (1970) a woman goes mysteriously missing on a trip to Germany. Sir Stafford Nye, a British diplomat, hunts for her; ever topical, Christie introduces a 'Nazism resurgent' sub-plot. *Nemesis* (1971) is the final Miss Marple mystery – the genteel detective is, like her creator, eighty and has retired to the village of St Mary Mead, but is still an indomitable investigator. *Elephants Can Remember* (1972) is a Poirot mystery. *Akhnaton* (1973) is a Christie curio, a mystery set in Egypt 1300 years BC – she was exploiting the Tutankhamun mania of 1972. *Postern of Fate* (1974) features the last appearance of Christie's heroic duo Tommy and Tuppence. Finally there was the aptly named *Curtain* (1975) – Poirot's curtain call. Christie waited only a few months to join him. *Sleeping Murder* was published posthumously, in 1976.

Christie's already massive popularity in the 1970s was boosted by two expensive movies: *Murder on the Orient Express* (1974), with Albert Finney as Poirot and *Death on the Nile* (1978), with Peter Ustinov doing the Poirot honours. It is a matter of fierce debate which of these plays the Belgian sleuth better – or should the award go to David Suchet, who took the role on TV from 1989 onwards? The queen's vacant throne would be worthily occupied by P. D. James and Ruth Rendell in subsequent decades.

The year of Christie's death, 1976, was the hottest ever recorded in Britain. That glorious summer, and the Montreal Olympics, together with some sterling performances by England in Test matches, produced a bumper crop of sports books. The 1976 British bestseller list included: *MCC: The Autobiography of a Cricketer*, by Colin

Cowdrey (England's former leader on the pitch); *Sailing: The Course of My Life* (by Edward Heath, England's former leader in the House of Commons); 'Fiery' Fred Trueman's cheekily entitled *Ball of Fire*; Tony Greig's *Cricket: The Man and the Game* (Greig was England's current captain); and Muhammad Ali's autobiography, *The Greatest*.

Other kinds of sport were also popular. The international non-fiction blockbuster of the 1970s was Alex Comfort's erotic manual *The Joy of Sex* (1972). The book would sell, year in year out, for a decade. Comfort takes a modishly hedonistic line on this most reliable of bestselling topics. No longer, as with fuddy-duddy Eustace Chesser, is sex a question of mechanical 'techniques'. No longer, as with the white-coated Masters and Johnson, or with Alfred Kinsey, is sexuality a clinical subject.

For the aptly named Comfort and his fellow 1970s swingers, sex was something to be enjoyed. Like good food, he suggested. The title alludes, mischievously, to Irma Rombauer's 1953 bestseller *The Joy of Cooking*; there is, of course, no copyright in titles. Comfort presents his advice as so many recipes for the middle classes to try out, as they might experiment with a new dish from Elizabeth David. His menu begins with 'Starters' (foreplay). It follows with 'Main Courses', 'Sauces and Pickles' (group sex, alternative orifices) and finishes with 'Problems' (troubleshooting for troubled shooters). Like *The Joy of Cooking*, Comfort's book was accompanied with helpful line drawings. As one commentator put it: 'The couple illustrated grope, suck, caress, and hump each other in all sorts of postures... the man is scruffily bearded and the woman has hairy armpits.' Children of the 1960s.

A shortcoming in *The Joy of Sex* was its male perspective. Comfort ruefully admitted that 'My wife says you can tell this book is written by a man.' Another objection was that it degraded intercourse by reducing it so many 'recipes'. The book's great success, however, was its internationalism. Sex, Comfort implied, was the universal language. When it came to coupling there was, after all, only one race, the human race.

Comfort was that distinctive variety of Englishman, the eccentric auto-didact. Born in 1920, he had been home-educated by his parents. In one of his home chemistry experiments, he blew the fingers off his left hand while constructing a bomb. He was always something of an anarchist. At Cambridge he studied natural sciences, but had a strong personal leaning towards things literary. Always out of step with his time (until the swinging sixties), he made a notorious name for himself after World War II by calling for the prosecution of the Allied commanders as war criminals for the saturation bombing of German cities and their civilian inhabitants.

A polymath – he was also a novelist and poet and had a PhD in biochemistry – Comfort conducted ground-breaking research in the 1950s and 1960s on gerontology, the biology of aging. He mass-produced academic papers and over fifty books on various subjects. On the side he translated the *Koka Shastra*, an Indian sex manual. But it was not until the 1970s that 'sexology' became his main line. His theory was that 'the way to find out about anything is to write a book about it', which he duly did.

Life changes followed. Comfort divorced and remarried shortly after *The Joy of Sex* was published. There followed a second volume, *More Joy of Sex*, in 1973. It testified to Comfort's personal preference for bondage and group sex. He associated himself in the 1970s with the Sandstone commune for sexual swingers in California, made famous by the 1969 movie *Bob and Carol and Ted and Alice*. In his bestselling survey of 1970s American sexuality, *Thy Neighbor's Wife*, Gay Talese recalled seeing Comfort, now in his venerable fifties, at Sandstone puffing on a cigar in the nude while inspecting copulating couples. 'After he had deposited the cigar in a safe place – he would join a friendly clutch of bodies, and contribute to the merriment.' It was less merry after the arrival of AIDS at the end of the decade. Comfort's views, as expressed in *The Joy of Sex*, were utopian. 'Sex,' he averred, 'must be physically the safest of all human activities.' All sex was safe sex. If only. It was good while it lasted, however. In the late 1970s the British Heart Association ran a TV ad promoting sexual intercourse as 'healthy exercise', with the added warning: 'But don't have a cigarette afterwards.'

The dominant flavour in Comfort's manual was hedonism. Sex was something to be enjoyed – by the 'cultivated' practitioner. This urge towards connoisseurship is found in the most instructional food guide of the decade, Egon Ronay's regular surveys of British cuisine. There was, with prosperity and improved education, an upward spiral towards better living. Even the huge sales of *The Highway Code* testified to rising living standards: Britain was moving, inexorably, towards Margaret Thatcher's car-owning democracy.

Sybaritic as Britain was becoming, things of the mind were not entirely neglected. The great non-fiction, self-improving popular book of the 1970s was Jacob Bronowski's *The Ascent of Man*. Bronowski was, arguably, the last of the great omniscient sages. Only a brain as well stored as his could have attempted *The Ascent of Man*: the totality, that is, of all human history and achievement. Kenneth Clark's aims in *Civilisation*, or Alistair Cooke's in *America*, were modest by comparison.

Bronowski was born in Poland in 1908, the son of a haberdasher. After World War I, the family settled in England. When young Jacob, known to his friends as Bruno, arrived in his new homeland he spoke no English: he would, in fact, have a lifelong European accent which added, mysteriously, to his authority as a 'thinker'. He was a natural polymath, as gifted in the sciences as in the arts. There was, for Bruno, no problem with the 'two cultures' which so worried C. P. Snow, whose 1959 booklet on the topic was a schools bestseller for decades. At university he read mathematics, won prizes and edited a literary magazine. In the inter-war years he pursued an academic career. During World War II he worked, appropriately enough, in Intelligence, where his mathematical skills were applied to making Allied bombing raids more efficient. He was one of those whom Alex Comfort would have had arraigned as war criminals.

Bronowski was, over this period, making a public reputation for himself on the *Brains Trust* programmes, which were a hit on BBC wartime and post-war radio. They transferred, seamlessly, to TV. On the Sunday afternoon TV *Brains Trust* Bronowski was – with A. J. Ayer, David Daiches, Alan Bullock and Marghanita Laski – a media star.

Bronowski had gone to Japan in 1945 with the British Chiefs of Staff Mission to study the effects of the atomic bomb on Nagasaki. This experience changed his life and directed his interests towards grand moral questions, outlined in his 1956 book *Science and Human Values*. He worked for UNESCO from 1947 to 1950, when he was appointed director of the Research Establishment of the National Coal Board.

In the early 1960s Bronowski had presented a series for BBC television called *Insight*, in which he examined for the lay viewer a range of scientific topics. His *magnum opus* would be the thirteen-part TV series *The Ascent of Man*, broadcast in 1973. It was published in book form the same year and was a runaway bestseller in the UK, topping the charts for three years and becoming the bestselling work of its kind ever. In the book's pages, as he had on screen, Bronowski ranged effortlessly over the whole panorama of human intellectual achievement from Pythagoras, through Shakespeare, Hegel, Michelangelo and Blake, to Einstein and Freud: from the Académie Française to Auschwitz.

Running through it all is Bronowski's principal contention that all knowledge, even scientific knowledge, is 'indeterminate'. It depends, vitally, on the human personality directing it. His own majestic intellect and humane personality dominated the programme, testifying to an encyclopedic knowledge that was not limited to a few specialisms. There was no question of researchers 'feeding' him. He was no mere 'presenter'. He knew what he was talking about. Bronowski fell ill during filming and died shortly afterwards in 1974, leaving *The Ascent of Man* as the highest point of his own life's achievement.

The prominence of 'Man' in Bronowski's title miffed feminists (but, the BBC retorted, would 5 million viewers have tuned in to 'The Ascent of Person'?). Feminism continued to develop its 'literature of their own'. Notable British bestsellers in the 1970s were Shirley Conran's sassy *Superwoman* (1975: 'for every woman who hates housework'). In women's fiction, Jilly Cooper and Molly Parkin launched their bestselling line of 'bonkbusters' ('Barbara Cartland without the iron knickers', as one saucy publicist called them). In America the flavour tended more towards the raunchy, with titles like Marilyn French's *The Women's Room*, Colleen McCullough's *The Thorn Birds* (both 1977) and Erica Jong's *Fear of Flying* (1973). Whatever else, women's fiction no longer feared offending male sensibilities.

In fact these women writers seemed positively intent on bringing a blush to the male cheek. Erica Jong's novel about Isadora Wing's quest for the 'zipless fuck' drew directly on the bawdy fiction of the eighteenth century on which the author had (in a previous more dutiful career) written an academic thesis. She was just thirty when her first novel, *Fear of Flying*, was published. In July 1987 she recalled that 'nobody was writing honestly in the 1970s about women and the variousness of their experience. What was missing was that a thinking woman could also have a sexual life.' And lively sex. Jong wanted to do for the woman's novel what Henry Miller had done for his male pals. Bawdy was the key. *Fear of Flying* was initially marketed as a 'literary' work before word-of-mouth made it a no.1 title, selling 3 million copies in its first year of publication.

Marilyn French's mode was more melodramatic. (She too had written an academic thesis – on James Joyce). The woman-hero of *The Women's Room* is a victim of the tyrant sex; man, that is. French had steeped herself in Simone de Beauvoir's *The Second Sex* and, as the allusive title of her own book indicates, she opposes Virginia Woolf's quietist view that all a modern woman needs for fulfilment is 'a room of her own'. Much more is demanded. As French put it, 'My goal in life is to change the entire social and economic structure of western civilization – to make it a feminist world.' She elaborated her goal of an ideal manless world in a second novel, *Bleeding Heart* (1980), which had considerably less éclat than its predecessor but established her as the most hard-hitting of the decade's feminist novelists.

Colleen McCullough's *The Thorn Birds* was written by an Australian and sold via the American market to the world. In America it was touted by its publishers as 'the number one international bestseller of 1977–9' and 'the publishing legend of the decade'. The typescript attracted a pre-publication bid of almost $2 million from Avon Books for the paperback rights. On one level, *The Thorn Birds* is a Leon Uris or James Michener style epic about the historical emergence of modern Australia. Within this historical sweep it combines elements of the popular 1970s 'bodice ripper' (a genre dominated by Avon's other discoveries, Rosemary Rogers and Kathleen Woodiwiss). In the steamiest episode in *The Thorn Birds* a priest, Ralph de Bricassart, is carried away into carnal lust – setting up generations' worth of complication when the object of his passion, Meg, is impregnated:

> Did he carry her to bed, or did they walk? He thought he
> must have carried her, but he could not be sure: only that she
> was on it, he was there upon it her skin under his hands, his
> skin under hers. Oh, God! My Meggie! How could they rear
> me from infancy to think you profanation? Time ceased to

tick and began to flow, washed over him until it had no meaning, only a depth of dimension more real than time.

McCullough, in a later interview, was engagingly candid about the commercial (and masculine) pressures which induced her to write this tosh: 'My editor told me that the second half of the book needed a damn good love scene, and there is nothing I dislike writing more. Love-making is such a non-verbal thing. I hate that explicit "he stuck it in her" kind of thing, because it is boring. You can only say "he stuck it in her" so many ways.' Would that all romancers were so honest.

British feminism had, by the 1970s, acquired its own voice with the formidable entrance on the scene of Germaine Greer. In the 1960s she was a lecturer at the University of Warwick: a 'new' university and a centre of radical action in that decade, regularly 'occupied' by demonstrating students. Greer had been born in Australia in 1939. At university in Sydney, she associated with a bohemian-anarchist group called Push ('pushy' was an epithet that never frightened her). One of Push's doctrines, reportedly, was a contempt for monogamy. Greer was subsequently one of the wave of brilliant young antipodeans who flocked to the UK in the 1960s. They included the connoisseur-comedian Barry Humphries, the film director Bruce Beresford and the young jack of all literary trades Clive James.

At Cambridge, Greer completed a PhD on Shakespearian comedy. She was, in the mid-1960s, a regular contributor to *Oz* (a determinedly outrageous 'underground' magazine with, as its name indicated, a core of Australian contributors) and its American equivalent, *Suck*. Strikingly photogenic, she posed as well as wrote for the magazines. *The Female Eunuch* was published in 1970 in the UK. As the title indicated, the basic thesis was that women had been traditionally and methodically disempowered. Liberation lay through a reclaiming of sexuality; in this, Greer reconnected herself with sexual radicals such as D. H. Lawrence. Her rhetoric could blow walls down. Eunuchs other women might be, but Greer had, as Hemingway would say, *cojones*. One of her axioms (much admired by her great antagonist Norman Mailer, the 'prisoner of sex', as he called himself) was that no woman who did not know the taste of her menstrual blood could consider herself 'liberated'.

*The Female Eunuch* became a bestseller in the UK. When the paperback came out in 1971 the publisher, Paladin, was obliged to reprint every month to keep up with demand. Sales were stimulated by a brilliant cover illustration which epitomized Greer's polemic in a single, vivid image of the female anatomy as a one-piece swimming costume hanging on a peg. Packaging was important in the marketing of Greer's book and got it into innumerable women's hands. The downside was that clever commercial packaging attracted accusations of 'hype', a pejorative term which began to circulate in the 1970s book trade. It is derived from hyperbole, or overstatement, with a hint of hypodermic syringe and drug pushing. Accusations of being a hyped-up creature of publicity (a media junkie) followed Greer's meteoric career. She personally distanced herself from *The Female Eunuch* circus. In her sequel, *The Whole Woman*, published in 2000, Greer claims that in the 1960s and 1970s she, like many of her sisters, swallowed 'the lie of the sexual revolution'. She disowns much of her earlier work as a feminist's juvenilia – scaffolding that she needed to get to where she now is.

*The Female Eunuch* was the UK's first feminist bestseller in the USA. McGraw-Hill paid $29,000 for the hardback rights; Bantam paid $135,000 for the paperback rights. However, unlike Betty Friedan (whose background was in old-fashioned political activism), Greer could not mobilize or organize. As she later said:

> When I wrote it, I didn't care if someone bought one copy and everyone read it or if they printed a book as big as Eaton Square and let people walk around it, reading. I won't give that money to taxes. For CS gas. To rule the people. I tried to form a foundation for women, a centre where they could come and read about themselves, maybe get a bed if their husband's left them. They called that a tax dodge. I tried to incorporate myself. No good.

Greer embraced the one career left to her: bestselling author.

It was, among the enlightened, another mild cause for complaint that Bronowski's *The Ascent of Man* was not merely male chauvinist but Euro-centric. The first courses in, and departments of, black (or

African-American) studies had sprung up in the USA in the wake of the 1964 Civil Rights Act. A notable spur to the emergent discipline was Alex Haley's phenomenally successful book and TV mini-series *Roots*.

Haley (1921–92) was brought up in the South. He left school at fifteen, attended college for two years and then joined the United States Coast Guard as a messboy (blacks were, during the early years of World War II, prohibited from front-line active duty). After twenty years in the military, mainly as a service journalist, Haley retired in 1959 and took up full-time writing. He became an assignment writer for *Reader's Digest* and later was associated with *Playboy*, where he inaugurated the 'Playboy Interviews' feature. Out of the magazine's interview with the activist Malcolm X came Haley's first book, *The Autobiography of Malcolm X: As Told to Alex Haley* (1965). It became a bestseller. Haley realized that he had an unusual dual ethnicity: he was a black writer in a white reading world. He could talk both to a Black Muslim like Malcolm X and to the white folks in the suburbs.

At this mature point in his career Haley embarked on a hugely ambitious venture: to recover a 'history' for the black millions of America whose history had been brutally erased by slavery. To find, that is, an ethnic value for Malcolm's 'X'. Haley had, in his youth, heard stories about his own and other families. In the mid-1960s he embarked on research into his maternal ancestry. He consulted linguists to trace the dialects of his family back to their native African languages. He investigated the maritime records of slave ships in Britain and America. Most momentously he travelled to The Gambia, where he met the 'griot' (tribal archivist) who told him of sixteen-year-old Kunta Kinte, who had been captured by slave traders, seven generations ago, while hunting for wood for a drum in the forest. Kunta was, allegedly, Haley's distant maternal ancestor. He had discovered his African roots.

In 1976 Haley published *Roots: The Saga of an American Family*, the seven generations of Haley's family from Kunta to Alex. It was never quite clear how much fiction was mixed in with the author's 'faction'. ABC produced a twelve-part TV mini-series of the book in 1977 which broke all records in America, with 130 million viewers. As a book, *Roots* sold over 1½ million copies in its first six months.

It is credited with inspiring a boom in black studies in American schools and colleges. Haley was awarded a National Book Award and a Pulitzer Prize for the book. *Roots* made the bestseller lists in the UK, but the veracity of Haley's account was questioned by the *Sunday Times* 'Insight' team. The book also attracted accusations and legal action for alleged plagiarism.

Without it, however, there would probably have been no Oprah Winfrey, no *The Color Purple* and, arguably, no Nobel Prize for Toni Morrison. Haley created a space where American black literature could grow and thrive.

# 4

The 80s

TWO FEATURES STAND OUT from the parade of 1980s British best-sellers. The more striking of these was the booming vitality of the home book trade. Production, consumption and distribution of books were expanding, despite all the previous decade's jeremiads about the death of reading. Between 1977 and 1980, annual turnover of the industry as compiled by the Association of British Publishers rose from £110 million to £170 million. Title growth over several decades had been even more dramatic. The number of new titles, including reprints and new editions, issued in 1947 had been 13,046. In 1960, it was 23,783. In 1970 it rose to 33,489. And in 1980 the total soared to 48,158. By the end of the century, it would be into six figures. The British book trade was bursting its seams, every year.

In British high streets, meanwhile, the retailing of books was being rationalized along American lines in uniform 'chain' outlets: W. H. Smith and Waterstone's would eventually domi-nate. Exit the old 'carriage-trade' British bookshop; enter the American bookstore with all the customer amenities of the supermarket. As the decade advanced, newly available computer systems would take over stock control – that bane of the book trade, with its half a million titles in print. The first item on computers to figure in the bestseller lists was *The Computer Book* by Edward de Bono, the sage of 'lateral thinking' in 1982.

Books, all this is to say, were more like other medium-price com-modities than they had been in the 1960s, when the British publishing industry successfully defended its retail price maintenance, the so-called Net Book Agreement, under the slogan: 'Books are Different'. In the 1980s they were less different. This process would lead, in 1994, to the abolition of the NBA – something that had been in place as a stabilizing mechanism in Britain (but not in America) for a hundred years. What it had meant, essentially, was no discounts, and hence a low level of retail competition. Very English, very un-American.

The other striking feature of the decade is the 'flavour' of the books preferred by the discriminating but eager buyers who thronged the new bookshops. The 1980s were, above all, a golden time for British comic writing. Books designed to amuse display the same vitality and buoyant national genius that are evident in, say, Ealing film comedy of the 1950s or stage drama of the Restoration period.

British bestseller lists in the early 1980s were dominated by Douglas Adams's sf (science fantasia, that is, not science fiction) series, beginning with *The Hitch-hiker's Guide to the Galaxy* (1979). Adams's title (he had a knack for catchy titles) spoofs the numerous how-to books which since the 1960s had proliferated as 'bibles' for every kind of leisure activity from potting plants to planting pot. Another bestseller of 1981, *101 Uses for a Dead Cat* by Simon Bond, sold almost a million copies in three years. There was money in spoof. In fact, Adams's title is misleading. The narrative itself is more in the nature of Munchausen updated, a comic *voyage extraordinaire* for modern times.

Adams (1952–2001) was educated at a minor public school and read English at Cambridge. He must also have read a lot of science fiction. At university he steeped himself in the Footlights revue comedy which had earlier generated *Beyond the Fringe*, Pete and Dud, and – more recently and most zanily – *Monty Python's Flying Circus*. Adams himself credited Python and the Beatles as his principal 'literary' influences. Behind them, one can also detect the radio *Goon Show*, that most original comic innovation of the British post-war period. Whatever the pedigree, Adams's was a quintessentially English line of wit.

On leaving university (where he had vainly hoped, as he later said, to be John Cleese – only to discover that the post was already filled by John Cleese) Adams scripted for TV one or two *Doctor Who* episodes when the series was in its most inventive phase starring the long-scarfed Tom Baker. He then drifted into writing late-night comic radio drama for the BBC. It was one of their graveyard shifts. Supposedly, Adams would turn up in pyjamas and dressing-gown for the recording session.

*The Hitch-hiker's Guide to the Galaxy*, for which Adams received the unprincely stipend of £1000, first went out for insomniacs in 1978. Its serial episodes, accompanied by surreal sound effects, caught on and became a cult hit. Pan offered him £1500 for a paperback original version. Adams was on his way. When it was published with a print run of 60,000, *The Hitch-hiker's Guide to the Galaxy* went straight to the top of the charts. In three months it had sold 750,000 copies.

Radio, it seemed, could still make bestsellers. After the BBC picked up his 'Lake Wobegon' monologues from America, Minnesotan Garrison Keillor would also become a popular author in the UK in the 1980s. Keillor's dry, Twainian rural humour was as much to British taste as to that of his compatriots.

Adams's invention begins, typically, with a joke against the 1970s disaster scenario (films like the 1979 *Meteor*) and the town-planning (so-called) that was currently defacing England. Earth, in Adams's fantasy, is about to be demolished to make way for a Galactic Motor-way ('a hyper-spatial express route'). No one has troubled to inform the population of this unimportant planet. Arthur Dent has two minutes to escape.

Leaving the debris of earth behind him, Arthur embarks on an aimless ramble through the universe accompanied by his extra-terres-trial Sancho Panza, Ford Prefect, who has been writing a hitchhiker's guide for fifteen desultory years. Arthur's companion is named after the unsexiest car produced, even by Dagenham, in the post-war period. He also has with him Zaphod Beeblebrox (a joke on the 'Beeb', or BBC), a two-headed, three-armed ex-hippy and Zaphod's girlfriend, Trillian. Picaresque encounters of more than three kinds ensue.

Published as a book, in 1979, *The Hitch-hiker's Guide to the Galaxy* topped the British bestseller lists for two years. Success sur-prised and rather worried the author. He had not aimed this high. 'Success', Adams said, was like 'orgasm without foreplay.' He was never sure he liked it (success, that is). It seemed wrong to him that this most modest of enterprises should hit any jackpots. It was something that worried another connoisseur of the less than triumphant, Stephen Pile, whose *Book of Heroic Failures* (1979) also became a superseller in 1980. When everyone and their girlfriend bought it, Pile's book seemed, somehow, to contradict itself. Like *The Hitch-hiker's Guide to the Galaxy*, it was not designed for the big time. All Pile wanted was to fail with style (the true 'British disease'). He none the less followed up with a (successful) sequel, *The Return of Heroic Failures*, in 1988. It was dedicated to Quin Xiang-Yi 'who in 1846 was given the title "distinguished failure" in recognition of his twenty years spent failing the Chinese Civil Service entrance exams. Buoyed up by this honour, he went on to fail several times more.'

Like Pile, Adams found himself on a treadmill. *The Hitch-hiker's Guide to the Galaxy* inspired a 'trilogy' (a total of five books, by Adams's erratic count), the further titles being: *The Restaurant at the End of the Universe* (1980), *Life, the Universe and Everything* (1983), *So Long, and Thanks for All the Fish* (1984), *Mostly Harmless* (1992). Adams also published a couple of novels based on his lugubrious detective Dirk Gently, including the delightfully named *The Long, Dark Teatime of the Soul* (1988), and a comic dictionary, *The Meaning of Liff* (1983, co-authored with John Lloyd). Adams was, by the middle of the decade, a superseller. In November 1985 *Dirk Gently's Holistic Detective Agency* and its sequel were auctioned among publishers and drew a winning bid of $2.3 million.

The founding idea in Adams's array of books, all of which sold extravagantly, was simple. Britain, when it came to space exploration, nowadays punched well beneath its weight. Arthur's family Ford space vehicle (no USS *Enterprise*, this, going boldly where none has gone before) can be read as a kind of rueful coming to terms with Britain's also-ran status as a competitor in the space race.

In H. G. Wells's *The First Men in the Moon* (1901) there had been no question that the first flag planted on the moon would not be the Union Jack; nor that, like most of planet earth, it would not be coloured imperial red on the astral maps. Schoolchildren in the 1950s had glued their ears to the family radio set to follow the adventures of Jet Morgan and his *Journey into Space*, and had spent their pocket money on the exploits of Dan Dare in the *Eagle* (this comic published Adams's first story, all two hundred words of it, when he was twelve-years old. The young author received ten bob, or 50p.)

Those dreams of a British foot making that giant leap for mankind were just dreams, it now transpired. There would be no British Luke Skywalker; no British astronauts other than those invited as freeloaders (or hitch-hikers) by the USA or the USSR. It was a sad comedown. But comedy could, none the less, be wrung out of such heroic failures. The recurrent device in Adams's stories is anti-climax. The main advice passed on by Dent to his faithful readers, for example, is that 'a towel is the most massively useful thing an interstellar hitch-hiker can have'. In *Life, the Universe and Everything*, the great secret alluded to in the title is revealed to be '42'.

Adams was forty-nine when he died in May 2001 – there was no more numerical neatness in his life than in his universe. There was, however, a lot more money latterly than the BBC had given him in 1978. The (much belated) fifth volume of his trilogy was eight months in the *New York Times* bestseller list. He was, reportedly, offered a $2 million advance for the sixth instalment of the Dentiad epic. At the time of his death, Adams's worldwide sales were estimated at 14 million; only Isaac Asimov and Arthur C. Clarke had sold more works of science fiction – and where were the laughs in their books? (Asimov, Adams once said, read like an American Express brochure.)

A pioneer of internet adaptation, Adams had devised a bestselling interactive electronic game, Starship Titanic, and a website, allusively called www.h2g2.com. A Hollywood film was in prospect – it has yet to appear, but Adams's style of comedy clearly influenced the style of the 1997 hit *Men in Black*. Douglas Adams died on an exercise bike, in Malibu, of a heart attack: going nowhere at high speed. The unlikeliness of it would have pleased the creator of the *Hitch-hiker's Guide*.

Alongside Arthur Dent in the early 1980s besteller lists is Sue Townsend's equally amiable, and ultra-English, Adrian Mole. Adrian first became famous aged, as he pedantically recorded, 13¾, with his *Secret Diary* (1982).

As a paperback, Townsend's comic book led the field in the mid-1980s, taking the top spot from Adams. Like Arthur Dent, Mole endeared himself to young readers – an emergent force in the market, if not as dominant in books as in popular music. But the diary's appeal extended well beyond this readership. Spotty, greasy-haired, wretchedly bourgeois, maladroit, unhappily parented (father George drinks, mother Pauline is a less than virtuous wife), Adrian is an anthology of early adolescent angst. His birthplace, Leicester, does not help. He lusts after the unreachable Pandora Braithwaite, glamorous daughter of the accountant at the local dairy, and fantasizes hopelessly about what treasures lie beneath her blouse. Alas, Adrian will always get the booby prize, not the prize boobies, in life. He toys with the idea of gay sex. He is, guiltily, a self-abuser.

The secret diary records Adrian's little rebellions. He wears red socks to school, and is 'excluded' for socialism. In an existential phase, he paints his bedroom black. But Blyton's 'Noddy' patterns, from his childhood days, protrude through the Sartrean hue (there is a symbol in this, if only he could put his finger on it). He writes 'modern' poetry, which editors universally reject. His ode to Pandora is typical Mole:

My young love,
Treacle hair and knee socks
Give my system deep shocks.
You've got a magic figure:
I'm Roy Rogers, you are Trigger.

He attempts to look after the aged and cranky Bert Baxter. Philanthropy fails, like everything else. His hold on the high culture he aspires to is insecure: for instance, 'when Rembrandt painted the Sistine Chapel in Venice', and he thinks Evelyn Waugh is a woman writer. He will never be as educated as he wants to be; but he will, unfortunately, be educated enough to know that he is not truly educated.

The diary was hugely successful. In 1985, Townsend's *annus mirabilis*, Mole titles took over the two top spots in the paperback list and the top spot among the hardbacks. Adrian's diaries were, by now, the least secret things in Britain. The first volume was the bestselling paperback of the 1980s. The book was translated into sixteen languages and sold over 5 million copies worldwide. It went on to inspire a successful TV series which in turn sold more copies of Townsend's book.

In terms of literary pedigree, Adrian can be seen as the etiolated descendant of the 1950s Angry Young Man, the rebel without a cause, the runaway Holden Caulfield. But Adrian will never, like Caulfield, have an episode with a hooker in a New York hotel. A fumble with Pandora is the highest he can aspire to. And, as it turns out, he doesn't even achieve that modest goal. He has to fumble with himself. An unheroic failure.

Unlike Salinger, Townsend followed her hero through subsequent life. Readers grew up and will presumably grow old with him. *The Growing Pains of Adrian Mole* (1984) brings the hero forward into still stormier years of adolescence. His parents are now separated (were they ever anything else?) and in different, but equally pointless, relationships. Adrian is still plagued by acne and no Pandora.

There followed *The True Confessions of Adrian Albert Mole* and *The Wilderness Years*. Finally, we rejoin Adrian in *The Cappuccino Years*, in the late 1990s. He is, at one point, an offal chef. Pandora is one of Blair's Babes. Ne'er the twain shall meet. Sex has not been kind to Adrian Mole. Aged thirty-four and the inevitable fraction, he is a 'single father'. His Nigerian wife has left him. At least his marriage was fashionably post-colonial. His mixed-race son, Glenn, is excluded from school for calling Tony Blair a 'leading twat', during a civics discussion on the bombing of Afghanistan. Beats red socks.

Sue Townsend, the creator of Mole, was a new kind of bestselling author and as much a child of her time and place as is Adrian of his. She was born in 1946, working-class, and brought up in a 'prefab' (somewhat less grand than even a council house) in Leicester (a city somewhat less than grand). She left school at fifteen to work in a factory, then as a shop assistant and subsequently as a petrol station attendant. The 1960s and 1970s were not, for her, liberated decades. She separated from her husband and raised three children on income support. She was, however, an indomitable self-improver. 'I was a print slut,' she recalls. 'I would read anything, anytime, anywhere: the *Beano*, the *Spectator* and the Kellogg's cereal packet.'

It paid off. At the age of thirty-five Townsend won a Thames TV playwrights' award and embarked on a writing career. This led to Adrian Mole and bestsellerdom. She got ideas for the Mole books from hanging out in youth clubs and overhearing kids say things like: 'I can't live without her, Nigel.' Even with success, life remained tough. She suffered a heart attack, aged thirty-nine, in 1986 and was diagnosed as diabetic, which would lead to virtual blindness by the 1990s.

Apart from the comic pathos of Adrian, it is Townsend's sharp depiction of the comedy of class in English life that distinguishes her work. In 1991 she wrote another bestseller, *The Queen and I*, in which a deposed House of Windsor ends up residing on a council estate, a neighbour of Alf Garnett and his kind. In other hands, it would have been a crass conception. Townsend made it deliciously (and unmaliciously) comic. In 1988, Townsend was given £30,000 sponsorship by the trade unions NUPE and NALGO for her play about the breakdown of the National Health Service, *Ear, Nose and Throat*. It was a long way from *Doctor in the House*.

On the face of it, Adrian Mole descends lineally from Nigel Molesworth and the comic world of the 1950s *Down with Skool* books. But Nigel's St Custards, like St Trinians, is a boarding 'skool' – a minor public school, in fact. Nigel's second volume was called *How to Be Topp* and Molesworth is, as *The Times* liked to call its readers in the 1980s, a 'top person'. Mole is many rungs lower on the British social ladder – a ladder on which there is no 'room at the topp' for Adrian and his kind. He is, none the less, as much an anti-hero for his time as Joe Lampton. And, like Braine's Joe, symbolically so. The centre of the reading public was, in 1980, more proletarian, less gen-teel, less upwardly mobile than it had been thirty years before. Books, as always, were following the money. The Moles nowadays had as much of it (for books, anyway) as the Molesworths.

As a revisionary writer for children Townsend can be usefully aligned with the author/illustrator Raymond Briggs, whose proletarian Father Christmas, created in 1973, has an outside lavatory and drops his aitches. His thoroughly working-class *The Snowman* was published in 1978 and successfully filmed in 1982. It remains his most popular, and most cheerful, work. Briggs could, on other occasions, be less cheerful. In his comic book *When the Wind Blows* (1982) he introduced the child reader to the realities of nuclear annihilation. The council house couple Jim and Hilda (who ultimately succumb to radiation sickness, despite taking all the measures advised by the authorities safe in their underground bunkers) are based on Briggs's own milkman father and lady's maid mother. In his gothic *Fungus the Bogeyman* (1978) Briggs did for the illustrated children's book what *Last Exit to Brooklyn* had done for fiction (''Orrible' books for children would, thereafter, become a popular sub-genre). It was Briggs's great trick, however, to retain even in his most visceral conceptions a core of working-class emotional warmth.

Briggs wrote solely for children – or for adults reading to children. There emerged in the 1980s a crossover market. Kit Williams pro-duced for it an illustrated book called *Masquerade* (1980), which is less story than fable: Moon falls in love with Sun and employs a clever hare called Jack to help him with his suit by tracking down the jewel that will win his lover's heart. So far, so fabulous. The gimmick was that if some reader actually cracked the riddle contained in the narrative, they would be directed to an actual 22-carat gold hare, buried somewhere in the British Isles. It was both book and treasure hunt (in fact the hunt lasted two years before the precious hare was found). Was *Masquerade* a book for gold-hungry adults, or for adventure-hungry kids, or both? Whichever, it sold 300,000 in its first two years of publication.

There were other notable bestsellers in the 1980s which developed new lines of comic writing. Clive James (b. 1939) dealt tenderly and side-splittingly with his Australian childhood in *Unreliable Memoirs* (1980), a bestseller in both hardback and (even more widely) paperback two years later. Unlike Adrian Mole's self-portrait, James's was non-fictional – although no less universal in its depiction of the plight of the sensitive child caught in the traps of a lower middle-class environment. It was James's achievement, like his compatriot Barry Humphries with his monster of the Melbourne suburbs, Edna Everage ('Dame Edna', as she would one day be), to satirize and, in a strange way, love what he satirized.

The comedy in Dirk Bogarde's first volume of autobiography, *A Postillion Struck By Lightning* (1977) had been more suave ('elegant' was the epithet which invariably attached itself to the veteran British film idol). It was followed by three more volumes: *Snakes and Ladders* (1978), *An Orderly Man* (1983) and *Backcloth* (1986). All made the bestseller lists. In 1980 Bogarde (1921–99) embarked on another career, in fiction writing, with *A Gentle Occupation* (1980), *Voices in the Garden* (1983) and *West of Sunset* (1984). They too sold solidly. With the success of his memoirs Bogarde was following in the footsteps of actor David Niven, who had initiated this popular mini-genre a decade earlier. The face one knew so well from the outside, on the cinema screen, now displayed its interior to us. None would do it better than these two with the possible exception of Alec Guinness – another world-class raconteur, his publishers gratefully discovered.

The practical jokester Henry Root (the *nom de lettre* of William Donaldson) had two titles simultaneously in the bestseller list of 1980: *The Henry Root Letters* and *The Further Letters of Henry Root*. The pseudo-author was a semi-retired wet-fish merchant based in the midlands (Donaldson's background was Winchester and Cambridge –

although he was not entirely a product his educators could be proud of, as his *in propria persona* memoirs subsequently revealed).

A ferocious Thatcherite (had not her father been, like him, a small tradesman?), Root whiles away his retirement writing letters to the high and mighty. Among the recipients are HM the Queen (accompanied by the slogan, 'Royalists demand the return of the Rope!'), Mrs Thatcher ('Keep up the good work!'), TV presenter Esther Rantzen, the Chief Constable of Manchester, football manager Brian Clough, impresario Lord 'Lew' Grade and newsreader Angela Rippon. Root would ensure replies by enclosing with his rabid and deliciously crass utterances a one-pound note (or in special cases, a fiver). Invariably, the money would be returned with some banal reply (Rantzen, after much prodding, sent back a letter – in return to his calling her a fat fool – with sincere thanks for his 'support'). Root also got the president of Magdalene College, Cambridge politely to decline £5 as the fee for accepting Root's fifteen-year-old 'boy' as an undergraduate. Things were not done that way, it was patiently explained to the Midlands fishmonger (and what fun they must have had about it, that evening, at high table!). Root's jape was, of course, seditious. He made the high and mighty look pompous and took them down a peg or two. Readers (from their lowly place on the pegboard) loved his mischief. Between them, the two volumes of Root letters sold 150,000 copies in hardback (at £4.50) in 1980.

In fiction, the savage extravaganzas of Tom Sharpe (b. 1928) returned to the black comedy pioneered in the 1930s by Evelyn Waugh. Sharpe's first novels had satirized South Africa, from where he had been deported in 1961. He got his revenge with *Riotous Assembly* (1971) and *Indecent Exposure* (1973). In these novels Sharpe did the seemingly impossible. In the aftermath of the Sharpeville massacre and the imprisonment of Nelson Mandela he made hilarious comedy out of apartheid: his series hero, Konstabel Els, an Afrikaaner sadist, is a monster of tastelessness – but funny.

In the 1970s, as a loyal readership mobilized about his fiction, Sharpe satirically anatomized various English institutions. No cow was too sacred. On his return to Britain, in the early 1960s, he had taken up employment at an East Anglian college of further education. He immortalized himself, and his experiences, in the Henry Wilt trilogy. Wilt, a lecturer at Fenland College, is condemned to teach 'Meat One' (i.e. literature to moronic day-release butchers' apprentices). He plots to kill his wife Eva. Divorce, Fenland-style. It goes wrong. With a blow-up sex doll under his arm, he practically castrates himself, urinating in the rose bushes (Sharpe's fiction works up to such improbable climaxes with amazing narrative logicality).

The political chaos produced by the late 1970s Winter of Discontent attracted his comic bile in *Ancestral Vices* (1980). Like the British satirists, Sharpe's political views tended towards Toryism. In matters of class he was, however, the least deferential of analysts. With its comic gallery of Petrefacts, *Ancestral Vices* indicated what would be Sharpe's most profitable target in the 1980s – the British toff. *The Throwback* (Lockhart Flawse – the product of generations of intensive inbreeding by the Flawse dynasty) rode high, as a paperback, in the 1980 paperback lists, as did *Vintage Stuff* (1982), a satire on the Bentley-owning classes.

The high point of Sharpe's 1980s popularity was itself a throwback – the 1987 TV adaptation by the congenial campus novelist Malcolm Bradbury of Sharpe's satire on moribund Cambridge and its cadaverous dons, *Porterhouse Blue*, first published in 1974. One would need a sensibility of stone not to laugh at the intricately described sequence of misadventures that results in the college quad being filled, like a sudsy washing-up bowl, with inflated condoms. Farcical as it was, Sharpe's depiction of an England paralyzed and ossified by its revered institutions and traditions bit deep. The South Africans were probably wise to deport him. He was an uncomfortable novelist to have around. But funny. And Britons, in their seditious mood, lapped up his novels in the 1980s.

Sharpe's fiction, like that of Adams and Townsend, takes as its subject D. H. Lawrence's 'England, my England' which has, mysteriously, transmuted into 'England, her England'. Her inside Number 10, as Arthur Daley, a 1980s folk-hero and avowed Thatcherite, would have said. The prime minister's great mission, as she declared, was to return Britain to 'Victorian values' – the moral 'basics', as her luckless successor, John Major, would call them.

But what, precisely, were Victorian values? George MacDonald Fraser had been making bestselling comedy out of that question since the launch of his Flashman series in 1969. 'Flashy' was, of course, the bully in Thomas Hughes's nineteenth-century novel *Tom Brown's Schooldays*. He it is who roasts the saintly hero over a slow fire in order to extract a sweepstake ticket from him. Eventually, after being brought back drunk to school on a shutter, Flashy is expelled from Rugby by the 'Doctor' (Thomas Arnold, the inventor of the British public school system: the cornerstone of Empire).

Flashy's adventures begin with his hangover. He seduces his father's mistress, ends up serving in the first Afghan War, learns the ninety-seven ways of Hindu love and wins the Victoria Cross (having, as it happened, displayed truly heroic cowardice in the face of the enemy). We follow Fraser's Victorian anti-hero through ten more books (and two big-budget film adaptations). He marries and is royally deceived by his minx of a wife, Elspeth. He becomes Sir Harry, he gallops with the Light Brigade into the valley of death. He has a 'Prisoner of Zenda' escapade in Bismarck's Prussia. He rides in America with John Brown, the great emancipator (Flashy, however, takes care that his body won't lie mouldering in the grave).

Fraser published five Flashman novels in the 1970s, but only two in the 1980s. They are, however, among the strongest in the series: *Flashman and the Redskins* (1982) and *Flashman and the Dragon* (1985). In the first Flashy sets off with the 'forty-niners, going West. By a series of adventures he is inducted into the Sioux nation – he picks up languages as readily as lesser rogues pick up STDs. He is now a redskin. The novel breaks for a quarter of a century. Returning to the West, through various shifts of fortune Flashy ends up with Custer at Little Big Horn. As always, he survives. There is a touching moment when he discovers a son, whom he fathered, all those years ago, among Sitting Bull's warriors.

The charm of the series is its pseudo-authenticity. Allegedly Fraser has been recruited by their new owner to 'edit' the Flashman papers, which turned up fortuitously in Leicestershire in 1965. All through the 1970s and 1980s, the novelist received letters from readers who assumed Flashman was indeed a real historical personage: Fraser had pulled off a kind of unintended Henry Root stunt. His detailed knowledge of the Victorian era is impressive; the books are, apart from anything else, the most enjoyable of history lessons. But the marrow of the Flashman books is their play with Victorian values, as they have descended to the present day.

On this subject, Fraser's novels are both subversive and unexpectedly affirmative. When the chips are really down (when, for example, European women and children are being massacred in the Indian Mutiny) Flashy acts as honourably as Scud East or Tom Brown himself would have done. He will 'roger' anything in skirts but never descends to rape; on a couple of occasions he is, however, himself a victim. He genuinely loves Elspeth and little Harry – the boy, at least, is worthy of his love. But he never believes the codswallop and bull that his 'betters' hand down to him. He is too much the old soldier for that. Not for him the rigid moral simplicities of the British public school ('Play up, and play the game!', 'Queen and Country!'). The point Fraser makes – subtly, persistently and wittily – is that Victorian values are more complex than modern politicians like Margaret Thatcher would have us believe. You can't extract your personal morality from a party-political manifesto.

Thatcherism was elevated to something like a state religion after the Falklands War of 1982. The main effect of that famous victory was to stop the pendulum of post-war British politics swinging. A term of Labour followed by a corrective Tory term – that had been the even-handed preference of the British voter since 1945. Mrs Thatcher, victrix on the hustings, at the dispatch box (against whatever duds the opposition could muster) and on the battlefield ('Attila the Hen'), would lead the country for longer, and more decisively, than any post-war premier.

The Falklands War itself left little residue in the bestseller lists of the time. It came and went so fast that books, with their ten-month 'lead time', could not catch up with the yomping marines and para-troops who won the day, in days, at Goose Green. Victory year, 1983, saw *The F-Plan Diet*, *Jane Fonda's Workout Book* and *Wisden's Cricketer's Almanac* topping the lists. Jack Higgins's *Exocet*, named after the French missile which almost did for the British expeditionary naval force, was the only thriller to exploit the conflict with any great sales success. As with *The Eagle Has Landed*, British victory was – we were to deduce – a damned close-run thing.

In non-fiction there were two 1982 publications from HMSO which enjoyed brisk sales, *The Falkland Islands: The Facts* and *The*

*Falkland Islands: The Lessons*. The marine directory *Jane's Fighting Ships* found itself more than usually in demand over 1982–3. But even first-hand accounts of the conflict, such as Max Hastings's *The Battle for the Falklands*, were somewhat passé on arrival in 1984.

In terms of popular books, the favourite son of Thatcherism was Jeffrey Archer (b. 1940). His amazing career – in authorship and everything else – is well known from his own (famously unreliable) versions, from the publicity attending his two great court cases in 1987 and 2001, and from various unauthorized biographies, notably Michael Crick's.

Having bluffed his way (with no A-levels) first into Brasenose College, Oxford, and then into Parliament (as the youngest ever MP, he falsely claimed) Archer was ruined by injudicious investment. You cannot, as they say, bluff the market. Ever resourceful, he resolved to write his way out of debt. You can, God knows, bluff the reading public. The resulting novel, as drastically rewritten by the publisher's editorial team, was a bestseller entitled *Not a Penny More, Not a Penny Less* (1975). The narrative is, patently, a revenge fantasy on those rogues – cleverer rogues than him, damn them – who hoaxed him out of his cash.

Archer succeeded. He paid off his debts with his pen. It was, arguably, the most admirable achievement in his many-sided career. In the 1980s, rehabilitated as an honourable man (the word 'honour' is suspiciously frequent in his fiction), Archer embarked on a method-ically integrated strategy in authorship. His model was John Buchan, the Brasenose man (just like Jeffrey, if you stretched a point) who wrote thrillers on the side, got himself made Baron Tweedsmuir (like Baron Archer of Weston-super-Mare) and ended up Governor General of Canada. Archer, famously, aimed higher: 'When I was three, I wanted to be four; when I was four I wanted to be Prime Minister'; alas, not in this lifetime.

A staple Archer theme (see, for example, *As the Crow Flies*, 1991) is rags to riches: he specializes in fables of dizzying upward social mobility. Another Archer standby is the hundred-to-one outsider making it, by sheer chutzpah, to the top of the slippery pole; as, for example, does the first woman president of the USA, Florentyna Kane, in *The Prodigal Daughter*, the bestselling paperback novel of 1983.

The allusion to the first woman premier of the UK was transparent. Nor did it go unnoticed. Mrs Thatcher declared herself a fan of her loyal party colleague, Jeffrey.

If a woman without inherited privilege can do it, why not a young chancer from the West Country with three O-levels? The corridor of power in Archer's fictional universe is never a destination, as it is in C. P. Snow. It invariably leads to the top position of all – Downing Street or Pennsylvania Avenue. Presidents and premiers figure centrally in nine of Archer's first ten novels. He is obsessed, to the point of drooling, with high political office. Only Benjamin Disraeli, in English fiction, is more so. Disraeli, of course, did make it to the top of the slippery pole.

The strangest feature of Archer's fiction is its eerily prophetic quality. His novels foretell his imminent disasters with the doom-laden prescience of the soothsayer in *Julius Caesar*. *First Among Equals* (his most naked 'Jeffrey becomes prime minister' fantasy) came out shortly before the Monica Coghlan scandal in 1986 which destroyed his (second) political career. In that novel, a contender for the nation's highest office learns that the *News of the World* has offered £100,000 to his wife for his 'unexpurgated' private life. He buys her off. Barely was the novel out of the bestseller lists (boosted by a TV adaptation) than the press were running stories that the novelist paid £2000 to Ms Coghlan, a low-grade prostitute.

Famously, Archer took on the tabloid press in 1987 and won. He emerged £500,000 richer, his reputation 'spotless' (like his back, *Private Eye* joked: Coghlan had alleged acne rash under the Archer vest). Only Dick Francis, among British bestselling novelists, outsold him in the 1980s. *Kane and Abel*, Archer's saga of a lifelong duel between two American magnates, was the second bestselling paperback of 1981 – Douglas Adams pipped him to the top spot. *The Prodigal Daughter* (the irresistible rise of the Kanes, in the second generation) was the no.1 hardback in 1982 and the top paperback novel the following year.

*First Among Equals* was the third bestselling hardback novel of 1984 and the third top paperback of the following year (two Adrian Mole titles outdid him). *A Matter of Honour* was the no.2 hardback in 1986 and the top paperback in 1987. Archer's collection of short stories (one of which was plausibly accused of having been plagiarized), *A Twist in the Tale*, made no.7 in the hardback list for 1988, which was a strong performance for a collection of short fiction. The book featured in the top ten in both hard and paperback form in 1989. As Alex Hamilton records: 'For the first time in British publishing history, if you except the Bible, a book of short stories has sold more than a million copies in a year. In a country which has produced so many brilliant storytellers, it is bizarre that its author should be Jeffrey Archer.'

It is a gross simplification to picture a single British reading public. Many groups go to make the whole, some of them at complete variance with each other. Chalk and cheese, bestseller and best fiction run, like separate veins, through the market. On occasion, they run together. Throughout the 1980s, in another part of the literary field from Archer, the Booker Prize winners (and, in some cases, the runners-up) were figuring in the lists. The first to do so was Iris Murdoch's *The Sea, The Sea*, the 1978 winner. In 1981, William Golding's *Rites of Passage* and Anthony Burgess's (runner-up) *Earthly Powers* both featured as hardback bestsellers. In 1982, Salman Rushdie's *Midnight's Children* was high among the bestsellers of the year. So too, in following years, were Thomas Keneally's *Schindler's Ark* (1983), Paul Scott's *The Jewel in the Crown* (1984), Anita Brookner's *Hotel du Lac* (1985), Kingsley Amis's *The Old Devils* (1986) and Penelope Lively's *Moon Tiger* (1987). Never had so much good, new British fiction done so well. As the trade magazines record, sales of these titles – in hardback in the first year of publication – were routinely 50,000 plus.

America's upward spiral during the 1980s was different from that of the UK. Notable among US bestsellers in this decade were the defiantly African-American autobiographies, poetry volumes, recordings, and public performances of Maya Angelou. Born Marguerite Johnson in 1928, Angelou was fostered in Arkansas and barely survived a horrific childhood – rape (aged eight, by a 'friend' of the family), double discrimination (as a black woman), and grinding poverty. Largely self-educated, she involved herself in the 1960s with the Civil Rights activism of Martin Luther King. She also worked in Africa as a politically engaged journalist in that continent's diverse struggles for freedom from European colonialism.

In 1970, the first (childhood) volume of her five-part autobiography, *I Know Why the Caged Bird Sings*, was a bestseller. The book was critically acclaimed for its brutal honesty about growing up black in the old South and was the subject of a two-hour TV special on CBS. Angelou's life-story was continued in two 1980s volumes, *The Heart of a Woman* (1981) and *All God's Children Need Traveling Shoes* (1986). The author's often proclaimed motto is Terence's *homo sum; humani nil a me alienum puto* – or, as she puts it, 'I am human, and nothing human can be alien to me.'

Honours were showered on Maya Angelou in later life. In 1981, she was appointed a professor of American Studies at Wake Forest University in North Carolina. By the end of the decade she was the most famous black woman in the world – with the possible exceptions of Oprah Winfrey and Nina Simone. She was, without question, the most famous black woman author. At the request of President Clinton (whose favourite writer she reportedly is) Angelou wrote and delivered a poem at his 1993 presidential inauguration.

In the 1980s, as in the 1990s, American bestselling novels were not automatically top titles in the UK. An exception was Tom Wolfe's *The Bonfire of the Vanities*, which topped the American charts in 1987. One of the reasons for the discriminating British reader to be attracted to Wolfe's satire (based, consciously, on Thackeray's *Vanity Fair)* is its dealing – openly to the point of tastelessness – with race. More particularly, with the breakdown of race relations (as Wolfe saw it) following the institutionalization of Political Correctness, a phrase heard everywhere in the late 1980s. The narrative is built around an enigma. What happened on the Bruckner Boulevard in New York's South Bronx? Was Sherman McCoy – hopelessly lost in his Mercedes sports car with his equally sporty mistress – about to be mugged by two black youths ('Hunters! Predators!' thinks Sherman, reflexively) approaching him? Or were they, with their neutral 'Yo! Need some help?', good Samaritans, simply offering to assist a broken-down motorist? We never know. What we do know is that, in their desperate haste to escape, Sherman and Maria kill one of the youths. And, inexorably, Sherman is then destroyed by the city's race-relations industry. One of the reasons that Wolfe's novel so appealed to myriad British readers who had never been closer to New York than watching *Kojak* on TV in the 1970s was that he broached a topic apparently taboo in popular British fiction of the decade. Or any other decade, presumably.

Even more surprising a testament to the growing sophistication of the British leisure reader was the runaway success of Umberto Eco's *The Name of the Rose* in 1984. Eco (b. 1932) was an Italian, a post-structuralist and a literary critic. Three strikes, one would have thought, against his writing a bestselling popular novel for the British reading public. None the less the publisher, Secker & Warburg, could not keep up with the demand for this hyper-enigmatic tale of a fourteenth-century monk's sleuthing (Sherlock Holmes-style; lest we miss the point, he is called William of Baskerville), only to discover the cosmic indeterminacy of things. Eco's proclaimed aim was to 'free the reader from the burden of interpretation'.

However baffling all this was, one could at least rest assured that *The Name of the Rose* was read by those who bought it, or at least struggled through, from Prime to Compline (the narrative is arranged around 'liturgical hours'). It was, by contrast, extremely unlikely that the hundreds of thousands who bought Stephen Hawking's *A Brief History of Time* in 1988–9 got beyond the first few pages. Brief this survey from big bang to black hole might have been. Easy it was not.

Whatever else, the fact that this most abstruse work of theoretical physics should have topped the hardback non-fiction list witnessed, as did the triumphant parade of Booker Prize winners, to an upward spiral of taste in reading matter – a spiral in which aspiration exceeded intellectual grasp. Even if they only wanted something to display on their coffee tables, large numbers of the British were, by the end of the 1980s, addicted not just to good books but to challengingly good books. Pessimism about the uses to which the reading public would put their literacy were confounded.

Pessimists had also predicted, with the rise of TV in the 1950s, that the box would kill the book as the automobile had done for the horse and carriage. Exactly the opposite happened. The 1980s saw a remarkable burst of synergy between viewing and reading. It would be a decade notable for book–TV tie-in projects and reciprocity between screen and page, page and screen.

In some cases it was simply a case of books spring-boarding off from some broadcast series, as with *The Life of Brian*, a 1980 bestseller. The Python troupe (whose nucleus, like so much British post-war comedy, had been formed at university) first achieved international success with the BBC. They went on to make films, partly financed by ex-Beatle George Harrison, who admired their surreal humour. *The Life of Brian*, a spoof fifth gospel chronicling a pseudo-Christ as an ingenuous Palestinian schlemiel, was the book of the film. Its blasphemy practically did for Mary Whitehouse and other defenders of the Christian faith.

There were, in the 1980s, a string of bestselling books which were, like the Monty Python biblical spoof, simple off-loads from the most popular TV programmes. ITV's update of Ripley's 'Believe it or not', entitled *Arthur C. Clarke's Mysterious World*, furnished a (dire) spin-off bestseller in 1980. In 1981, *Not the Nine-o'clock News* furnished the BBC with two concurrent bestsellers in the same year (no.3 and no.6 in the paperback list), piggy-backing on the popular and sparklingly fast-paced comedy programme.

Most spectacularly, in 1986, *The Complete Yes, Minister* earned the BBC third place in the fiction annual bestseller list. *Yes, Prime Minister* (the latest scripts, novelized) came in at no.10. The following year *Yes, Prime Minister: vol. 1* was the top-selling title. *Yes, Prime Minister* held on at no.4. The series was, along with Jeffrey Archer's *oeuvre*, a favourite of the prime minister, who consented to appear as herself in a specially written sketch.

The *Yes, Minister* and *Yes, Prime Minister* series, with their Whitehall ju-jitsu between politician Jim Hacker (Paul Eddington) and Sir Humphrey Appleby (Nigel Hawthorne), his civil servant (civil master, that is), marked a high point in the history of British TV comedy. Many would say it was the highest: certainly it was said in the obituaries of Eddington in 1995 and Hawthorne in 2001. They represent what might be called the velvet edge of British political satire; the razor edge found its expression in the savage puppetry of TV's *Spitting Image* and in Michael Dobbs's 1989 portrait of a modern Machiavelli, Francis Urquhart, in *House of Cards*, adapted as an Emmy award-winning TV series the following year.

The BBC in particular now had routine bestsellers spun off from high-profile natural history series. Peter Crawford's *The Living Isles* did well in 1986. But the blockbuster presenter-author was David

Attenborough with *Life on Earth* (1980), *The Living Planet* (1984) and *The First Eden* (1987). They sold immensely: *Life on Earth*, for example, was seventy-eight weeks in the bestseller lists and cleared 250,000 copies. What were all those purchasers looking for? Attenborough's boldly ambitious series undertook to answer, head on, Douglas Adams's sly questions about 'Life, the Universe and Everything'. As always, people wanted to know the meaning of life – even if, like Monty Python, they laughed at the idea.

Natural history had always done well on the screen. But TV, it transpired, could make even the dustiest academic disciplines sexy. Archaeology was the most surprising example. *In Search of the Trojan War*, by the charismatic Michael Wood, was a tandem screen and book hit in 1985. Talking heads, shovels and the occasional 'reconstruction' went down surprisingly well. At the small end of things the BBC explored, profitably, new lines in hobbyism among its viewing public. The Corporation had a hit book, as well as a successful programme (the founder of a successful genre, in fact), with Geoffrey Smith's *Indoor Garden* (1980). Outdoor gardening would prove even more popular. The welly-boot-and-garden-fork bestseller would feature strongly in British bestseller lists for the rest of the century. They alternated between 'experts' (as in Alan Titchmarsh's *Avant Gardening: A Guide to One-Upmanship in the Garden*, 1984) and the hopeful amateur (such as Susan Hampshire's *Trouble-free Gardening*, 1989).

Dramatic adaptation could breathe life into a dead book, as with Vera Brittain's *Testament of Youth*, which, decades after going out of print, entered the paperback bestseller list in 1980 when it was revived by a BAFTA award-winning mini-series. Being optioned for such a series was second only to having Steven Spielberg buy your rights, which the tycoon did for two 'quality' novels of the 1980s: J. G. Ballard's *Empire of the Sun* and the Booker-winning *Schindler's Ark* by Thomas Keneally. Publicity about the author's death in the same year as his winning the Booker Prize for *The Jewel in the Crown* (1978), together with a television adaptation six years later, made Paul Scott's *Raj Quartet* the top hardback fiction title of 1984. It was not, in the event, the apocalyptic year that George Orwell had foreseen, but it was an appropriate date on which to commemorate the petering out of

Empire. In 1989, the BBC did a Jules Verne (and created both a best-seller and a TV superstar) by sending Michael Palin *Around the World in 80 Days*. In 1992 the Corporation would send him from *Pole to Pole*, and later in the decade *Full Circle*, around the Pacific rim.

The power of the TV engine to 'make' megaselling authors is nowhere more evident than in the career of Delia Smith (b. 1937). Smith had begun her career as a media-cook in the pages of the 1970s *Evening Standard*. Her early books were quick-and-smart efforts, addressed to the young woman like her, rushing back on the tube or train from work with no idea what to rustle up for her man. They had titles like *How to Cheat at Cooking* (1973) and *Frugal Food* (1976).

Smith was, in the late 1970s, taken up by the BBC. Her confident, unshowy, above all British style suited the Thatcherite 1980s. *Delia Smith's Cookery Course* (published as a companion book by the BBC) topped the paperback bestseller list in 1980 and successive volumes of her 'course books' featured in the lists most years in the decade. Her great skill was not to 'show' you how to do it, as did her contemporary Keith Floyd, but to educate – without condescension. She was not a chef; nor was she a literary stylist, like Elizabeth David. She was a woman just like any other who knew a few culinary tricks she was willing to pass on. At the start of her career she was famously described as 'the Mary Quant of cooking'; by the 1980s she was more the Mrs Beeton of her times.

The BBC's maximal viewing figures were gained with the royal weddings, of which there were two in the decade. Both that of Lady Diana Spencer to Prince Charles in July 1981 and that of Sarah Ferguson to Prince Andrew in July 1986 were Klondikes for opportunists in the book trade. *An Invitation to a Royal Wedding* was rush-printed by Colour Library International in days after the announcement of Charles's forthcoming nuptials. It clocked up sales of 150,000 in weeks. *Debrett's Book of the Royal Wedding* (published in May 1981 – they clearly had advance warning) was as 'Establishment' as such publications could be. It dominated bestseller lists over the summer, selling 160,000 copies in a couple of months.

A less stuffy response was offered in the no.1 non-fiction bestseller of two years later, *The Official Sloane Ranger's Handbook* (1982), subtitled 'The First Guide to What Really Matters in Life'. The book's coverlines include: 'Why it really matters to (1) wear navy blue (2) eat jelly with a fork (3) read Dick Francis and the *FT* (4) giggle in bed'. Chapter headings cover: 'Crucial dresscodes; Single sex; Money matters; Sloanes in the loo'. The rules of the Sloane universe are: 'God is a Sloane and Heaven is SW7'. There was a spin-off industry in such things as *The Official Sloane Ranger Diary*.

'Sloanes', like 'dolly-birds' in the 1960s and 'crumpet' in the 1950s, were the pattern of attractive young womanhood – albeit rich and upper-class. What the so-called 'official' handbook contained could be summed up in a single word. 'Diana'. The Diana 'look' – fresh, *sportif*, sensibly short-haired, tall and slim-limbed – was an object of emulation for young women of the decade. Diet books which promised 'thinner thighs' (preferably in under ninety days) were automatic bestsellers.

There were, in the 1980s, a profusion of books by British dieticians which promised not just to reduce weight but to sculpt the young, female body into something like that of the admired Princess. Ideally, they were embellished by the picture of a glamorously sculpted authoress. They included *Flatten Your Stomach* (1988) by Ann Dugan and Audrey Eyton's *F-Plan Diet* (1982), together with *The F-Plan Diet Calorie and Fibre Chart*. Eyton's magic bullet was the exact opposite of Dr Taller's two decades earlier: potatoes all the way. The spud could make you look like Diana. Or, at least, flat-stomached and whippet-thighed.

Other books which were buoyed up to bestseller rank by the first wedding were Robert Lacey's *Princess* (1982) and Susan Maxwell's *Princess of Wales* (1982). *The Country Life Book of Diana Princess of Wales* by Lornie Leete-Hodge combined two formulas. (Edith Holden's *Country Diary* was still selling phenomenally well. It only dropped out of the lists in mid-1981, after 150 appearances and over 2 million sales.) As events would later prove, Diana was neither countrified nor, by any stretch of the term, an 'Edwardian Lady'. Sloane Ranger, through and through.

When she married, 'Fergie' wrote the foreword to the non-fiction bestseller of the year, *One Day for Life*, a rhapsody on her forthcoming union with the third in line to the throne. Unfortunately her marriage would, like Diana's, fall short of any lifelong arrangement.

The mood of the country was, as a result of the royal weddings, more pro-Windsor than at any time since the Coronation. Not only were there beautiful young women again on the balcony at Buckingham Palace, but Prince Andrew was a bona fide Falklands hero. He had flown Sea King helicopters in combat: Fergie would later invoke this in her sadly less than bestselling children's books based on Budgie the Helicopter. Prince Charles actually topped the bestseller lists in 1980 with his children's book *The Old Man of Lochnagar*, loyally illustrated by Hugh Casson. Written during the long summers at Balmoral for his younger brothers, it recounts the adventures of an old man who lives in a cave by the Loch. It contains such royal inventions as underwater haggis (Charles had always loved *The Goons*) and a grouchy grouse.

As has happened in every decade since World War II, new genres established themselves in response to the ever-changing British reading public, answering its new demands and the new conditions of the age (the Me Decade, as it would be called). There was, by the mid-1980s, a clearly defined gay and lesbian niche market for books; bookshops would often designate them as 'Erotica', to the irritation of some consumers. Quentin Crisp's *The Naked Civil Servant*, with its amazing opening: 'As soon as I stepped out of my mother's womb, I realized that I had made a mistake', was a classic in this division. The book had been published in 1968, but took off with the Thames televisation in 1975 and Crisp's subsequent elevation to 'one of the stately homos of England'. This niche would, as time went on, provide a home for fiction as good as Alan Hollinghurst's *The Swimming Pool Library* (1988).

The women's market, now clearly defined and self-motivated, made a success of the Virago imprint – a new publishing house, run by women for women – which set out to resurrect the historical canon of women's writing, or, to put it more bluntly, books consigned to oblivion by a male-oriented literary culture. Virago was World's Classics with a feminist twist – and so successful that the orthodox publishing industry decided to buy it. The imprint, and its founder Carmen Callil, were eventually absorbed into Chatto & Windus.

In March 1982, on the initiative of the literary agent Carol Smith, the publishing house Fontana launched their 'Nightshades' list with *Shockwaves* by Thomas Tessier and *Takeover* by Rosalind Ashe. They were nicknamed 'weepie creepies' – ghost and horror stories mixed with love. Their inspiration was the extraordinary success of the V. C. Andrews books in the USA, following her 'incest and horror' super-seller *Flowers in the Attic* – a kind of Anne Frank crossed with Peter Blatty concoction. Andrews died in 1986 but, mysteriously, the books kept coming: just like Freddy Krueger, Michael Myers or Jason, she was the superseller that wouldn't die.

New genre hybrids were forever being created. Some succeeded. In the 1990s, for example, Black Lace had considerable success combining the Mills & Boon formula of women's romance with medium-hard pornography. It was a logical extension of Jilly Cooper's more playful reformulation of women's romance in her trilogy of bonkbusters with their smart, upper-class, horsey settings: *Riders* (1985; dealing with showjumping), *Rivals* (1988; the world of TV) and *Polo* (1991). These 'shagging in the shires' romances, as one reviewer irreverently labelled them, sold massively. A vague tincture of Windsor, as glamorized by Diana, attaches to them.

If one calculated the ratio of copulation to wordage, Jackie Collins would probably outdo even Jilly Cooper. Collins (b. 1939) had her first success in 1968 with *The World is full of Married Men* – a title which suggested (perhaps misleadingly) a saving sense of irony in the author's florid narratives. Jackie followed up with *The Stud* (1969) and *The Bitch* (1979) which were made into gloriously trashy films starring the author's sister, Joan Collins. Both sisters had made the move from London to Tinseltown as effortlessly as chameleons change colour. Jackie's biggest successes in the 1980s were the partnered melodramas *Hollywood Wives* (1983) and *Hollywood Husbands* (1986). As in all her fiction there is much inventory of the trappings and accoutrements of high life on the West Coast: the clothes, the cars, the houses, the cosmetics. Cynics may suspect that 'product placement' at times swells Ms Collins's already huge advances. *An American Star* (1993; a sequel to *Rock Star*, 1988) has the distinction of being the first novel to feature in the American bestseller lists accompanied by a safe-sex warning advising readers not to attempt the bedroom exploits described therein. Collins successfully hybridized women's romance with Harold Robbins. The mixture worked. Or, at least, it sold.

A successful hybridization which took hold in America, but less successfully in the UK, was that between the hard-boiled detective story and the 'woman's novel' with its soft-boiled traditions. This resulted in Sara Paretsky's V. I. Warshawski series, launched in 1982 with *Indemnity Only*. The hero-narrator is a private eye, divorcée, bisexual, pro-choice, jogging woman of the time and a child of the mean Chicago streets. Paretsky wrote two Warshawski novels a year through the 1980s.

Paretsky's main rival in this tough–tender mini-genre was Sue Grafton, whose alphabetic series of crime novels feature West Coast sleuth Kinsey Milhone. *A is for Alibi* was published in 1983; at the time of writing, Grafton is running out of titular letters. This new breed of tough-guy women crime-busters would culminate, in the 1990s, with the astoundingly successful Kay Scarpetta series, by Patricia D. Cornwell. Scarpetta, unlike Paretsky's and Grafton's private eyes, is a CME, or Chief Medical Examiner – she solves crimes from corpses. Bad news if she takes your case.

In Britain in the mid-1980s another successful hybrid came into existence with Cyberpunk sf. This, too, drew on hard-boiled fiction, of the kind pioneered by Dashiell Hammett and Raymond Chandler in the 1930s. Into the mix was thrown 1940s *noir*, the wild science fiction of practitioners like Philip K. Dick, and, as the main ingredient, the wildest element of early 1980s youth culture, punk. Cyberpunk's leading practitioner, William Gibson, deserves a spot in the science-fiction hall of fame for his anticipation, in 1984 in *Neuromancer*, of what ten years later would be called 'the Web'. He calls it the 'Matrix' – a name which would be picked up, with Gibson's depiction, in the popular 1999 youth movie starring Keanu Reeves.

There were many new accents, fresh voices and modish twists in 1980s offerings to the British reading public. But the core of what sold best, as in previous decades, was the traditional, familiar commodity. Seventy per cent of bestsellers, Alex Hamilton estimates, were what he calls 'entertainment fiction' – rattling good yarns, as they were once called. The bestseller lists are heavy with products from the 'old firm' and 'usual suspect' authors. *James Herriot's Yorkshire* (1979) made eighty appearances in the weekly lists, selling 300,000 copies. *The Lord God Made Them All* (1981) did almost as well – and was, to boot, the bestselling British non-fiction title in the USA that year.

In 1980 another long-time favourite, Len Deighton, had a hit with his anti-Europe sf-satire *SS-GB*. In this 'alternative universe' fantasy, Germany wins World War II and renders the British economy, which in 1980 was still reeling from the disastrous Winter of Discontent, as sound as a bell. Unfortunately, German business efficiency includes a state-of-the-art British Gestapo. Deighton's gimmick was picked up a decade later in Robert Harris's even better-selling *Fatherland* (1992).

Other familiar names that crop up in this period include Frederick Forsyth with *The Devil's Alternative* (1980), a thriller about terrorism which sold, home and abroad, half a million copies in its first year, and *The Fourth Protocol* (1984), a thriller about 'briefcase nuclear bombs'. As usual, Forsyth was prophetic; with the downfall of the Soviet Union in 1989, these devices were indeed seen as a risk to world peace should they, as they do in this novel, get into rogue hands.

Catherine Cookson (1906–98), the bestselling mainstream women's writer of the decade – a supremacy she would cede to Maeve Binchy in the 1990s – had a string of hits: *Tilly Trotter* (1980), *The Black Velvet Gown* (1985), *A Dinner of Herbs* (1985) and *Bill Bailey* (1987). Each of these clogs-and-shawls sagas, as they were nicknamed, from Cookson's penchant for North Country historical settings, was part of a long *roman fleuve*. There would, for example, be three novels in the 1980s following the career of Tilly Trotter, probably the most loved of the author's creations. Typically the Cookson heroine, like the author, raises herself from the working class by self-education – or, in Tilly's case, tuition from the parson's daughter. By the 1990s, Cookson's ninety-plus novels would have sold an estimated 90 million worldwide, many of these in America. Clogs and shawls were everywhere.

James Clavell's homage to British imperial-commercial know-how, *Noble House*, set in Hong Kong, was the top hardback of 1981. Wilbur Smith, as in the previous decade, continued to please male readers with his lusty romances: *Men of Men* (1981), *The Leopard Hunts in Darkness* (1984), *The Burning Shore* (1985) and *Rage* (1987). John Gardner's 007 redux, *Licence Renewed* (1981), showed that there was life in the old Bond yet. John le Carré's anti-Zionist *The Little Drummer Girl*, the bestselling hardback of 1983, demonstrated something which had been almost forgotten: that a bestselling novel could also be politically engaged and controversial. And, of course, there were the sequels, second squeezings of earlier bestsellers. Shirley Conran, for example, came round again with her sub-Susann *Lace 2* (1985), the first instalment of which had been published in 1982.

One name was never out of the annual bestseller lists in the 1980s. Dick Francis's formulaic racing thrillers led the field, with *Whip Hand* (1979), *Twice Shy* (1981), *The Danger* (1983), *Proof* (1984), *Break In* (1986), *Hot Money* (1987) and *The Edge* (1988). How to explain the continued phenomenal success of Francis's books? They are not elaborately plotted and he writes at best competently. Right always prevails. Where his novels are strong, and this is the source of his appeal, is his detailed understanding of the mysterious world of racing. It is tempting to see Francis's popularity as an indirect consequence of the reform of the British gaming laws in the 1960s and 1970s; and the English passion for the 'sport of kings'. By the end of the decade Francis, now in his seventies, was still galloping like a three-year-old.

The adventure genre which rose above all others in the 1980s was the old standby, espionage. The spy thriller was given an immense boost by the BBC's mini-series *Tinker, Tailor, Soldier, Spy* (1979) and its follow-up, *Smiley's People* (1982). The world of spies had become even more complicated than what le Carré had portrayed twenty years before in *The Spy Who Came in from the Cold*. Now the atmosphere was foggy rather than frigid. The increasing moral complexity of spycraft was reflected in Arthur Hopcraft's BBC screenplay and powerfully communicated by Alec Guinness, whose performance as George Smiley earned him a BAFTA award.

In the television adaptation of *Tinker, Tailor, Soldier, Spy* le Carré's intricate narrative is necessarily pared down. An operation goes wrong in Czechoslovakia. George Smiley, retired from active work in the 'Circus' (the HQ of MI6), is recalled to dig out the mole. Treachery is everywhere, even in Smiley's bedroom. The novels and their TV versions are as much about the intricate corruptions of British life as about spycraft.

Fact as well as fiction was complicating the old certainties of what a 'spy' was – a brave man such as James Bond or Richard Hannay who went undercover for his country. At the end of the 1980s there were two censorship affairs which created unusual bestsellers. Peter Wright's *Spycatcher: The Candid Autobiography of a Senior Intelligence Officer* was submitted for publication in 1987. Wright (1916–95) was a former assistant director of MI5, and his erstwhile employers placed an injunction on publication in the UK. They were particularly incensed by the author's allegation (pure le Carré) that Roger Hollis, former Director-General of MI5, was a Russian mole. Wright also divulged that much of MI5's espionage had been directed against the agency's own countrymen: 'For five years [in the 1960s] we bugged and burgled our way across London at the State's behest, while pompous bowler-hatted civil servants in Whitehall pretended to look the other way.'

MI5 issued a booklet categorically denying Wright's allegations. Newspapers such as the *Guardian* and *Observer* which printed summaries of Wright's book, were 'gagged' by court order. *Spycatcher* could not be published in the UK, but it was published in the USA and smuggled back in tourist baggage. It was also published in Australia, where the British government (given the connections between Commonwealth law) felt they could prosecute, which they did through the British Attorney General. The case was contemptuously dismissed by the Australian judge. By this point, *Spycatcher* was the most famous book in Britain. In 1991 the issue went all the way to the European Court of Human Rights, which found unanimously that the British government had been in breach of European law with their ban.

The other censorship *cause célèbre* of the late 1980s was even more sensational. In 1988 Salman Rushdie (b. 1947), one of the most esteemed authors in Britain (winner of the Booker of Bookers in 1993 for *Midnight's Children*), published a novel called *The Satanic Verses*. The title refers to some verses in early versions of the Koran, apparently condoning polytheism, which were later expunged as a 'Satanic interpolation'. Had the holy book been 'revised'? To devout Muslims, the suggestion that the Koran could be changed by human hand was blasphemy beyond blasphemy.

Rushdie's novel, in his familiar 'magic realism' mode, does not give up its meanings easily. But the reflections on the holy writ of Islam were enough to provoke riots and deaths in India. On 14 February 1989 (Rushdie would find the Valentine's Day connection ironic) Ayatollah Khomeini of Iran issued a *fatwa* or religious ordinance: 'I inform the proud Muslim people of the world that the author of *The Satanic Verses* book which is against Islam, the Prophet and the

Koran, and all involved in its publication who were aware of its content, are sentenced to death.' A reward of $1 million was offered by an Iranian charity to whoever executed Rushdie. The novelist was obliged to go into hiding. His novel was publicly burned and defaced, and duly shot to the top of the fiction bestseller list in America and the UK. Rushdie himself saw the outrages against him, his publishers and even his readers as a vindication of his art: 'The speaking of suppressed truths is one of the great possibilities of the novel,' he told the *Third World Book Review*, 'and it is perhaps the main reason why the novel becomes the most dangerous of art forms in all countries where people, governments, are trying to distort the truth.'

Novels could, it seemed, shake the world. Or transform it. In November 1989, the Berlin Wall came down and with it the Evil Empire. Who did it? What did it? Arguably a popular novel. Tom Clancy (b. 1947), a Maryland insurance agent and US Navy buff – although his short-sightedness had prevented him from actually serving – had great difficulty placing his first adventure story, *The Hunt for Red October*. It told the tale of a Soviet submarine commander who intends to deliver his state-of-the-art vessel to the USA. Commander Ramius, like every right-thinking person, detests communism even though it can build good underwater weaponry. He forges a strange comradeship with his adversary, the American Jack Ryan, who is hunting him (as is the whole of the Soviet Navy). Ryan and Ramius, brothers under the uniform, finally bring the ship safe into American waters, after much excitement and derring-do.

Eventually *The Hunt for Red October* was accepted by the Naval Institute Press in Annapolis. They did not publish novels, but had recently done well with Tony Geraghty's books about the SAS and thought that Clancy's techno-thriller, which was very well informed about nautical hardware, would appeal to the same market. It came out in 1984. The book was put President Reagan's way, after which sales went through the roof. Over half a million sold in hardback in the year, and a million-copy first print run was ordered for the paperback edition.

Clancy was invited to the White House and, reportedly, further enthused Reagan with the idea of the '600-warship' navy (he was already enthused about the military applications of George Lucas's

*Star Wars* and, after watching *Rambo* in the White House cinema, had said, 'Now I know what to do about Gaddafi').

It is plausible that the expense of matching the USA, ship for ship (and chip for chip in space) was what finally persuaded Gorbachev to throw in his hand. Whether this is true or not, Clancy went on to write six more techno-thrillers in the 1980s – elevating Jack Ryan, in the process, to the most technologically savvy president of the United States since Jefferson.

# 5

BY THE END OF THE TWENTIETH CENTURY, the bestseller machine was in its full technological maturity. The universal computer chip allowed instant monitoring of sales, reader preferences and shifting tides of popularity. New devices, such as W. H. Smith's pioneering EPOS (electronic point of sale) system, enabled booksellers, like other merchandisers, to move to the 'just in time' practice of targeting the customer with pinpoint accuracy. Streamlined manufacture, distribution and retailing of books were, by the mid-1990s, reshaping patterns of consumption. Thirty years before, bookshops and public libraries were by and large patronized by two groups: the 'middle-class/middle-aged' and 'young readers'. Books were dusty or do-good things compared to LPs or the latest Hollywood blockbuster.

The retail revolution in bookselling made books as attractive as designer-label clothes. And, as with fashion, the young and upwardly mobile ('yuppies') were the hot market. By 2000 not only were they mobile, they also had them – invariably pressed to the ear as they walked, stylishly, through life. This group had money; they had their own assertively generational style; they were (thanks to the steady expansion of higher education) increasingly smart and literate. *Bridget Jones's Diary*, for example, contains jokes about F. R. Leavis and Salman Rushdie – the latter good-naturedly furnished a cameo appearance for the 2001 movie. 'Shiny happy people', as the rock group REM would call them, were now shiny happy book buyers.

Two gender-specific yuppie products emerged during the 1990s, labelled respectively lad-lit and chick-lit. Both were marketed, in the UK, with a 'pizazz' frankly envied by the American book trade. When in 1993, for example, the American author Dale Peck published his first novel, a post-modern effort about gay – 'ladette' – sex, the American edition was demurely entitled *Martin and John*. The British publisher

143

thought this sounded like a child's reading primer and brashly retitled it *Fucking Martin*. In other words, f*ck decorum. The book, by an unknown author writing for a niche readership, stayed for two months in the UK bestseller lists on the strength of the F-word.

Chick-lit (a genre which literary history can trace back, via Jane Austen, to the eighteenth-century 'mothers of the novel') is obsessively concerned with the thirty-something trials of combining career, independence and a (stable) relationship with the other sex. These books breathe an atmosphere of insoluble existential angst amidst a personal affluence which to Bridget Jones's great-grandmother would have seemed the riches of Croesus. How, the heroines agonize, to deal with surplus: the too many pounds, the too many cigarettes, the too many glasses of white wine, the too many credit card bills. How to do all this – and still be a woman? If chick-lit has an ideological foundation it is to be found in the 'lipstick feminism' of Naomi Wolf's *Promiscuities* (1997), with its subtitle *The Secret Struggle for Womanhood*. Some critics, mainly in American academia, dignified chick-lit as 'postmodern feminism'.

Arabella Weir's *Does My Bum Look Big in This?* (1997) owed much of its success to its vulgar-and-don't-care title: less post-modern than posterior-modern. Weir had begun life as a comedienne and a writer of comic pieces for magazines. She remained in this line of work for ten years – profitably, but without fame. Her break came with the TV programme *The Fast Show*, for which she wrote and performed her own sketches. As the archetypal 'insecure woman' she popularized the catchphrase about the size of her derrière. The spun-off 'diary' (narrated by 'Jackie') was embellished by a modishly outrageous cover – a naked leering Weir against a neon background. The book has the *de rigueur* raunchy jokes about knickers, one-night stands, Tampax and – of course – bums. The plot, so to call it, relates the heroine's men problems, mother problems, clothes problems and diet problems. Men problems dominate, each with their Homeric epithet: 'Attractive Andy', 'Perfect Peter', 'Keen John'.

The market leader in chick-lit was (and is) Helen Fielding, author of *Bridget Jones's Diary* (1996). Fielding was educated at Oxford and, like many of the best and brightest of her generation, went on to work in 'creative and media' – TV and magazine journalism. Her first novel,

*Cause Celeb* (1994), was based on experience filming documentaries in Africa for *Comic Relief*. She subsequently wrote what became a cult column for the *Independent* newspaper.

Bridget Jones, the most famous heroine since Jane Eyre, is an over-weight, over-thirty and over-self-indulgent office worker in London (somewhat less well educated than her author, one deduces). Bridget longs to be a 'stick insect' and possessed of a bottom a little more like two snooker balls. But her bottom remains obstinately bigger than ideal; and the rest of her life less than ideal. She dreads dying alone in a bedsitter and being devoured by Alsatians.

As Bridget's diary opens she is thirty-two (that crossroad age for women), a size 12, taking in 2000 calories a day (much of it in illicit white wine 'units'), buying too many lottery tickets (a symptom of her desperate optimism) and determined to take charge of her life. This means three visits a week to the gym, avoiding relationships with 'misogynists, megalomaniacs, adulterers, workaholics, chauvinists or perverts. And, of course, learning to programme the VCR.' A typical entry in the diary runs: '130 lbs. – how is it possible to put on 4 pounds overnight? Could flesh have somehow solidified becoming denser and heavier? (repulsive, horrifying notion); alcohol units 2 (excellent) cigarettes 21 (poor but will give up totally tomorrow); number of correct lottery numbers 2 (better, but nevertheless useless).'

The plot of *Bridget Jones's Diary* artfully rewrites Jane Austen's *Pride and Prejudice*. (Following the box-office success of the 1995 film *Clueless*, which recasts Austen's Emma Woodhouse as a Californian 'valley girl', there was a vogue for this gimmick.) Like Elizabeth Bennet, Bridget Jones becomes involved with the enigmatic Mark Darcy and the cad Daniel Cleaver. In her fantasy love-life she lusts after Colin Firth, who played Mr Darcy in the TV adaptation of Austen's novel (in the film, Firth plays Mark: a kind of 'Bridget meets postmodernism' joke). Fielding is clear on where she deviates from her source: 'Jane Austen was also writing about dating, but in her day the rules were very clear, whereas now it's a quagmire of bluff and counterbluff.'

*Bridget Jones's Diary* is genuinely funny; as funny, for example, as *Lucky Jim* was for its time, class and gender. The heroine's neologisms quickly became common usage among the young, hip and female:

'singleton' (i.e. spinster), 'fwittage' (think d*mwit), 'v.gd.', 'mentioni-tis' (when you can tell someone has a crush on someone because their name keeps coming up, irrelevantly, in conversation), 'smug marrieds'. Bridget's most endearing virtue is that quintessentially British thing, pluck – she compares well in this respect to the wet, anorexic American chick Ally McBeal. Bridget is a modern woman, consciously breaking away from the womanhood represented by her mother whose generation thought pickles on toothpicks hot stuff. Endearingly, the novel is dedicated to Fielding's own mother, 'for not being like Bridget's'. She is also savvier and, for all her angst, more competent than the 1990s version of the 'dumb blonde', the Essex Girl (the misogynistic *Essex Girl Joke Book* was a bestseller in 1991).

None the less, doctrinaires among Bridget's sex complained that the diary, with its monotonous stress on consumerism, dieting, fashion and sexual subservience to Alphaman, represented an 'insult to femi-nism'. Fielding retorted that she was merely writing comedy: no one accused Bertie Wooster or Jim Dixon of being insults to the male sex, did they? From another quarter a concerted attack was launched on the whole genre in 2001 by Beryl Bainbridge and Doris Lessing, matri-archs of British fiction. For Bainbridge, chick-lit was merely 'froth' and 'a waste of time'. Why this cult of frivolity? Were clever young women, Lessing pondered, writing about 'helpless girls, drunk and worrying about their weight, just in order to get published?' Of course they were. Fielding stuck to her guns, arguing that her fiction was truer to the lives of her readers than, say, *Anna Karenina* or even *Pride and Prejudice*. Bridget was the woman of the age.

The film of *Bridget Jones's Diary* was released in April 2001, with Renee Zellweger in the lead. It was, on the face of it, a strange choice of star. She was a slim Texan who had to fatten herself up and learn the heroine's alien dialect – Sloane, Estuary, English posh. In the event Zellweger put on the pounds and did the voice admirably. By the time the movie came out, the original diary had sold an estimated 5 million worldwide. Fielding had by now published the *de rigueur* sequel: *Bridget Jones: The Edge of Reason* (1999). Bridget at last has a boyfriend. She also (in between stints in jail and other disasters) lands an interview with Colin Firth. Can life offer more? Doris Lessing, of course, would think it can; or, at least, it ought to.

With Fielding's sales triumph the genre established itself. Chick-lit was, by the end of the decade, everywhere. In Alex Hamilton's *Guardian* round-up of the top 100 bestsellers of 2001 there are seven chick-lit titles: *Sushi for Beginners*, by Marian Keyes (no.6), *One Hit Wonder*, by Lisa Jewell (no.55), *Honeymoon*, by Amy Jenkins (no.76), *Talking to Addison*, by Jenny Colgan (no.81), *My Favourite Goodbye*, by Sheila O'Flanagan (no.86), *Millie's Fling*, by Jill Mansell (no.91) and *Olivia's Luck*, by Catherine Alliott (no.98). More pervasively, the genre conditions such popular TV programmes as *Sex and the City* and *Friends*. The international success of the Spice Girls (with their battle cry 'girl power'), and the cult of 'Posh Spice' (Victoria Beckham, whose book on motherhood, *Learning to Fly*, was a 2001 bestseller) can also be plausibly aligned with the trend.

It would not be far-fetched to cast Diana as the ultimate chick of the decade. Following her separation from Charles, Andrew Morton (b. 1954) was commissioned to write the unhappy Princess's 'true story'. He was well qualified to tell it as it really was. Morton was no courtier, and no Crawfie. His CV included *Andrew, the Playboy Prince* (1983), *The Wealth of the Windsors* (1989) and *Diana's Diary* (1990). Morton was smart, had his 'sources' and was as irreverent as any tabloid hack. Diana had liked his 1990 biography of her and made contact through trusted intermediaries (the ubiquitous 'close friends'). Thereafter Morton, codename 'Noah', was, by royal appointment, her 'deep throat'.

Morton's 'true story' came out, in a storm of publicity, in June 1992. The book scandalized and, it must be confessed, titillated with its revelations of Charles's cruelty and flagrant adulteries, her bulimia and suicide attempts. *Diana* shot to the top of the bestseller list and perched there for months. Rupert Murdoch's newspapers had been pushing a republican line for some time and they gleefully serialized the more explosive segments. The House of Windsor shook (literally as well as figuratively – Windsor Castle was badly damaged in a fire in 1992). In December, Buckingham Palace announced that the couple had separated. It had been, the Queen declared, her *annus horribilis*. But not for the book trade.

The Prince mounted a counter-attack with an 'authorized' biography, written in collaboration with Jonathan Dimbleby. *The Prince of*

*Wales* came out in November 1994 and was another huge bestseller, although the people's sympathy remained overwhelmingly with the people's princess. In a TV interview with his biographer a few months earlier the heir to the throne huskily admitted adultery – but only after the marriage had 'irretrievably broken down', he claimed. And why had it broken down? Diana's instability, it was implied. Charles intimated that he had only married Diana to please his father. In the same year, 1994, Anna Pasternak published her bestseller *Princess in Love*, based on 'love-rat' James Hewitt's confessions and letters from Diana (she 'adored' the cad, she later confessed). Diana gave her side in an interview on BBC's *Panorama*, with Martin Bashir, in November 1995. She said she had no designs on the throne (beyond wanting it for her son William, of course) but wished to be the 'queen of people's hearts'. More people watched the interview than had watched the royal wedding. She won many hearts.

The couple divorced in August 1996. Diana received a reported £20 million settlement and lost her title of HRH. The fifth act of this unprecedentedly public royal drama was played out when, on 31 August 1997, Diana was killed in a high-speed car crash with her playboy lover, Dodi Al Fayed, hurtling through the early-morning streets of Paris, pursued as always by a scavenging pack of paparazzi. It was, in terms of British public reaction, the biggest event of the decade; bigger, by far, than Desert Storm. There had been 'celebrity lives' before; Morton himself had written a clutch. This was the biggest-ever celebrity death.

*Diana, Her True Story* had, by 1997, sold 5 million copies worldwide. Her death enabled Morton to reissue the story – with still more 'truth'. He now revealed that he was not Diana's biographer but her ghost writer. The title of the new edition was followed by the addition 'With New Material Including Her Own Words'. Those words were transcripts of the six audio cassettes she had sent him, in response to his questions while preparing the first edition. The transcripts make up a kind of 'dark memoir' from the early trauma when her mother (a 'bolter' by nature) decided to 'leg it', leaving her children behind her. The tapes revolve obsessively around Diana's self-doubts, self-hatreds, self-abuse (bulimia, principally) and total self-preoccupation. In one memorable vignette she recalled walking down the aisle at St Paul's on her wedding day and seeing the 'third person in our marriage', Camilla Parker-Bowles, in a grey suit and pill-box hat (looking the frump she was, it was implied). The new edition of Morton's book sold even more copies than the first, as the British people went into hysterical convulsions over the death of 'their' princess. Morton, now the undisputed chick-biographer of the English-speaking world, went on in 1999 to do *Monica's Story* (Monica Lewinsky, that was) and *Posh and Becks*. The Princess of Hearts, a Jewish American Princess and Princess Spice.

Nick Hornby (b. 1957) established himself as the doyen of lad-lit early in the decade with his string of topsellers: *Fever Pitch* (1992), *High Fidelity* (1996), *About a Boy* (1998) and *How to be Good* (2001). Hornby had worked for some years as an English teacher, and retains the morose personality that often accompanies that job. His strongest allegiance is to Arsenal FC (he lives locally in Highbury) and pop music (which, nowadays, he reviews with his left hand for the *New Yorker*). He has deep London roots and at the same time cultivates a kind of MTV supra-nationalism. It is a flavour of the decade and much to the taste of his book-buying contemporaries, whatever soccer team they support or band they listen to.

In his fiction Nick Hornby concocts what he calls 'comedy of depression'. He cites, as the major influence on his fiction, Anne Tyler's melancholy *Dinner at the Homesick Restaurant* (1982) and Lorrie Moore's *Self Help* (1985) and *Like Life* (1990). In British writing he acknowledges a debt to Roddy Doyle. (Doyle was the bestselling of all the Booker Prize winners with his *Paddy Clarke Ha Ha Ha* of 1993, the story of a 1960s Dublin childhood.) More deferentially, Hornby admits to having been influenced by Martin Amis. With novels like *Money* (1984) Amis had forged a new 'demotic' vernacular for autobiographical fiction, which Nick Hornby has gratefully adopted. But Amis, of course, is high-brow. Hornby situates himself in the yawning gulf between Jackie Collins and Michael Ondaatje. His are not books one would be ashamed to be seen reading on the underground. But they might not be the books one would leave prominently on one's coffee table if Melvyn Bragg were coming round for supper.

*Fever Pitch* is, as the title intimates, about soccer fandom (what was it Bill Shankly said? 'Football is not a matter of life and death.

It's more important than that'). Hornby has an almost religious reverence for what soccer means. The 'Saturday game', he recalls, was the sole medium of communication between himself and his dad in childhood; it was how they bonded. In *Fever Pitch* every event in the hero's not very wonderful life is linked to a memorable Arsenal game. Like other writers of his generation, Hornby is forever looking for a 'taxonomy' that will make sense of his life. Here it is the 'match report' (a device E. Annie Proulx also uses in her 1993 novel *The Shipping News*). From another angle, *Fever Pitch* stands up politically for the maligned football fan. We are not, the novel proclaims, the 'hooligans' about whom every British home secretary waxes indignant. As the author says in his introduction: '95 per cent of the millions who watch games every year have never hit anyone in their lives.'

*High Fidelity*, Hornby's second novel, anatomizes mid-life crisis (crisis, it must be said, of a rather tepid kind). Rob Fleming is encountered at the Dantean age, thirty-five, the owner of an LP store (like himself, an obsolete commodity), with an unfulfilling love life behind him. His existence revolves around self-lacerating angst. Does he, Rob wonders, enjoy 'having sex', or 'having just had sex'? He collects records which, like Krapp's tapes, preserve his past in vinyl. They are, he says, an 'autobiography'. But what good, in the cosmic scheme of things, is the archive of Rob Fleming? He orders events in his life, past and present, by making 'top ten' lists. The novel opens with him glumly charting his top ten break-ups. Despite the almost claustrophobic North London atmosphere of the novels (much less glitzy than Hugh Grant's Notting Hill, in the 2000 movie of that name), Hornby's books have been popular in the USA. None more so than *High Fidelity*, which was made into a big-budget film (also released in 2000). The setting was relocated to Chicago, with John Cusack as an American Rob. Hornby approved. He was writing about the human condition, not the plight of Highbury man.

In *About a Boy*, the responsibilities of life are weighing more heavy. This is a novel about fatherhood and 'maturity'. It completes the Hornby trinity: Arsenal, pop music, paternity. Hornby extends his range, and the domain of lad-lit, still farther in *How to be Good*. This story is narrated by a woman, Katie Carr, unhappily married to David. They have two children. She is a doctor. He writes a column called

'The Angriest Man in Holloway'. In other words, he is peeved for a living, permanently at war against the 'wankers' everywhere around him in the London streets. He has a particular peeve against women with headscarves, dog owners in parks and the pensioners who clutter up London buses. He doesn't, Katie spitefully thinks, have the balls to be homophobic or fascist. All he has is anger and nowhere to put it. During the narrative David sees a faith-healer and miraculously undergoes a life change. He becomes 'good'.

Lad-lit (itself a loose category) can be broadly divided into bad-lads and good-lads. Hornby is of the first party. So too is Tony Parsons (b. 1955), another connoisseur of popular music, whose novel *Man and Boy* (his first work of fiction) was the fourth-bestselling paperback of 2001, selling almost a million copies. The story – artfully heart-warming, occasionally tear-jerking – deals with the mutual love of thirtyish Harry Silver and his four-year-old son. Harry is a media person. His marriage breaks up after his reckless single night of infidelity. His wife takes off. He is left, a single father, with the task of 'bonding'. The 'lad' becomes a man.

Parsons followed up with *One for My Baby* (2001). It too was a year-long bestseller. A more complex and fraught story of love relations in a lower-class London setting, it was less affirmative than its predecessor. The hero, Alfie, is a descendant of Bill Naughton's hero immortalized in the 1966 film by Michael Caine. Different decades, different Alfies.

Martin Amis had pioneered the bad-boy strain of lad-lit with novels such as *Dead Babies* (1976). His lead was followed by Iain Banks with *The Wasp Factory* (1984), a novel which reviewers likened to the 'video nasties' about which Mary Whitehouse was currently exercised. Technically, *The Wasp Factory* is both bad-chick-lit and bad-boy-lit, since the hero/heroine (who regards murder as a phase one has to get through, like acne) eventually discovers himself/herself not to be a castrato after all, but... oh, well, forget it. Bad-boy-lit was exploited most successfully by Irvine Welsh (b. 1961). His book, *Trainspotting* (1993), features a gang of Edinburgh juvenile villains – laddies from Hell. Nihilistic, work-shy layabouts, they live (if it can be called that) for drugs, rock and roll (Iggy Pop, preferably), brawling, Jean-Claude van Damme movies and brutish sex (unprotected, of course; AIDS will wipe them out if the heroin doesn't. Who cares?). Particularly obnoxious is Begbie, a psychopathic sadist and drug dealer, who likes to punch his pregnant girlfriend in the stomach by way of domestic discipline. The hero, so to call him, is Rents – Mark Renton, a university dropout who intersperses his rampages with reflections from Kierkegaard. Welsh's novel went through fourteen printings in three years. It was further boosted in 1996 by Channel 4's prizewinning film directed by Danny Boyle.

There was money in bad-lad-lit, and Welsh inspired numerous imitators; but none, however nauseating they tried to be, approached his sales success – nor, after *Trainspotting*, did he. If nothing else, *Trainspotting* made Edinburgh settings cultishly fashionable, something exploited by one of the more interesting new crime writers of the 1990s, Ian Rankin, whose Inspector Rebus is only slightly less debauched and nihilistic than Welsh's Rents, even though on the other side of the law. Rankin became the bestselling British detective novelist of the late 1990s. The Edinburgh tourist office must have hugged themselves when they saw the weekly bestseller lists with another Rankin or Welsh title riding high.

From whatever angle one approached the 1990s entertainment industry, of which the book trade was now a central component, its subject matter and its target were palpably younger. Every generation, it seems, feels the need to recycle Conrad's *Heart of Darkness*, that voyage into the interior blackness of the human condition. William Golding had done it in the 1950s for middle-aged readers like himself. *Apocalypse Now*, Francis Ford Coppola's 1979 film, had recycled Conrad for thirty-year-olds – those, that is, who ten years earlier had been burning their draft-cards. Alex Garland's *The Beach* did Conrad for the late 1990s. Garland, twenty-six years old and British, published this, his first novel, in 1996. Its target audience, like its heroes, was the twenty-somethings celebrated by Douglas Coupland in his 1991 book *Generation X: Tales of an Accelerated Culture*.

The story of *The Beach* is simple. A drunken Scot in Bangkok known as Daffy Duck gives the hero, Richard, the map to a 'paradise island' before killing himself. Richard and some fellow backpackers set off to find it, which they do after much travail. It turns out to be hell on earth, the heart of darkness. *The Beach* was filmed in 2000, directed (as had been *Trainspotting*) by Danny Boyle, and starring the most beautiful of the film industry's lads, Leonardo DiCaprio – the characters having been transposed into Americans to maximize audience appeal. The movie received mixed reviews, but it kept the novel (already a bestseller) selling strongly.

The end-of-decade phenomenon which most vividly characterized the frenetic new tempo and vast new scale of the book industry was even younger: eleven-year-old Harry Potter. And close behind J. K. Rowling's boy wizard came a slew of other megaselling books which seemed properly to belong in the children's or the teen-market niches: Terry Pratchett's interminable 'Discworld', J. R. R. Tolkien, and Philip Pullman (whose *The Amber Spyglass*, the final part of the *His Dark Materials* trilogy, won the Whitbread Prize for fiction in 2002, the first 'children's book' to be so honoured).

Tolkien's fiction had been around for half a century. The books had not changed, but their readership had. In the 1960s readers of *The Lord of the Rings* had mostly been in their mid-twenties. In 2002, when the film came out, surveys showed the average age of 'Tolkies' to be twelve. Pratchett, on the other hand, clearly benefited from the sword-and-sorcery computer-game boom. By 2001, in America, the revenue from computer games overtook that from TV and was closing in fast on the movie industry; games based on Pratchett's Discworld were market leaders. Books and toys were merging into a single, seamless product range.

Why did children's books cross over into the adult market? Because, critics suggested, they dealt head on with big metaphysical questions about good and evil, the meaning of life and the human condition. This is the essence of another crossover bestseller, Jostein Gaarder's *Sophie's World* (1991), a fable built round a girl's Socratic inquiries into the nature of the universe. Meanwhile, chick-lit and lad-lit were obsessing about the size of their bum, sexy deodorants and which was the seventh-best doo-wop number of 1964.

Of all these phenomena, Potter was the most phenomenal. The genesis of the series is well known. J. K. Rowling (b. 1965) – the initials were used so as not to put off little boys with a 'girly' name like Joanne – a single mother, graduate (classics, Exeter), unemployed teacher and flat broke, found herself on a long train journey from

King's Cross. She conceived a seven-part serial story. On arrival at Edinburgh, she started writing it.

Instalment One of her septet, *Harry Potter and the Philosopher's Stone*, was turned down by three publishers before being taken on by Bloomsbury for £10,000. They brought it out as their lead children's book in June 1997. It took off respectably, selling 30,000 in six months, and won prestigious prizes. Word of mouth (potent among younger readers) made it first a bestseller and then an unstoppable superseller. When the second Potter book, *Harry Potter and the Chamber of Secrets*, came out in July 1998 it shot to the top of the UK bestseller lists ahead of John Grisham and even Terry Pratchett. This one needed no word of mouth. Warner Brothers bought the film rights. Rowling was awarded an honorary doctorate by St Andrews University in acknowledgement of her achievements for child literacy.

Harry is a waif whose parents die (killed, he later discovers, by the villainous Voldemort). He is fostered out to an unkind uncle and aunt, the Dursleys, in their unlovely middle-class house in Privet Drive. They lodge him in a cupboard under the stairs. Young Dudley Dursley makes his life hell. Eleven-year-old Harry is, to be honest, an abused child:

> Perhaps it had something to do with living in a dark cupboard, but Harry had always been small and skinny for his age. He looked even smaller and skinnier than he really was because all he had to wear were old clothes of Dudley's and Dudley was about four times bigger than he was. Harry had a thin face, knobbly knees, black hair and bright-green eyes. He wore round glasses held together with a lot of Sellotape because of all the times Dudley had punched him on the nose.

Miraculously (would that all abused children were so lucky) Harry discovers himself to be a wizard. An owl comes to tell him the good news – though a social worker might, perhaps, have been more appropriate. He is instructed to depart on the Hogwarts Express from Platform 9¾ at King's Cross for his training at the School for Witchcraft and Wizardry. So the epic, and Harry's long quest to avenge his parents, begins. By 2002, four out of the seven instalments had appeared and J. K. Rowling, happily remarried, was well on the way to being a billionaire.

There was no backlash or satiation, just inexorably mounting enthusiasm and sales madness. When *Harry Potter and the Goblet of Fire* was published in June 2000, queues formed overnight outside British bookshops. The shops made a special event of the release, and opened, for the first time in history, on the stroke of midnight – the witching hour. Amazon.com reported that demand for the title was eight times higher than for anything else they had ever sold over the internet. The US first printing of 3.8 million copies (the largest in publishing history) was exhausted in weeks; sales for the Potter books in the USA were already well over 20 million; 35 million worldwide and still soaring. The UK print run was a similarly unprecedented 1½ million. The film came out in 2001, to huge acclaim. No one, anywhere it seems, has a bad word for Potter other than Christian fundamentalists in the USA who saw in J. K. Rowling's innocent designs 'sheer evil' and a 'lack of respect' for adults.

By the end of the twentieth century, the most popular male writer in Britain was Terry Pratchett. He and J. K. Rowling went title for title against each other in the lists. A writer with roots in the working class, Pratchett was born in 1948. Although he passed his eleven-plus, he declined a grammar school place on the grounds (as he later put it) that 'woodwork would be more fun than Latin'. Not that he was unbookish. His first sf story was published when he was thirteen. Pratchett left school without any A-levels and went to work as a journalist on the local Buckinghamshire newspaper. His first book, *The Carpet People*, was published in 1971. It sold well enough to encourage him to write *The Dark Side of the Sun* (1976) and *Strata* (1981), while still pursuing his day job of journalistic and, latterly, PR work.

By this time Pratchett was planning what would become Discworld, loosely inspired by Isaac Asimov's *Foundation* trilogy and George Lucas's six-part *Star Wars* epic. Discworld is a flat disc reposing on the back of four giant elephants (once there were five) who stand on the back of a giant space turtle, Great A'tuin. Unlike Atlas, the turtle never shrugs. The disc is bordered by a circular waterfall of ocean. Much description is lavished on the exotic cosmogony of Discworld: its seasons, satellites, circadian rhythms and regions from warm spots to icy Hublands. There are four points of the disc: Rimwards, Hubwards, Turnwise and Widdershins. The first Discworld novel, *The Colour of Magic*, was published in 1983. It was serialized on *Woman's Hour* (as Douglas Adams and Garrison Keillor had demonstrated, radio was still a powerful popularizing medium for books). At this point Pratchett was taken up by Gollancz, the country's most prestigious publisher of sf, and the leading paperback publisher Corgi. They put a major promotional effort behind the Discworld novels, which were soon flowing from Pratchett's pen at the rate of one or more a year. *The Light Fantastic*, came out in 1986. On the strength of its reception, Pratchett devoted himself to full-time authorship.

From that point Pratchett's career was meteoric. By the early 1990s he was figuring in the bestseller lists, and towards the end of the decade it was customary for him to have two or more titles cresting the annual paperback charts. His novels were overwhelmingly popular with the cohort of newly computer-literate younger readers; those, that is, who lived with discs if not on them. The twenty-sixth volume in the Discworld series, *Thief of Time*, was the bestselling hardback novel of 2001. Set, as usual, in the seething city of Ankh-Morpork, it features a clockmaker, 'Death' (a character, not the last fact of life), the Fifth Rider of the Apocalypse (like Zeppo Marx, he left early before the others got famous) and the usual cast of Pratchettian fantastics.

However hard he tries, Pratchett has found it impossible to saturate the market. In 1996, for example, he brought out his third 'Johnny Maxwell' title, *Johnny and the Bomb*; *Feet of Clay*, a Discworld mystery; a portfolio of Discworld illustrations by Paul Kidby; *Hogfather*; a paperback edition of *Maskerade*; and a computer game version of Discworld. By the end of the decade he had thirty-odd works in print, all selling healthily. He is estimated to have sold some 10 million copies of his works in the 1990s.

The supernatural was everywhere in the British bestseller lists of the late 1990s. A Martian would have assumed, from bookshop windows in any high street, that the country was being converted wholesale to paganism. So strong was the appetite that a whole new kind of outlet, the so-called New Age bookshop, proliferated to satisfy it.

In the orthodox bookstore, one author among all others could be relied on to sell big every time. Stephen King had featured high on every annual UK bestseller list which Alex Hamilton had been assembling for the *Guardian* since 1979. By 2002, the American master of horror had had more no.1 hits on the *New York Times* weekly list than any other living author. By the end of the century it was estimated that some 300 million copies of his works had been sold, worldwide. Among novelists, only Agatha Christie had done better – and she had taken decades longer to do it.

During the 1990s King, as always, pumped out a title a year. Ignoring the works he did under a pseudonym, his bestsellers included *Needful Things* (1991), the tale of a horrifically magic antique shop in his favourite Castle Rock location; *Gerald's Game* (1992), in which a wife finds herself alone after a sex game, chained to a bed in a cabin in the woods; *Dolores Claiborne* (1992), a new territory for King, a whodunit murder mystery; *Insomnia* (1994), a horror novel about (unsurprisingly) insomnia; *Rose Madder* (1995), more new territory – a novel about wife battering; *The Green Mile* (1996), a superseller, even by King standards, about capital punishment and ESP, which with a boost from the Tom Hanks-starring film sold over 2 million in the UK; and *Desperation* (1996), about the traffic cop from hell, literally. During the 1990s King pioneered the e-novel, with his World Wide Web-published *Riding the Bullet* (1999) and *The Plant* (2000).

The 1990s had been a good decade for him – until, that is, a camper van crashed into him in June 1999 as he was taking his evening stroll. King almost died. Despite his horrific injuries and painful convalescence, he remained king of the charts. *Bag of Bones* (1998), a story of revenants in a New England resort town, was still selling well. In the aggregate top ten figures in the UK for fiction he figures twice in 2001, with the sequel to *The Talisman* (*Black House*, co-written with Peter Straub) and *Dreamcatcher* (extra-terrestrial vampires descend to invade the bowels, literally, of America). In February 2002 King announced his retirement. No one believed him. Resurrection is one of his favourite themes.

Wilbur Smith, who for years had specialized in big-bicep male-action adventure stories, was at the end of the decade, also riding high with King-like tales of the supernatural. *Warlock*, a sequel to his earlier novel *River God*, was the second-bestselling adult hardback fiction title of 2001 – second only to Terry Pratchett's *Thief of Time*, itself no masterpiece of literary realism. Smith's romance is set in ancient Egypt and features Taita, the warlock of the title, who is adept in the lore of the primitive gods. A titanic contest between dark and light, goodness and evil, ensues – the soul of young Prince Nefer is at stake. With a change of setting to modern New England, this is much the same as the plot of King's *Dreamcatcher*.

Two titles by Joanne Harris continued to feature high in the fiction paperback bestseller lists of 2001. *Chocolat* (1999) and *Blackberry Wine* (2000) comprise the first two parts of the author's 'gastronomic/sorcery' or 'grub and magic' trilogy. Harris, a former schoolteacher, had written two 'gothics' before *Chocolat*. She had read modern languages at university and knew France well. In *Chocolat* a witch does battle with a priest for the soul of a French village. The situation of *The Exorcist* is reversed; the witch is now the good guy. Her weapon is chocolate (the wicked food?). The novel was boosted in 2001 by a film adaptation starring Juliette Binoche and Johnny Depp which slipped smoothly down the public gullet.

In *Blackberry Wine* a blocked writer, Jay Mackintosh, buys a derelict farmhouse in the same French village of Lansquenet. Ghosts appear. The inevitable witch, Marise, enters his life. A bottle of magic wine unlocks his past. A third novel, *Five Quarters of the Orange* (2002), completes the sequence. Set in a village on the Loire during the German occupation, it features a widow, her three children and a soldier, Tomas. Things turn out disastrously. Long after the war the only surviving child returns with a new identity, intending to set up a crêperie-restaurant. The past, however, cannot be exorcized until she works through her mother's witching-book of recipes (i.e. spells). Food again figures as the novel's central metaphor.

There are multiple ingredients in Harris's fictional brew. Prominent is a kind of ecological correctness, a love of the natural and wholesome things of the earth. The author confesses that she 'enjoys making my own incense and growing and using herbs'. Magic is another key ingredient. All the astrology decanted on to the British population in the studiously un-Christian millennium year had, one assumes, stimulated an appetite for supernatural explanations of the cosmos.

As the century came to an end, Britain was palpably undergoing a huge swerve away from established religion – as dramatic, in its way, as the swerve from sexual orthodoxy in the 1960s. With the feminist interventions of the 1960s the figure of the witch or wise old woman was rehabilitated into something heroic and valuable. There is also in Harris's fiction a strong tincture of the tourist brochure and the *Michelin Guide*. The concoction sold wonderfully well.

In the 1980s, a new style of travel book had become popular. Its principal practitioners were Paul Theroux and Bruce Chatwin in the UK; William Least Heat-Moon in the USA. The stress was less on old-fashioned travelogue than on 'personality'. The travellers were 'accidental tourists', in Anne Tyler's phrase. They were not 'exploring', like John Blashford Snell or Ranulph Fiennes. Nor were they 'experts' like Wilfred Thesiger. They did not do dangerous things like Redmond O'Hanlon. These accidental tourists wander in interesting places and make interesting observations. They are connoisseurs of the quirky. Their voyages are not thematized like Michael Palin's BBC-sponsored expeditions but random pilgrimages. Thanks to the package holiday, travelling was, most readers felt, no big deal now anyway. In the 1990s, most Britons had 'seen the world': been there, done that. Boarding the jumbo at Gatwick one didn't feel like Thor Heyerdahl. More like self-loading freight.

This line of casual-anecdotal travel writing was developed in the 1990s by Bill Bryson, and for a more select public by W. G. Sebald. Both of them were 'insider-outsiders'. Bryson was 'an American with a British soul'; Sebald was a German who fell in love with (of all places) East Anglia. Their stance (home and away) is summed up by Bryson's 'I'm a stranger here myself'. Stranger, but never a 'foreigner'.

Bryson was born in 1951. He comes (as they say) from Des Moines, Iowa ('*somebody* has to', his first travel book tells us). He came to Britain in the early 1970s, as a college drop-out and hitch-hiker (those heroic figures of the decade). Vietnam was one of the things he left behind. Young Bryson took a part-time job at a mental institution and fell in love with one of the nurses (having a psychotherapist around the house has been invaluable, he jokes. All authors should be so lucky.) Over time he also fell in love with the English. He admired their national gift for irony. He picked the device up, wiring for himself new neural circuits. He was the 'special relationship' incarnate.

What British readers particularly like about Bryson is that he accepts the smallness of his expat domicile. It is 'Little England', a 'small island'. No continental superpower. But the American writer knows, loves and (most gratifyingly) admires little old us. We still matter, his books reassure us, despite the microscopic dot we represent on the world map.

Before he became famous Bryson freelanced in journalism and wrote articles and books on language usage such as *Mother Tongue* (1990). They were – unusually for books on linguistics – amusing as well as informative. Bryson could make a bus timetable funny. By the 1980s he was happily married, an English resident with four Anglo-American children. He was not rich and his opportunities for globe-trotting were limited. Not that it bothered him. As he records: 'I never set out to be a travel writer. I got into it entirely by accident. The first book, *The Lost Continent*, was essentially a kind of memoir. I'd been living in England for a long time, and after my dad died I decided to come home and travel around America, to look at the country and see how it had changed, and how I had changed, in the years that I'd been living away.'

That first effort, *The Lost Continent* (1989), became the best-selling travel book of the decade. 'Travel' is perhaps the wrong word: 'ramble book' might be more accurate. The author just got in his car and drove, rediscovering the vacation experiences of his youth and childhood. Surprisingly, it got him into some trouble in his (other) home country. Compatriots found Bryson's 'English' humour alien and offensive. Particularly his 'comforting' himself, on being pushed by senior citizens in the queue to get into Roosevelt's house in Warm Springs, Georgia, with the thought that the old geezers 'would soon be dead', along with their president. As Bryson complains, exasperatedly: 'Americans are painfully literal. They [not, one notes, 'we'] don't understand irony.' His later books, however, are palpably softer-hitting. America may be 'literal', but it's a big market.

If Bryson has a favourite place, it's what he calls 'the middle of nowhere', or, as expressed in the title of his 1993 book about Europe, *Neither Here Nor There*. In 1996 Bryson, his children now growing up, moved back to live in New Hampshire. There, presumably, he is known as an Englishman with an American heart. He has said he

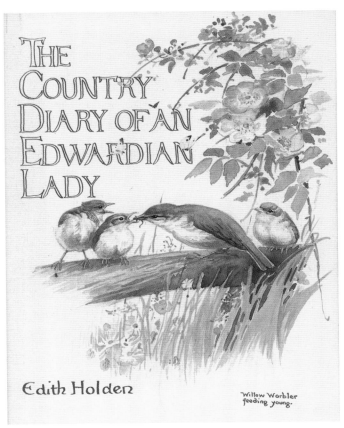

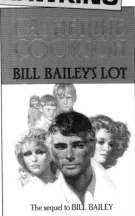

**Above** Edith Holden's illustrated diary of 1906 capitalized on an appetite for nostalgia. It was the bestselling non-fiction title of the late 1970s, featuring in the lists for three years.
**Below** Andrew Morton's biography really does appear to have been Diana's true story, as the world discovered after her death in 1997.

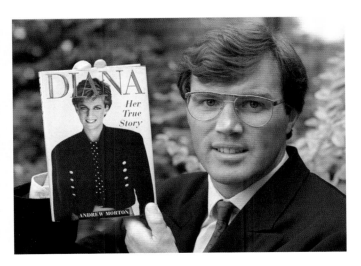

**Above, top to bottom:**
How to bag the best grass at Glyndebourne was just one essential tip passed on by *The Official Sloane Ranger Diary*; Hawking's *A Brief History of Time* – has anyone without a PhD got past page seven?; Catherine Cookson's North Country clogs-and-shawls sagas made her one of the world's bestselling authors of the twentieth century.

**Previous pages** Once a heart-throb, later a distinguished film actor, Dirk Bogarde revealed a third and possibly even more impressive talent for autobiography and fiction writing in the last decades of his life. **Above** Jackie Collins pushes one of her gloriously trashy 'bonkbusters' with pizazz. Note how big the author's name is compared with the title.

**Opposite top** Eye to eye? Perhaps not. Kingsley Amis wins his Booker Prize in 1986. Son Martin is still waiting for his. Between them they represent two generations of British bestsellers at their classiest.

**Opposite bottom left** Stephen King with what he calls the world's best word processor: a Waterman pen.

**Opposite bottom right** 'I want to free you from understanding what my books mean.' Umberto Eco: Italian, post-structuralist, literary critic and bestselling author of *The Name of the Rose*.

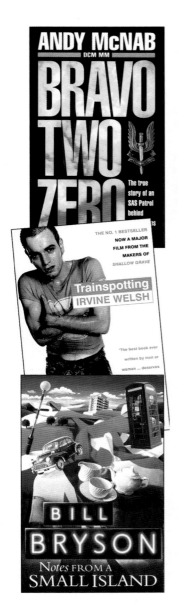

**Above, top to bottom:**
Andy McNab pioneered the
Gulf War SAS thriller – the
patrol was a disaster, but
the book was a triumph;
*Trainspotting* did nothing
for tourism in Edinburgh,
but it made Irvine Welsh an
internationally bestselling
author; the American, Bill
Bryson, did a lot for British
tourism with his quirky
survey of Blighty.

**Above, top to bottom:** Ubiquitous on the London Underground, the paperback edition of *White Teeth*; the first of Dave Pelzer's trilogy of childhood suffering was a surprise top-selling title of the 1990s; Terry Pratchett's twenty-first Discworld instalment, *Jingo*.

**Opposite top** Vikram Seth looks pleased, and well he might – despite its length, his novel *A Suitable Boy* was a huge bestseller.
**Opposite bottom** John Bayley's account of his wife Iris Murdoch's descent into Alzheimer's disease enjoyed considerable sales success, further boosted by a film adaptation released in 2002.
**Above** Zadie Smith's post-colonial saga of the Asian diaspora, *White Teeth*, won prizes and sold half a million copies.

**Above** The appeal of the Harry Potter books to girls and boys of all ages – and a good many adults – has put their author J. K. Rowling (inset) on track to become fiction's first billionaire.

wants to be buried in 'Thornton-le-Beans'. Before returning to his own continent he made a farewell trip around Britain and subsequently wrote *Notes from a Small Island* (1995; it was adapted as a TV series in 1999). The first thing he did, on arrival in America, was to go for a 'walk in the woods' – the Appalachian trail which snakes 2000 miles from Maine to Georgia. He didn't do the whole trail – too much beer and too many doughnuts. But he did the book (1998). It was followed by *I'm A Stranger Here Myself: Notes on Returning to America After Twenty Years Away* (1999). He was no longer 'a tourist who wrote books'; he was a tourist who had come home.

Now that Bryson is a hot property his employers pressure him to synchronize his books with public events that will give them some extra lift. *A Walk in the Woods* coincided with the trail's seventy-fifth anniversary. *In a Sunburned Country*, his 'Australian' book, appeared simultaneously with the September 2000 Olympics in Sydney.

Another 'different' kind of travel book which proved surprisingly popular during the 1990s was Peter Mayle's *A Year in Provence* (1991). Neither tourist, emigrant nor retiree (although a little bit of each, having given up his job in advertising), Mayle wrote a humorous month-by-month chronicle of his, his wife's and his two dogs' awkward cultural transplantation. It became a bestseller, selling half a million copies in paperback, and was adapted for TV.

If nothing else, *A Year in Provence* testified to the huge prosperity which had transformed Britain in fifty years. In 1950, a week in Blackpool (or, if you were that way inclined, a 'dirty weekend in Brighton') would have been the realistic extent of a getaway – unless you applied for the £10 assisted passage to Australia. In 1950 'emigration' meant the quest for a better life. In the 1990s the 'expat experiment' meant a luxurious twist to the 'good life'. No longer did the British middle classes have to savour France through Elizabeth David's recipes. They could buy the country: or, at least, a country house in Provence, the Dordogne or Burgundy.

The great war of the 1990s, against Iraq, had relatively little fall-out in the bestseller lists other than creating a new flavour of military-male-action thriller based on the feats of the SAS. Foremost in this valorous squad was Sergeant Andy McNab, whose autobiographical account of a cock-up heroically survived (that archetypal subject in

British military narrative), *Bravo Two Zero* (1993), was the bestselling book to be produced by the war. It went on to sell 350,000 in hardback in 1994. The story it tells is stark. In 1991 an eight-strong SAS squad had been dropped behind enemy lines to take out Saddam's Scud missiles – the kind of mission romanticized in innumerable movies. This was no movie. Three of the group were killed, others were captured and tortured, and the mission failed utterly. McNab (a pseudonym, one assumes) returned to tell the tale after the necessary Ministry of Defence vetting. On becoming a civilian he followed up with the 'inside story' of the SAS, *Immediate Action* (1996), defying attempts by the authorities to gag him. Even more profitably, he embarked, with *Remote Control* (2000), on a string of SAS thrillers based on a series hero, Nick Stone. 'Chris Ryan', another member of Bravo Two Zero, weighed in with his version of the patrol, *The One That Got Away* (1995). It was less than complimentary to McNab – these warriors seemed to be as eager to zap each other as the enemy. But men, as John Gray's 1993 bestseller put it, are from Mars. They like to scrap with each other.

These 'Special Forces' romances, documentary and fictional, satisfied a British need. The SAS, an elite regiment no more than a few hundred strong, bore out – if you believed McNab, Ryan and the more excitable elements in the tabloid press – Paul Brickhill's thesis in *The Dambusters* that British 'quality' made up for the greater *matériel* and numerical superiority of Britain's enemies. It was a dangerous illusion; but it sold books.

The late 1990s vogue for military history such as Anthony Beevor's *Stalingrad* (1998) seems plausibly connected to the barrage of military information, notably via the front-line cameras of CNN, which the public received during the 1992 siege and bombardment of Iraq. For the first time in media history, from Baghdad newscasts one could feel without any personal risk what it was like to be 'inside' combat – under a rain of Tomahawk missiles. The success of Sebastian Faulks's novel of the World War I, *Birdsong*, which sold almost 250,000 hardback copies in 1995, may also distantly owe something to Desert Storm. Tom Clancy's consistently top-selling techno-thrillers (always more popular in the USA than in the UK), with their breathless admiration for US military hardware and its invincibility, certainly benefited from the US 'turkey shoot' on the Basra road. America had at last purged the Vietnam Nightmare. No more *Catch-22*. From now on it was B52 all the way.

Computers now ran war. They also, increasingly, ran everything. It was in the 1990s that another ubiquitous screen, that of the VDU, joined the movies' big screen and TV's small screen. By the end of the decade the majority of American households and almost half of those in the UK were 'Web-connected'. The internet interacted dynamically with the book trade. There were simple explanatory books, from *The World Wide Web for Dummies* (and an array of similar titles for book-buying dummies) to Bill Gates's guru pronouncements in *The Road Ahead* (1995), which sold almost a million copies worldwide, familiarizing people with the 'first mover' advantage and making Mr Microsoft (already the richest man in the world) even richer. The e-book, despite Stephen King's gallant experiment, has yet to take off. The main incursion of the internet into the book trade was the phenomenal growth of the 'electronic bookshop' and the 'first mover' in that field, Amazon.com. America, of course, led the field.

The UK in the 1990s had nothing quite like Oprah Winfrey, whose daytime talk show featured regular book spots, inspiring 'Oprah's Pick' stands in bookstores across America and on Amazon's web pages. The reading-group movement which Oprah principally addressed did, however, take off in the UK. A group of people would get together and set themselves books to read and discuss. Typically, their choice was stimulated by some high-profile television adaptation of a classic text. There was a constant stream of these through the 1990s, beginning with Jane Austen (every one of whose six major works was given colourful TV or film treatment), going through Thackeray, Dickens and Mrs Gaskell, and ending in 2001 with Trollope's *The Way We Live Now* (a new version of *The Forsyte Saga* is promised for 2002). Each of these adaptations inspired a surge of reading interest, group and individual, in the source book.

The fruitful interactions between television and the book trade, the page and the small screen, grew, consolidated and diversified during the 1990s. The TV celebrity cook spot was a contested prime-time arena – followed by the celebrity gardener, the celebrity interior designer, the celebrity historian, the celebrity astronomer and, on the talk-show circuit, the celebrity celebrity. At the end of the decade the TV kitchen was dominated by the trinity of Nigella Lawson, Delia Smith (thirty years at the top) and Jamie Oliver (the so-called Naked Chef, looking as if he had just wandered off the set of *Men Behaving Badly*).

Ever since its inception as a mass medium in the 1950s, television, along with the longer-established radio channels, has acted as a pervasively influential popular educator. In the 1990s tie-ins inspired a boom in historical series, which as surely as day followed night (or the evening's prime-time transmission) sold tons of books. The first part of Simon Schama's epic series *A History of Britain* (2000) had a companion volume which topped bestseller lists for weeks. So, in the same year, did David Starkey's Channel 4 programmes on British queens. Peter Ackroyd, whose 1991 biography of the Great Inimitable had become, over the years, one of the bestselling books in its class, weighed in with his one-man, one-voice radio dramatization of *The Mystery of Charles Dickens* in March 2002. Millions watched (or listened); tens of thousands bought.

As always, detective fiction and TV worked well together. In the UK, the late John Thaw's sensitive interpretation of the agonized Oxford detective and would-be don, Inspector Morse, sold millions of copies of Colin Dexter's novels. Another happy media marriage was that between saga and mini-series. An outstanding example from Channel 4 was Peter Hall's adaptation of Mary Wesley's *The Camomile Lawn*. Wesley belonged to the venerable cohort of distinguished British women writers which included Victoria Holt, P. D. James, Ruth Rendell and Rosamunde Pilcher and who, as the advertisements put it, did not get older but got better. Born in 1912, she was educated at the London School of Economics. During World War II she worked in the War Office, and afterwards travelled widely. Amazingly, her first novel, *Jumping the Queue*, was not published until she was seventy. If everyone has a novel inside them, hers was well seasoned.

*The Camomile Lawn* (1984) opens with a description of the lawn of the title, stretching from a fine house in Cornwall to the cliffs. It is high summer, 1939. Five cousins have gathered at their aunt's house for their annual reunion. The world is about to change. But the lawn, like the earth in Ecclesiastes, abides. There follow multiple plots, sub-plots and interweavings of destiny. Of course, the narrative is really about England. Does it survive? Or is it, like the phoenix, reborn out of its own destruction? Or is it, horrible thought, decaying?

Wesley was a woman of mature years, writing 'lady-lit' (as one might call it) for a mature female readership. Other writers, too, catered for that large, book-hungry, highly literate market. Leading the field were Joanna Trollope and Maeve Binchy. Trollope (b. 1943) made it into the bestseller lists relatively late (if not as late as Wesley) with *The Rector's Wife* in 1991. She then wrote *The Men and the Girls* (1992), *A Spanish Lover* (1993), *The Best of Friends* (1995), *Next of Kin* (1996), *Other People's Children* (1998) and a series of other popular, but less bestselling, works under the *nom de plume* Caroline Harvey. Her fiction, which, like Wesley's, adapts well to TV, typically features intricate complexities of marital or family crisis in the upper-middle classes – Aga Sagas, as they were irreverently nicknamed. Trollope's popularity consolidated during the decade, culminating with *Marrying the Mistress*, the seventh-bestselling novel of 2001 (by Alex Hamilton's count) with some half a million copies sold. It tells the story of a superannuated judge who crowns forty years' service in the courtroom and in the marital bedroom by proposing to ditch the family Aga and make an honest woman of his long-term mistress. Moral turmoil of a genteel kind ensues.

In the same 2001 list Maeve Binchy is several places above Trollope. She comes in at no.3, close on the heels of Rowling and Grisham, with *Scarlet Feather*, a novel which sold 1½ million copies in the year. Binchy was born in Ireland in 1940 and taught in various girls' schools there until 1969, when she joined the *Irish Times* as a journalist. In the 1980s she began to turn out a stream of bestselling novels. In the 1990s the stream became a flood. *The Copper Beech* (1992), *The Glass Lake* (1995), *Evening Class* (1997) and *Tara Road* (1999) were all no.1 bestsellers. Like Trollope's, her work adapted well for TV and *Circle of Friends* (1992) was successfully filmed. She favours Irish settings of the not too distant past and 'everyday' crisis and melodrama. *Scarlet Feather* is a typical high-quality Binchy which tells of Cathy and Tom Feather, who study together at cookery school and set up their own catering business called Scarlet Feather. Sub-plots, involving other characters, criss-cross in a sprawling, loose-weave narrative.

Probably the best woman's romance of the decade, certainly the cleverest, was the Booker Prize-winning *Possession* (1990) by A. S. Byatt (b. 1936). Byatt's success with both a mass readership and discriminating readers arose from a canny blending of genres. Subtitled *A Romance*, the novel draws on the story-telling skills of Georgette Heyer, a novelist Byatt admires and on whom she has written perceptively. While never surrendering its page-turning appeal, *Possession* displays, as ostentatiously as any campus novel, Byatt's prodigious learning and her mastery of contemporary literary theory. The novel has a strong narrative line. A post-doctoral research student discovers a letter which seems to uncover a clandestine love affair between two Victorian poets. We travel backwards in time to the Victorian era, and forward to the denouement of the mystery.

There was a growing market for the smart novel for smart (mainly women) readers, such as Zadie Smith's *White Teeth* (2000). Smith's book was extraordinarily ambitious for a first effort and, like Rushdie's early work, notably *Midnight's Children*, or Vikram Seth's 1994 bestseller *A Suitable Boy*, was grandly post-colonial in its design. From North London, it stretches back in history to the origins of the Asian diaspora which has created so-called multicultural Britain. How, exactly, did we get here? Smith's novel asks. The heroes are Archie Jones and Samad Iqbal, who served together in a 'Buggered Battalion' during World War II. The narrative follows their post-war careers, and with it the history of post-war Britain. *White Teeth* was, after *Scarlet Feather* (a different, and softer-edged, saga), the top-selling novel of 2001. Its success (half a million copies sold by 2002) was a heartening sign of the growing maturity of a large segment of the market for popular fiction.

A genre which grew to dominate the non-fiction bestseller lists of the 1990s was, as best one could name it, the 'dark memoir'. Essentially, these books revolve around childhood suffering, frequently involving social deprivation and abuse, heroically survived. A precursor is *Wild Swans* (1991) by Jung Chang, a Chinese-born writer living in London. The memoir tells of her family's survival, generation after generation, under war, persecution, exile and myriad other disasters. The book became, surprisingly perhaps, a favourite with UK A-level boards.

The dark memoir genre emerges in its full-blown character with *Angela's Ashes* (1998) by Frank McCourt (b. 1930). His book opens in

Depression-era Brooklyn. The hero does what millions of Irish Americans dream of doing – he goes back to Ireland. Back, however, as a four-year-old child to grinding poverty in the old country. Frank grows up with his mother's family in Limerick. Angela is indomitable, but ostracized because of her marriage to an Ulsterman – a drunkard to boot. Ireland is not the romantic turf sung about in Irish American pubs. The memoir opens with a glum universal truth: 'Worse than the ordinary miserable childhood is the miserable Irish childhood, and worse yet is the miserable Irish Catholic childhood.' The McCourt household crumbles into squalor, with rags on their backs and a pig's head as their Christmas 'treat'. As he grows up, Frank dreams of returning to America. It ends when the hero is nineteen. McCourt followed with a sequel, 'Tis (1999), following the author-narrator's career; eventually, he will end up a teacher of creative writing. Both volumes were huge bestsellers, boosted by Alan Parker's 1999 film of Angela's Ashes.

The dark memoir was taken into still darker places by Dave Pelzer. The first book of what would be a trilogy, A Child Called 'It', became the third-bestselling non-fiction title of 2001, selling 750,000 copies in the UK and multiples more in Pelzer's native USA. The second part, The Lost Boy, sold half a million copies in 2001 in the UK. Together, these titles put Pelzer out in front of everyone except J. K. Rowling.

Pelzer was that iconic figure of the 1990s, a child-abuse survivor. He was, by his own account, lucky. He is reckoned to be the third-worst victim in California state history. The other two, being dead, are unable either to contest the claim or to write bestselling books. The abuser, in Pelzer's case, was his mother (there is, in places, a distinct feel of Christina Crawford's 1970s bestseller, Mommie Dearest, in his memoirs). His rescue from probable death at his mother's hands happened in March 1973. The twelve-year-old Dave had gone through what was, for him, routine preparation for school. His hands had been dunked in corrosive ammonia for some venial dereliction with his household chores. He was lucky. On other occasions his arms were held over blazing gas flames, scarring them for life. That day his face was slapped and his head banged against the kitchen counter. He had been denied food for twelve hours – apart from what he could scavenge from the dirty dishes which he was set to wash. Sometimes he would be starved for as long as ten days on end or forced to eat dog turds; the household dog was, of course, well fed. It was not easy for Dave to eat, anyway, since most of his teeth had been knocked out. His torso, underneath his shirt, was a mass of weals. His stomach was still scarred by a knife wound inflicted by his chronically drunken mother. At home he was known as 'it'. None of his four siblings was abused or neglected.

The Pelzer household had fallen apart when his father, a fire-fighter with a taste for strong drink, walked out. His mother took her rage out on 'it'. Why him and not the other children? According to Pelzer, the explanation is 'child-selection'. The perpetrators 'pick on a child that they can control and get away with. She picked on me because I was shy, and I believe that she thought I was slow, and I was clumsy.... So she picked on me, and a relationship formed.' In an interview he had with his mother shortly before her death she told him, candidly, that she wanted to kill him but couldn't work out what to do with the body.

On 12 March 1973 the school authorities finally stepped in, and Dave Pelzer was put in foster care. He went on to have a good life in the United States Air Force and thereafter in civilian life. Twenty years later, now married, and the father of an eight-year-old son, Pelzer wrote up his experiences as A Child Called 'It' (1993), The Lost Boy (1994) and A Man Named Dave (2001). The cumulative sales of these books were enormous. Needless to say, the books grow out of the long course of therapy that put him together again; and the fact that he married a literary agent helped put the books together. At the end of the trilogy he finds that he can, at last, forgive his mother.

Why were the Pelzer books so phenomenally popular? Why, moreover, did they appeal so far from the dreary California suburbs that originated them? One reason, clearly enough, is 'male payback'. For years, men had been confronted with the uncomfortable fact of their violence against women and children. Men battered wives, inspiring the setting up of refuges. Within families the perpetrators of incest were exclusively male and preponderantly father on daughter (or older brother on sister). Paedophiles? One hundred per cent male. Pelzer was simply levelling the score. Mothers could be bad guys too. The data is unavailable, but it is probable that, as with Robert Bly's Iron

*John*, the 'recover your masculinity' bestseller of 1992, the readership of Pelzer's trilogy was overwhelmingly male, resentful and deeply insecure.

The topselling non-fiction hardback of 2001 in the UK was *Billy*, the 'life study' of comedian Billy Connolly. It sold 600,000 in hardback in the three months leading up to Christmas 2001, stimulated by an exceptionally lively performance by the Scotsman on the Parkinson talk show. The author was Pamela Stephenson, comedienne turned psychotherapist and, of course, Mrs Connolly. Billy, like Dave, was abused as a child – but, unlike Dave, sexually. As an adult he plunged into alcoholism and violence: parts of the book read like Irvine Welsh. Underneath the hilarity of his stage persona, one apprehends, was always torment. But Billy 'survived'. What did he survive? Being himself.

A rung or two below *Billy* on the 2001 hardback non-fiction list, at no.7, is George Best's alcoholic odyssey from soccer superstardom to jail, *Blessed*. 'Bestie' too, we discover, has survived. Survived to write bestselling books and appear on talk shows – not, alas, to star on the soccer pitch. The best and least self-pitying of this genre are Martin Amis's *Experience* (2000) and Lorna Sage's description of growing up unloved and an unwed sixteen-year-old mother, *Bad Blood* (2000). Amis went on to become the country's most controversially famous novelist; Sage went on to become, before dying prematurely in January 2001, a distinguished academic. Survival plus.

The appetite for suffering undergone and survived was, as the 1990s drew to an end, insatiable. John Bayley's trilogy of domestic agony during Iris Murdoch's descent into Alzheimer's and Teletubby addiction enjoyed considerable sales success in the last years of the decade. Bayley, as the last volume (*Widower's House*, 2001) records, survived widowhood to marry again. The film of the first part of the trilogy, *Iris*, was released in 2002 and starred Judi Dench as old Iris and Kate Winslet as young Iris.

Lad-lit, chick-lit, the dark memoir and SAS thrillers were all newcomers to the 1990s bestseller lists. There they joined familiar ranks of old friends and usual suspects. In 1991, Alex Hamilton noted that five names had been on every list of fastsellers he had compiled since 1979. His 'Formidable Five' were Catherine Cookson, Dick Francis, Danielle Steel, Victoria Holt and Stephen King.

A sixth name would be added during the decade. From *The Firm* (1991) onwards, John Grisham (b. 1955) had established himself as the most 'bankable' of American blockbuster writers. Publishers loved his thrillers – not just because they sold millions of copies (which they did, invariably, in hardback, softcover and audiobook form) – but because his stories adapted unfailingly into hugely profitable films with Hollywood's biggest stars. Grisham was the king of tie-in. The films went on to boost both backlist and future sales of Grisham books. The ball never stopped rolling. It was perfect reciprocity. *The Firm* was filmed in 1993, starring Tom Cruise and Gene Hackman; *The Pelican Brief* (1992) in 1994, starring Denzel Washington and Julia Roberts; *The Client* (1993) also in 1994, starring Susan Sarandon and Tommy Lee Jones; *The Chamber* (1994) in 1996 starring Gene Hackman and Faye Dunaway; *The Rainmaker* (1995) in 1997, starring Matt Damon and Danny DeVito. The sums generated by the Grisham phenomenon amounted to billions.

The formula behind this money machine was simple. *LA Law* crossed with *The Godfather*. In all Grisham's thrillers, an idealistic young lawyer decides he is mad as hell and can't take it any more. He rebels against the Establishment of American law (seen, in *The Firm*, as intrinsically criminal). In so doing, the Grisham hero saves his soul and purifies America. These novels responded, romantically, to a period dominated by petty litigation and with high-profile trials, like O. J. Simpson's, polluting the reputation of the courts and the justice system. The same factors explain the popularity of David E. Kelley's legal-soap TV series, *Ally McBeal* and *The Practice*.

Why Grisham should have been as popular as he was in the UK is more mysterious. We have different law. He is not a great writer, nor an ingenious deviser of plots; Scott Turow and John Mortimer, in his 'Rumpole' books, are more inventive. None the less, in Alex Hamilton's aggregate list of the country's 'fastsellers' of 2001 Grisham comes second, outstripped only by Harry Potter. *The Partner* (1997), *The Street Lawyer* (1998), *The Testament* (1999), *The Brethren* (2000) and even Grisham's semi-autobiographical recollection of growing up in Arkansas, *The Painted House* (2001), topped British bestseller lists, often selling over a million in their first editions. One assumes that the films had something to do with it.

Other American blockbusters were to British taste in the 1990s. In the 1980s Thomas Harris (b. 1940), a journalist who wrote books on the side, had established himself as a classy writer of hard-boiled crime novels. The modish feature of *Red Dragon* (1981) and *The Silence of the Lambs* (1988) was his fascination with serial killers and profiling, something picked up in the successful British TV series *Cracker*.

*The Silence of the Lambs* is constructed around the hunt for a sadistic serial killer nicknamed 'Buffalo Bill', who likes to flay his victims and make himself leather garments out of their skin. A young FBI agent, Clarice Starling, is helped in her profiling by an even more horrific mass murderer held in highest-security custody, Hannibal ('the cannibal') Lecter. An evil genius and connoisseur of fine wines and good food (not all of it human), Lecter had also appeared marginally in *Red Dragon* and would, in 2000, get a novel all to himself, *Hannibal*. *The Silence of the Lambs* offers a new twist on the old adage, 'set a monster to catch a monster.' A subtle duel of wits develops alongside the murder hunt. For every clue Lecter divulges, Clarice must reveal something intimate about herself – more specifically, as Hannibal immediately intuits, her childhood trauma. She, too, is being profiled.

The book version of *The Silence of the Lambs* sold well, but not spectacularly: nothing, that is, to elevate Harris above, say, Jonathan Kellerman, James Patterson or Martin Cruz Smith. What propelled his thriller to supersellerdom was a movie tie-in that won five Oscars and a cleverly whipped-up Anglo-American sales mania not seen since *Jaws*. The 1991 film was directed by Jonathan Demme, who chose to throw the focus on Lecter – played by Anthony Hopkins, who subsequently won the Oscar for Best Actor. Hopkins hammed up his part magnificently ('A census taker once tried to test me. I ate his liver with some fava beans and a nice Chianti'). Lecter is as horrible as, but more 'real' than, the slasher-film hero-villains Michael Myers or Jason (he wears an allusive ice-hockey mask in one scene). It was 'Hannibal the Cannibal' who made the film a 'must-see', and with it *The Silence of the Lambs* a 'must-read' book.

A problem, from the entertainment industry's point of view, was that Thomas Harris was a slow producer – if only he could have been put in a bag and shaken up with Terry Pratchett. It was ten years before a sequel could be wrung out of his muse. *Hannibal* the book was released in 2000, and the film a few months later. Ridley Scott directed and Hopkins starred, again, in the title role at a reported fee of $15 million. In this much-awaited sequel, Lecter is on the loose in Florence where he is being stalked by his sole surviving victim, Mason Verger (or what remains of him; Hannibal induced him to scrape off his face; in revenge, he wants Hannibal devoured alive by wild boars).

Michael Crichton is a more fluent, and diverse, writer than Harris. Ever since his breakthrough into the bestseller lists in 1969 with *The Andromeda Strain*, Crichton had been consolidating his reputation as the most scientifically informed of popular novelists. His unusual background was a useful apprenticeship to his writing career. Born in 1942, he attended the Harvard Medical School. In the classic American self-help tradition he paid his way through college writing pulp fiction under the ironic pseudonym 'Jeffrey Hudson' (the name of history's most famous dwarf; Crichton stands a Brobdignagian 6 ft 7 inches tall). He made the *New York Times* bestseller list under his own name with *The Andromeda Strain* while in his last year at medical school. After graduation, and some research at the Salk Institute, he followed his left hand and gave up science for scientific romance.

Crichton specialized in narratives featuring hard and knowledgeable science. He also took an early interest in theme parks. He not only wrote, but financed, produced and directed the cult movie *Westworld* (1973). It depicts a fantasy Disneyland of the future in which patrons can inhabit 'worlds' like the cowboy West which are populated by androids, who then start killing the customers. *Westworld* was the first movie to use digitized imagery, forerunner of computer-generated imagery, which would, at the end of the 1990s, make possible such 'spectacle' movies as *Gladiator* (2001) without Cecil B. DeMille's 'cast of thousands'. A few computer scientists could handle it.

During the 1980s Crichton became fascinated by computer technology; his 1994 novel *Disclosure*, about female-on-male sexual harassment, introduced a mass readership to the complexities of virtual reality. His other hits included *Congo* (1980), a Rider Haggard-type fantasy about intelligent apes in Africa, with inevitable touches of Conrad to darken things. Crichton had a bigger hit in 1992 with *Rising Sun*, about the Japanese 'takeover' of the USA (for them, World War II is not over until they win).

Crichton had his biggest hit of all (the biggest hit of the decade, it would be) with an update of his theme-park-of-the-future fantasy *Westworld*. *Jurassic Park*, published in 1990, is, like its predecessors, larded with expert exposition of such mysteries as chaos theory and bio-genetics. The film rights were acquired by Stephen Spielberg, the producer-director with the touch of gold.

Spielberg respected the general outline of *Jurassic Park* but, as usual with him, realigned it to favour the 'child's-eye view'. The narrative is simple. A palaeontologist (ancient bone hunter) and his palaeobotanist (ancient plant hunter) girlfriend are summoned by an eccentric millionaire (ancient cash hunter) to help out in a theme park he has developed. Jurassic Park is a zoo for dinosaurs, cloned through genetic engineering. The magic elixir is dinosaur DNA recovered from mosquitos, preserved for millions of years in amber: nonsensical, scientists inform us. The park is located on an island off Costa Rica. Of course, as in *Westworld*, it goes awry. The dinosaurs run amok. Human hubris is punished. There are some things we must not meddle with, as the bioethicists never tire of telling us.

The film, with its irresistible advertising slogan 'An adventure 65 million years in the making' pioneered the full resources of CGI to reproduce the dinosaurs with uncanny realism. Released in June 1993, it was, both in the USA and Britain, the biggest box office success in film history, earning its makers a billion dollars. Michael Crichton got $2 million for the rights. *Jurassic Park* inspired websites, computer games and a state-of-the-art ride at a theme park, Universal Studios (no one, to date, has been eaten by T-Rex). And, of course, sequels. Crichton, the most restlessly creative of popular writers, went on to devise and produce the television series *ER*, which in 1995 won eight Emmys.

Spielberg, it seemed, could make an international, all-time record-breaking hit out of anything. In 1994, he retitled Thomas Keneally's 1982 Booker Prize-winning novel *Schindler's Ark* as *Schindler's List* and turned it into the biggest film of the year. Who else could have done this with the story of a handful of Jews saved from the Third Reich's gas chambers by an inscrutably egocentric businessman? The critic Theodore Adorno famously proclaimed that writing poetry after Auschwitz was 'barbarous'. Spielberg demonstrated that you could make unbarbarous movies about the Holocaust if you chose the right novel to start from.

There is something of the juggernaut about books like *The Silence of the Lambs*, *Jurassic Park*, *Schindler's List* (as repackaged by Spielberg) or the latest John Grisham. One feels one must throw one-self beneath their wheels. What remains fascinating, even in this most rationalized of book-trade eras, is the unexpectedness of many best-sellers – the fact that they seem to come from nowhere. Who, for example, would have expected an unknown writer's book about nautical navigation to become a runaway bestseller? But that is what Dava Sobel's *Longitude* did in 1998. It created a new genre, the 'biography of a thing' – books on cod, the potato and the lead pencil followed; most, alas, were not bestsellers. Who could have predicted (certainly not the wise old men or even the young computer whizzes of the book trade) that a murder mystery, translated from the Danish, about a Greenlander would be a 'popular novel' outside Copenhagen? None the less, Peter Høeg's *Miss Smilla's Feeling for Snow* (1993) topped the UK fiction bestseller lists – the first Scandinavian novel to do so since, presumably, Hans Christian Andersen.

The diaries of Alan Clark were a surefire bestseller. But who expected *Memoirs of a Geisha*, confected by a young American Japanophile, to sell 4 million copies in the USA in 1997 and half a million in the UK? (The Japanese market was highly unimpressed by the novel.) The most surprising British novel to sell in the millions in the 1990s was Louis de Bernières's serio-comic story of love and partisan conflict set in wartime Cephalonia, *Captain Corelli's Mandolin* (1994). With worldwide sales of close on 3 million by the end of the decade, and a terrible film adaptation, this technically ambitious work testified either to the perversity or, more likely, to the inexorably advancing sophistication of the British reading classes since 1945.

Surveying popular books, as Richard Hoggart did in the 1950s, can be a depressing exercise: so much schlock, dreck and pointless writing. But there are also pearls. Above all, it is the wonderful unpredictability of what will rise to the top that fascinates the observer. Who knows what the next decade's bestsellers will be? One thing is certain. They will be something else. And there will be even more of them.

# Notes

## 1945–59

p. 11 '... "expurgations" of dubious material.'   An account of the publishing career of *Love without Fear* is given in Roy Porter and Lesley Hall's *The Facts of Life* (New Haven, 1995). Quotations are from the 1947 edition of Chesser's sex manual.

p. 13 '... because it imprisons her in her sex.'   Simone de Beauvoir, *A History of Sex* (the second volume of *The Second Sex*, 1953 repr. 1965), p. 25.

p. 14 '... "The Great Husband Hunt".'   The phrase and subsequent information about women's romance is taken from Mary Cadogan, *And Then Their Hearts Stood Still* (London, 1994).

p. 14 '... when the shocked hero smothers her with frantic, anxious kisses.' Quoted in Joseph P. McAleer, *Popular Reading and Publishing in Britain: 1914–1950* (London, 1950), p. 112.

p. 16 'Her novels, typically, sold between 70,000 and 100,000 each ...' This and other details are taken from Jane Aiken Hodge, *The Private World of Georgette Heyer* (London, 1984).

p. 17 '... who doesn't allow her heroine to go to bed with anyone until she's married him.'   Quoted from an interview between Mary Cadogan and Barbara Cartland in *And Then Their Hearts Stood Still*, p. 198.

p. 19 '"... where it is not considered pretentious, or bad form, to care about food".'   Elizabeth David, *A Book of Mediterranean Food* (London, 1950 rev. 1965), p. 12. Biographical details are taken from Artemis Cooper, *Writing At The Kitchen Table* (London, 1999).

p. 20 '... onions, garlic, herbs, and brightly coloured southern vegetables.' *A Book of Mediterranean Food*, p. 1.

p. 22 '... and admitted later that he had "never read the *Odyssey*".' J. P. Morpurgo, *Allen Lane: King Penguin* (London, 1979), p. 216.

p. 23 '"... John Gunther's *Inside America* and various travel guides."' Quoted in Steve Holland, *The Mushroom Jungle: A History of Postwar Paperback Publishing* (London, 1993), pp. 129–30. I have drawn on Holland's expertly informed account in the following discussion of Hank Janson.

p. 24 '... loyalty, honesty, kindliness, and all the things that children should be taught.'   Quoted in Robert Druce, *This Day Our Daily Fictions* (London, 1992), p. 18.

p. 28 '"... are outnumbered in this not too amicable world."' Paul Brickhill, *The Dambusters* (London, 1951 repr. 1978), p. 498.

p. 28 '... and finally an air detective at Scotland Yard.' See the *DNB* entry on W. E. Johns, by P. B Ellis and Piers Williams, reprinted in J. A. Sutherland (ed.), *Literary Lives* (London, 2001), p. 182.

p. 31 '"More history for children to learn in a hundred years."' Quotations and references are from the 1993 reissue of Marion Crawford's *The Little Princesses* (1950), with foreword by A. N. Wilson.

p. 33 '... the world changed with the first performance of *Look Back in Anger*.' Tynan made this pronouncement in his 1958 essay, 'The Angry Young Movement' reprinted in *Tynan on Theatre* (London, 1961), pp. 54–62.

p. 33 '... encouraged the strange young intellectual ...' See Margaret Drabble, *Angus Wilson* (London, 1995), pp. 214–17.

p. 35 'But I looked well enough that morning ten years ago.' John Braine, *Room at the Top* (London, 1957), p. 1.

p. 36 '... because trouble it's always been and always will be.' Alan Sillitoe, *Saturday Night and Sunday Morning* (London, 1958 repr. 1993), p. 219.

p. 38 '... and yet thinks he has gone beyond his own class.' Richard Hoggart, *The Uses of Literacy* (London, 1957 repr. 1959), p. 250. Hoggart does not identify the quotations he cites, nor can I.

p. 40 'Golding had difficulty getting his first novel published ...' See Michael Howard, *Jonathan Cape, Publisher* (London, 1980).

p. 40 '"the cosy catastrophe"' Brian Aldiss coined the phrase in his *Billion Year Spree: The History of Science Fiction* (London, 1973). Elsewhere, he has memorably called Wyndham 'the Anthony Trollope of sf writers'.

p. 42 '... "clubland thugs" popular in 1930's low-brow fiction.' Good accounts of Fleming's *modus operandi* are given in John Pearson, *The Life of Ian Fleming* (London, 1966) and Andrew Lycett, *Ian Fleming: The Man behind the Mask* (London, 1996). The most entertaining critical account of the Bond novels, on which I draw, is Kingsley Amis's *The James Bond Dossier* (London, 1965).

p. 45 '"... the crude, snob cravings of a suburban adult".' Johnson's diatribe was first published in the *New Statesman*, 5 April 1958.

p. 45 '... and recruited disciples, including the young Alan Greenspan, for years afterwards.' In *The Passion of Ayn Rand* (New York, 1986), Barbara Branden estimates that by 1984 *Atlas Shrugged* had sold over 5 million copies.

p. 48 '"... that person would be Trevor Huddleston without a doubt."' Archbishop Tutu offered this tribute to a journalist on Huddleston's death in 1998.

p. 48 '... selling 20 million copies in twenty years.'   Details taken from Norris McWhirter, *Ross* (London, 1976).


## The 60s

p. 50 '... just as you might tickle and caress a giggling child – just that.' V. Nabokov, *Lolita* (London, 1959 repr. 1995), pp. 59–60.

p. 50 '"... and uglily savage: especially England and America."' D. H. Lawrence, '*À Propos of Lady Chatterley's Lover' and Other Essays* (London, 1961), p. 99.

p. 50 '... than a lavatory wall, or so the prosecution contended.'   For an account of the trial see J. Sutherland, *Offensive Literature* (London, 1982), pp. 10–31.

p. 52 'Could degradation sink further? (Yes, alas.)'   For an account of the *Little Red Schoolbook* see *Offensive Literature*, pp. 111–16.

p. 53 'And the Beatles' first LP.'   For a discussion of this poem and its background see Andrew Motion, *Philip Larkin: A Writer's Life* (London, 1993 repr. 1994), pp. 372–3.

p. 54 'He abhorred what he called "ghastly good taste".'   See Kingsley Amis's *DNB* entry on Betjeman, reprinted in *Literary Lives*, pp. 29–34.

p. 55 '... "to make the New Testament intelligible to an intelligent reader" ...'   See the *New English Bible* (Oxford and Cambridge, 1961), p. x.

p. 56 'Mills & Boon, always ahead of the curve ...'   For the history of this firm, and their successive and successful adaptations, see Joseph McAleer, *Passion's Fortune: The Story of Mills & Boon* (London, 1999).

p. 58 '... in the foliage of her pubis.'   One reviewer estimated that there is sex and/or sadism every seventeen pages of *The Carpetbaggers*. See J. Sutherland, *Offensive Literature*, pp. 30–1.

p. 59 '"Forty," she once said, "is Hiroshima."'   My account of Susann is drawn largely from Barbara Seaman, *Lovely Me: The Life of Jacqueline Susann* (New York, 1996).

p. 61 '... he ungallantly divulged in 2000.'   My account of Friedan's life is taken largely from Daniel Horowitz, *Betty Friedan and the Making of the Feminine Mystique: The American Left, the Cold War, and Modern Feminism* (New York, 1998). The 'ungallant' remark about their marital love life (or lack of it) is divulged on Carl Friedan's website, www.carlfriedan.com.

p. 62 '... burned alive all along your nerves.'   Sylvia Plath, *The Bell Jar* (London, 1963), p. 1.

p. 64 '... and *Where Eagles Dare* (1967).'   The comments on MacLean are expanded in my book *Bestsellers* (London, 1982), pp. 96–109.

p. 65 '... "of a certain ease and speed, which might be counted in its favour".'
Kenneth Clark, *Civilisation* (London, 1969), p. 2.

p. 67 '... "a couple of generals who might wish to turn the book's fiction
into a reality".'   See Anthony Aldgate, James Chapman and Arthur Marwick
(eds), *Windows on the Sixties* (London, 2000), pp. 75–6.

p. 68 '... like a set of patio lights.'   See Alvin Toffler, *Future Shock* (New
York, 1970 repr. 1971), p. 436.

p. 73 '... "he seems incapable of marshalling his thoughts on paper" ...'
Quoted in Alan Warren, *Roald Dahl* (New York, 1988), from which I also
take the anecdote about gambling with Truman. A fuller account of the
author is given in Jeremy Treglown, *Roald Dahl: A Biography* (London, 1994).

p. 76 '...McLuhan's writing looked as if McLuhan had never read it.'
See Philip Marchand, *Marshall McLuhan* (New York, 1989), p. 153.

p. 78 '... solemnly "grokked" before going out on their homicidal rampages).'
See Vincent Bugliosi, *Helter Skelter* (New York, 1969).

p. 78 '... (a rare woman author in the genre).'   For a discussion of the
publishing of sf in the 1960s see Patrick Parrinder (ed.), *Science Fiction:
A Critical Guide* (London, 1979), pp. 162–86.

p. 78 'All this extra-mural fame was somewhat bewildering to the Oxford
academic ...'   The fullest account of the author is given in Humphrey
Carpenter, *J. R. R. Tolkien* (London, 1977).

p. 79 'The "naked ape" episode was, apparently, the director's idea.'
In his novelization of the film *2001: A Space Odyssey* (London, 1968),
Arthur C. Clarke gratefully includes the 'man-ape' episode in his first chapter.
According to Vincent LoBrutto in *Stanley Kubrick* (London, 1998),
the director took his inspiration from Robert Ardrey's *African Genesis*.

p. 80 'She used George's diaries, photographs and warden's journals.'
My account is taken, largely, from Caroline Cass, *Joy Adamson: Behind
the Mask* (London, 1997).

## The 70s

p. 83 'The bestseller had always been an American kind of book.'   I deal
with the evolution of bestsellerism, and the accompanying 'lists', in the first
chapter of *Bestsellers*, pp. 10–30.

p. 83 'Reviewing American bestseller lists of the 1970s ...'   I have taken
the following examples from the *Publisher's Weekly* lists, as compiled on
www.caderbooks.com.

p. 85 'Puzo had sold out in style.'   See *Bestsellers*, pp. 38–9.

p. 87 '"They're as mysterious as any animal on earth."'  See Peter Benchley, *Jaws* (New York, 1974 repr. 1975), p. 117.

p. 88 '... has since been set up in Wight's house by the local council.' The best source on the world of James Herriot are the several websites devoted to him, e.g. www.thirsk.org.uk/herriot1.

p. 90 '... to tax exile in the Bahamas in the 1970s.'  A revealing portrait of Arthur Hailey is given by his wife Sheila in her book, *I Married a Bestseller* (London, 1978).

p. 92 'I seem destined to remain a quite damnably lucky amateur.' Frederick Forsyth, *The Four Novels* (London, 1982), p. vii.

p. 94 '... was the power behind her husband's pen.'  See Graham Lord, *Dick Francis: A Racing Life* (London, 1999). The 'revelation' provoked some useful publicity for Lord's unauthorized biography.

p. 98 '... although his remedies tended to be less drastic than exorcism.' I discuss the link between Spock and 'frighteners' of the 1970s in *Bestsellers*, pp. 59–73.

p. 99 'King was born in 1947 in Portland, Maine ...'  The following account is taken from the autobiographical chapters in Stephen King, *On Writing: A Memoir* (London, 2000), George Beahm (ed.), *The Stephen King Companion* (New York, 1989), and www.stephenking.com.

p. 101 '..."*Star Wars* is a movie for the kid in all of us" ...'  A full account of Lucas's theory of film-making is given in Dale Pollock, *Skywalking: The Life and Films of George Lucas* (London, 1983).

p. 103 '... her American sales were reckoned at half a billion.'  Figure taken from D. Riley and P. McAllister (eds), *The New Bedside, Bathtub and Armchair Companion to Agatha Christie* (New York, 1979 repr. 1986), pp. 1–2.

p. 105 '"... he would join a friendly clutch of bodies, and contribute to the merriment."'  Guy Talese, *Thy Neighbor's Wife* (London, 1980), p. 316. Talese offers a somewhat jaundiced view on 1970s 'liberation sexuality', as practised in Sandstone.

p. 109 '"You can only say 'he stuck it in her' so many ways."'  McCullough's observation on *The Thorn Birds* was made in an interview with the *Guardian*, 15 April 1977. The earlier quotation is from *The Thorn Birds* (London, 1977 repr. 1978), p. 354.

p. 110 '... scaffolding that she needed to get to where she now is.' The most recent (and unauthorized) account of Greer's career is Christine Wallace, *Germaine Greer, Untamed Shrew* (London, 1998).

p. 110 'I tried to incorporate myself. No good.'  From an interview with Robert Greenfield in the magazine *Rolling Stone*, 7 January 1971.

## The 80s

p. 113 '... it would be into six figures.'   The annual statistics of the British book trade are assembled, at the turn of the year, in the trade journal the *Bookseller*.

p. 114 '... and hence a low level of retail competition.'   For an account of the campaign to abolish the NBA see Terry Maher, *Against my Better Judgement* (London, 1997).

p. 115 'In three months, it had sold 750,000 copies.'   See Neil Gaiman, *Don't Panic: Douglas Adams and the Hitch-hiker's Guide to the Galaxy* (London, 1988 rev. 1993). As Gaiman points out, there is no unanimity on whether 'hitch-hiker' should be two words, half-joined, or one word. For consistency, I've used hyphens.

p. 118 'I'm Roy Rogers, you are Trigger.'   From the first secret diary. The entry, logically enough, is for St Valentine's Day, 14 February. In subsequent comments I have drawn from two interviews with Townsend in *The Times*, 13 October 1986 and 30 September 1988.

p. 126 '... who hoaxed him out of his cash.'   I draw in this section on Michael Crick, *Jeffrey Archer: Stranger than Fiction* (London, 1995 repr. 2000). See particularly pp. 192–5.

p. 128 '"... it is bizarre that its author should be Jeffrey Archer."'  Alex Hamilton in his annual round up of bestsellers in the *Guardian*, 11 January 1990.

p. 129 'We never know.'   I discuss this enigma in J. Sutherland, *Where was Rebecca Shot?* (London, 1998), pp. 134–7.

p. 137 'Seventy per cent of bestsellers, Alex Hamilton estimates ...' See the *Guardian*, 11 January 1990.

p. 138 '... a state-of-the-art British Gestapo.'   See *Bestsellers*, pp. 240–4.

p. 140 '"... while pompous bowler-hatted civil servants in Whitehall pretended to look the other way."'   See Peter Wright, *Spycatcher* (New York, 1987), chapters 20–3.

p. 141 '... "where people, governments, are trying to distort the truth."' The interview is reprinted in Michael Reder (ed.), *Conversations with Rushdie* (London, 2000).

p. 142 '... the most technologically savvy president of the United States since Jefferson.'   In *Debt of Honor* (New York, 1994), Clancy anticipates the tragic events of 11 September 2001, when Ryan assumes the presidency after a plane, piloted by hijacking terrorists, crashes into the White House.

## The 90s

p. 145 '"... a quagmire of bluff and counterbluff."'   From an interview with Helen Fielding, conveniently found on www.penguinputnam.com.

p. 146 '... "helpless girls, drunk and worrying about their weight, just in order to get published?"'   Lessing's and Bainbridge's comments are reported in an article by John Ezard in the *Guardian*, 24 August 2001.

p. 147 'In Alex Hamilton's round-up of the top 100 bestsellers of 2001 ...' See the *Guardian*, 29 December 2001.

p. 149 '... a grey suit and pill-box hat ...'   See Andrew Morton, *Diana: Her True Story in her own Words* (London, 1997), p. 42.

p. 152 '... who intersperses his rampages with reflections from Kierkegaard.' For Rents's strange preoccupation with the philosopher see *Where was Rebecca Shot?*, pp. 165–7.

p. 154 '... because of all the times Dudley had punched him on the nose.' J. K. Rowling, *Harry Potter and the Philosopher's Stone* (London, 1997), p. 11.

p. 155 '... "sheer evil" and a "lack of respect" for adults.'   The reception history of Rowling's books is fully chronicled in the many websites devoted to her work, e.g. www.harrypotter.warnerbros.com.

p. 159 '... the swerve from sexual orthodoxy in the 1960s.'   In newspaper accounts of the in-church manoeuvring to find a new Archbishop of Canterbury, in early 2002, it was estimated that no more than 1 million of the country's Anglicans regularly attended church.

p. 160 '... in the years that I'd been living away."'   Taken from an interview transcribed on www.powells.com/authors/bryson.html.

p. 171 'She, too, is being profiled.'   The most extensive analysis of Harris's fiction (albeit in a series entitled 'Short Books') is given by David Sexton, *Thomas Harris* (London, 2001).

# Index

# Index

# Index

# Index

# Index

# Picture credits

Reading in the bomb shelter © Hulton Getty; Graham Greene and Carol Reed © TimePix; *Love without Ending* courtesy Mills & Boon; *Sinister Rapture* courtesy Alexander Moring; *Hurrah for Little Noddy* courtesy HarperCollins Publishers; Agatha Christie © Hulton Getty; *French Country Cooking* courtesy Penguin Books; *The Cruel Sea* courtesy Penguin Books; *Casino Royale* courtesy Hodder & Stoughton; *The Little Sister* courtesy Penguin Books; Fanny and Johnnie Cradock © Topham; BBC adaptation of *Nineteen Eighty-four* © BBC; *Nineteen Eighty-four* newspaper cutting © *Daily Express*; *Lady Chatterley's Lover* queue © Topham; The paperback revolution © Hulton Getty; *The Catcher in the Rye* courtesy Penguin Books; John Wyndham © Camera Press; *The Day of the Triffids* courtesy Orion Publishing; *Dune* courtesy Penguin Putnam; *Odyssey* courtesy Penguin Books; Kubrick's *Lolita* © Moviestore; Tom Wolfe © Hulton Getty

Ian Fleming and Barbara Cartland © Mark Gerson; Colin Wilson © Hulton Getty; Sylvia Plath © Corbis; Topolski's portrait of Bronowski © BBC; *The Ascent of Man* courtesy BBC Books; *Civilisation* courtesy BBC Books; *The Naked Ape* courtesy Random House; Jacqueline Susann © Mark Gerson; *The Day of the Jackal* courtesy Transworld Publishers; Frederick Forsyth © Mark Gerson; *The Female Eunuch* courtesy HarperCollins; *Whip Hand* courtesy Michael Joseph; Forman's *One Flew Over the Cuckoo's Nest* © Moviestore; Germaine Greer © Hulton Getty; *Yes, Minister* courtesy BBC; *The Hitch-hiker's Guide to the Galaxy* courtesy Macmillan Publishers; *The Exorcist* courtesy Transworld Publishers; Alistair Cooke © Corbis; Jeffrey Archer © Rex Features; Salman Rushdie © Topham; *Jane Fonda's Workout Book* © Penguin Books

Andrew Morton © PA News; *The Official Sloane Ranger Diary* courtesy Ebury Press; *A Brief History of Time* courtesy Transworld Publishers; *The Country Diary of an Edwardian Lady* courtesy Michael Joseph; *Bill Bailey's Lot* courtesy Transworld Publishers; Dirk Bogarde © Alpha Photo Press Agency; Jackie Collins © Camera Press; Kingsley and Martin Amis © PA News; Stephen King © Rex Features; Umberto Eco © Rex Features; *Bravo Two Zero* courtesy Transworld Publishers; *Trainspotting* courtesy Random House; *Notes From a Small Island* courtesy Doubleday; Vikram Seth © Camera Press; Iris Murdoch and John Bayley © Rex Features; Zadie Smith © Camera Press; *White Teeth* courtesy Penguin Books; *A Child Called 'It'* courtesy Orion Publishing; *Jingo* courtesy Transworld Publishers; J. K. Rowling © Rex Features; *Harry Potter and the Philosopher's Stone* courtesy Bloomsbury Publishing (cover illustration by Thomas Taylor)